Exploring Buried Buxton

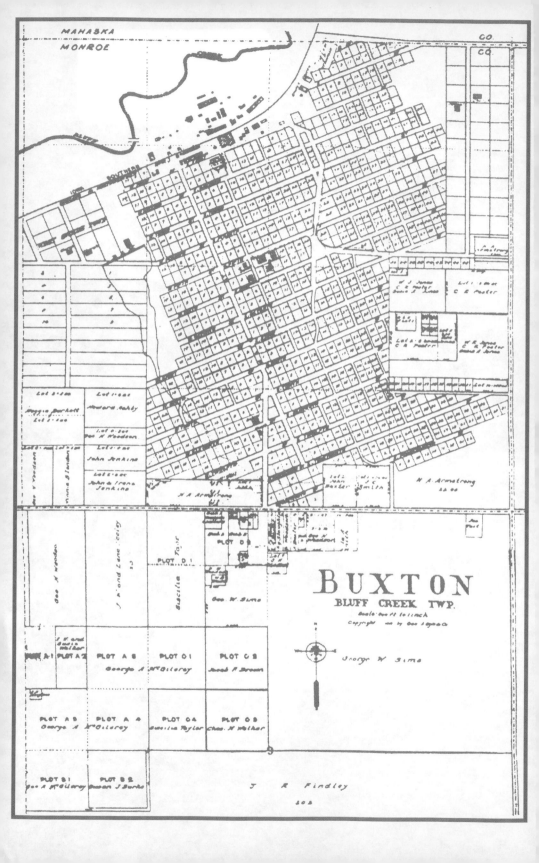

Exploring Buried Buxton

Archaeology of an Abandoned Iowa Coal Mining Town with a Large Black Population

DAVID M. GRADWOHL
& NANCY M. OSBORN

University of Iowa Press, Iowa City

DEDICATED TO
Dorothy Neal Collier

University of Iowa Press, Iowa City 52242
www.uiowapress.org
All rights reserved
Printed in the United States of America

The University of Iowa Press is a member of Green Press Initiative
and is committed to preserving natural resources.

Library of Congress Cataloging-in-Publication Data
Gradwohl, David M.
    Exploring buried Buxton: archaeology of an abandoned Iowa
coal mining town with a large black population /
David M. Gradwohl and Nancy M. Osborn.
    p.   cm.
    Includes bibliographical references and index.
    ISBN-13: 978-1-58729-574-4 (pbk.)
    ISBN-10: 1-58729-574-1 (pbk.)
    1. Buxton (Iowa)—Antiquities. 2. Afro-Americans—Iowa—
Buxton—Antiquities. 3. Excavations (Archaeology)—Iowa—
Buxton. 4. Cities and towns, Ruined, extinct, etc.—Iowa—Buxton. I.
Osborn, Nancy M. II. Title. III. Series.
F629.B98G73
977.7 '865—dc20   90-4804

07 08 09 10 11 P 5 4 3 2 1

Contents

Figures

vii

Preface

MOST PEOPLE have stereotypes about archaeology. They perhaps have heard about the "romance of archaeology" and have chuckled at cartoons showing pith-helmeted scientists going to faraway places to find treasures in Mesopotamia, explore the mysterious ruins of a Mayan temple, or discover the remains of ancient human fossils given a name nobody can pronounce. The discovery of King Tutankhamen's tomb contributed greatly to that exciting, though rather embellished, picture in the public's mind. It is also said that archaeology is a dirty business. Indeed it is. Any "romance" soon wears off in the "heat of the noonday sun" where, it is sometimes said, only mad dogs and Englishmen go.

The archaeological investigation of the Buxton townsite illustrates the truth as well as the exaggerations in these proverbial images. For us, as archaeologists at Iowa State University (ISU) in Ames, the site was close to home, not far away. We never thought of northern Monroe County near Albia and Lovilia as exotic, but in some respects it is. There was indeed the exciting challenge of making some sort of correlation between the location of Buxton's buildings, as photographed in 1912, and the initially desolate-looking fields and pastures we first viewed at the townsite in 1980. There was mystery about where a house once stood on Gobbler's Nob—where a woman, now in her seventies and living in Des Moines, recalled from her childhood playing with china dolls and watching her mother put up vegetables and fruits in stoneware crocks and glass canning jars.

Mapping the ruins of former buildings was interesting, if not romantic, as was digging down into a trash dump and finding broken stoneware crocks and Ball mason jars. But fieldwork is hard work and the pace is demanding. During July the heat of the noonday sun was intense in Iowa, and unseasonable rains interrupted planned work schedules. "Is *this* the romance of archaeology?" our students asked. Even the senior crew director, supposedly hardened to these sorts of field conditions after nearly thirty years doing archaeology in the prairies and plains, asked this question as he hurriedly made his way through cow manure in a feedlot, taking iron fence posts to cordon off an excavation unit before the onset of another torrential thunderstorm. Lightning struck a nearby silo and the electrical charge could be felt in the metal fence posts. Was this the place the archaeologist would "pass" and meet his Maker? So much for romance and idealized challenges!

In a real sense, archaeology is down to earth. The archaeologist looks at the past primarily through material objects, bits of buildings and pieces of pottery, which have been buried in the ground and preserved through time. Many things about the human past are mundane and often are not recalled by the living. But even the simplest artifacts left over from the past are a treasure trove to the archaeologist. The material evidence can also supplement and objectify the things remembered by people and perhaps their thoughts and visions as recorded in diaries and photographs. The more intangible parts of the historic past, of course, are more the domains of the historian, the sociologist, and other humanists and social scientists.

In that sense we, working on an interdisciplinary project, have attempted to present the archaeology of Buxton "from the ground up" – to articulate the material remains with the data acquired from archival studies and oral interviews, and to look at the broader significance of the Buxton experience to the people who lived there and to their children and grandchildren, who have heard about Buxton all their lives. A sense of urgency in recording the Buxton experience has been underlined by the recent deaths of several former residents who contributed information to this research project, among them Emanuel Blomgren, Jesse Frazier, Reuben Gaines, Jr., Bessie Rhodes Lewis, Martin Peterson, Hazel Chapman Stapleton, and Wilma Larson Stewart.

The cultural resources of the townsite, as well as the ultimate meaning of the Buxton experience, are significant beyond the former residents of that town to all Iowans, and perhaps to others across the nation.

Acknowledgments

THE recent Buxton project was undertaken by an interdisciplinary group of researchers at Iowa State University. That group worked in cooperation with members of the Buxton, Iowa Club Inc. under funding from the Heritage Conservation and Recreation Service (National Park Service), managed by the Division of Historic Preservation of the Iowa State Historical Department. Because of the large size and the interdisciplinary nature of the Buxton project, we are indebted to many people for the results of what we feel was a challenging and successful venture.

Dr. Adrian Anderson, Iowa's state historic preservation officer, is thanked with great gratitude for his vision and efforts in getting the original project launched. Aware of the paucity of well-documented cultural resources pertaining to the history of black people in Iowa, Dr. Anderson recognized the potential qualification of Buxton for U.S. Department of Interior research funds. He also gave needed guidance in putting together the research proposal, which ultimately was approved for funding beginning on 1 June 1980.

During the 1980–1982 contract period the project coordinator was Dr. Dorothy Schwieder, Department of History at ISU. Also working on the project were Dr. Elmer Schwieder, Department of Family Environment, and Dr. Joseph Hraba, Department of Sociology and Anthropology. These colleagues pursued the archival study and oral history phases of the interdisciplinary project and prepared a separate report on their investigations. We thank them particularly for including questions on material culture in their interview schedules with Buxton's former residents.

Other personnel at ISU greatly facilitated this research project. We wish to acknowledge the assistance of Dr. Daniel Zaffarano (vice president for research), Dr. Norman Jacobson (associate dean of the Graduate College), Dr. Wallace Russell (then dean of the College of Sciences and Humanities), Dr. Richard Van Iten (then associate dean, College of Sciences and Humanities, cross-disciplinary studies), Mr. Richard Hasbrook (contracts and grants officer), and Dr. Gerald Klonglan (chair, Department of Sociology and Anthropology). We especially appreciate the generosity of the ISU Graduate College in providing funds for a research assistantship during the tenure of the present project.

The research proposal submitted to the Heritage Conservation and Recreation Service was accompanied by a letter from the president of the Buxton, Iowa Club Inc. (Mr. Paul Wilson) to Mrs. Dorothy Collier (chair of the advisory board) pledging the assistance of the club in the proposed project. Mrs. Collier has pursued her task tenaciously. We also thank Ms. D. Chrystal Peavy, first vice president of the Buxton, Iowa Club Inc., for using her personnel management skills in the quest for interns to participate in the project, and for inviting us to discuss our archaeological discoveries at meetings of the club. We wish to thank all members of the Buxton, Iowa Club Inc. and all other former residents of the town who participated in the interview program conducted by the historians and sociologists on the research team, as well as those who contributed information directly to us in the field. In the latter case we especially acknowledge the assistance of Mr. Archie Harris, who was born in Coopertown, worked in Buxton's mines, and still lives in Section 4 of Bluff Creek Township. We are grateful to this gentleman for sharing with us his extensive knowledge of the past as well as his cheerful perspective on the present. The following individuals also contributed information pertaining to the Buxton townsite: Emanuel Blomgren, Gerald Chamberlain, William Collier, Alex Erickson, Joe and Nettie Keegel, Jim Keegel, Harvey Lewis, Martin Schipper, and Orville and Susie Schipper.

In terms of the archaeological field investigations, we are indebted to the landowners who permitted access to their properties and shared valuable information regarding the former community. We especially thank Mr. Pete Keegel, who not only allowed the preliminary surface survey of his property but kindly permitted the excavation of test pits and trenches in the downtown district of Buxton, which he and his family now own. Miss Mabel Blomgren and Mr. Loren Blomgren not only allowed surface surveys of their land, but also shared with us photographs, documents, and other information pertaining to East Swede Town. Mr. and Mrs. Raymond Carter, Mr. and Mrs. Case Keegel, and Mr. and Mrs. Jack Jones were also helpful in facilitating the archaeological surface survey of the Buxton townsite. Mr. Jones also donated artifacts to the project, and we express our appreciation for his thoughtfulness in that regard. Mr. and Mrs. Jack Harris allowed an inspection of portions of their property during the summer of 1980 and the spring of 1981. We particularly thank Mr. Harris for taking us on our first visit to the breached dam at the reservoir and for guiding us to the abandoned Buxton cemetery. Also assisting the field investigation of the townsite was Mr. Charles Wever, president of the Monroe County Historical Society and retired Monroe County Engineer, who helped us obtain plat maps of Buxton and aerial photographs of Section 4 of Bluff Creek Township.

Abundant information was collected at the townsite by students who literally sweated out long days in the field. Members of the 1980 field crew were Lori Fisher, Robert Gearhart, James Gifford, Rosemary Griffin, Marsha Miller, Charla Prange, Donna Randall, and Martha Stewart. In addition, we thank John Hotopp for his assistance in setting out baselines at the site, and Steve Mbutu for his help in cataloging artifacts at the laboratory on campus. During the 1981 field season the operations were more complex and the crew was larger—including paid workers, field school students, and interns. We are grateful for the hard work and diligence of James Gifford (field supervisor), Martha Stewart (field assistant), and other members of the crew: John Broihahn, Steven DeVore, Janice DeVries, Lori Fisher, Derek Frerichs, Robert Gearhart, Ralph Hanson, Steven Harsin, J. Charles Lockett, Marsha Miller, Charla Prange, Donna Randall, Olivia Smith, Carla Tollefson, Robert Thompson, Karen Turnmire, Nancy Wallace, and Susan Young.

During the summer of 1981 Barbara Morley assisted in the retrieval of archival data in Des Moines.

Personnel at William Penn College in Oskaloosa graciously provided dormitory housing and eating facilities for the 1981 field crew. We especially thank Mr. Harold Case (business manager) for his assistance in making these arrangements. Hanna Gradwohl not only accompanied us on our original visit to the Buxton townsite but also assisted in many ways, including the task of hauling heavy containers of artifacts from our field headquarters in Oskaloosa to the archaeological laboratory back on campus.

Martha Williams deserves applause for her gargantuan efforts in supervising the laboratory operations on campus, keeping the huge catalog of artifacts moving along, and drawing illustrations of selected specimens. These laboratory functions, as well as the initial laboratory preparation of field maps for publication, were also the accomplishment of James Gifford, Charla Prange, and Steven DeVore, who served as the Graduate College research assistant for the archaeological phase of investigations.

Back on campus two anthropology majors continued their interests in Buxton beyond their roles of field school student and paid laboratory assistant. Nancy Wallace undertook a study of her kinfolk's participation in the Swedish community at Buxton, and we thank her for sharing with us photographs and other information pertaining to the Peterson and Bergquist families there. James Gifford took on an analysis of artifacts exhibiting manufacturer's marks, and we thank him for contributing to our understanding of the economic and trade networks into which Buxton was woven. Thanks go,

too, to Sandra Wright and Alice Zwierzycki, our secretaries during the contract period, and to Rose Jordan, Linda Halleland, Melinda Howell-Vassey, Judy Hankins, Liz Carpenter, and Ramona Wierson for typing and proofreading our original manuscript.

During the past three years we have had the opportunity to discuss the Buxton archaeological investigations at a number of lay club meetings and professional conferences around the country. Marion Carter, who flew from Detroit to Tucson to hear one of our presentations, has contributed valuable information about Buxton as she remembers it when she lived there as the daughter of the prominent Dr. E. A. Carter. We are greatly indebted to her continuing support of our research efforts. We also thank her cousin, Lawrence T. Carter, for providing information stemming from his twenty years' life experience in Buxton.

Through professional meetings and other contacts, we also have had the opportunity to discuss the Buxton archaeological investigations with scholars studying black communities throughout North America. These discussions have provided insights into the archaeological investigations at Buxton and have pointed out the great potential significance of the data being assembled from the townsite. Contributions from the following individuals are particularly notable: Dr. Charles C. Irby (professor and former chair of the Ethnic Studies Department at California Polytechnic University in Pomona), Ms. Bertha Calloway (director of the Great Plains Black Museum in Omaha), Mr. Andrew Wall (head of Minority Programs at New Mexico State University in Las Cruces), Ms. Barbara Richardson of Tucson (author of the book *Black Pioneers of New Mex-*

ico: A Documentary and Pictorial History), Professor Gloria Smith (Black Studies Program and Political Science Department at the University of Arizona), and Dr. Jennie Rucker (professor of business and government at the Community College of Denver).

Other people were of additional assistance as this book was being prepared. We thank Jack Lufkin, who brought to our attention important archival materials, recently donated to his office at the Iowa State Historical Department, that pertain to Buxton. We also appreciate the editorial assistance and patience of Kathleen Glenn-Lewin during the final revision of this manuscript. Finally we gratefully acknowledge the efforts of Daniel F. Griffen, Jr., executive director of the Iowa State University Research Foundation (ISURF), who assisted us in a number of matters and facilitated ISURF support for the publication of this book.

Above all, we express with respect and affection our debt to Dorothy Neal Collier, to whom this book is dedicated, for her many formal and informal contributions to the Buxton archaeological project. Through her we are able to comprehend something of what the Buxton experience meant to her childhood and to the lives of her parents, George and Alice Mobilia Neal. Through her we can understand at least part of the heritage that she has transmitted to her children: Lillian, Dorothy Ann, Richard, Irving, Mary Jane, Kenneth, and William. Through her we have been inspired to pursue the significance of Buxton by way of the present archaeological investigations and to think of the meanings beyond. We hope that many others will be inspired by her and will fathom the broader meanings of the Buxton experience.

DAVID M. GRADWOHL
NANCY M. OSBORN

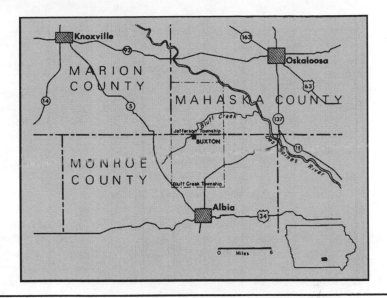

1. Location of
Buxton within
Bluff Creek
Township,
Monroe County,
Iowa. (Adapted
from a 1941
Federal Works
Agency Iowa
transportation
map)

Exploring Buried Buxton

BUXTON, IOWA, was a coal mining town that existed in Monroe County throughout the first quarter of the twentieth century (see Fig. 1). This town was established in 1900 by the Consolidation Coal Company, a subsidiary of the Chicago and North Western Railroad. For at least 20 years the miners, many of whom were black, commuted daily by train from Buxton to the outlying mine operations. There they dug coal for their patron company, whose continuous needs provided relatively stable employment for the miners and for the support businesses and professional people who also resided in Buxton. Ultimately the Consolidation Coal Company changed its base of operations, and the inhabitants of Buxton were forced to move on to other mining communities or to cities

2. Photographic overview of Buxton, looking toward the southeast sometime prior to 1908. *Left foreground,* the water tower at the residence of the mine superintendent; *center,* the first company store and the main YMCA building; *extreme right,* Main Street; *right center horizon,* the high school and water tower. (Courtesy of the Iowa State Historical Department)

where they took up new lives and different economic pursuits. The townsite was abandoned during the 1920s and the land was quickly reclaimed for dry land farming and stock raising activities.

Some things about the Buxton settlement are known historically through written documents, including census records and newspaper accounts; photographic evidence (see Fig. 2), including formal portraits and snapshots; and the remembrances of former residents, which constitute an oral history of the former community. As was typical of many mining towns, Buxton's residents included white people of various national origins and ethnic backgrounds. This community's population was unusual, if not unique, however, in its large component of black people, which counted not only miners but also merchants, accountants, secretaries, school teachers and principals, physicians, dentists, druggists, and lawyers, in addition to men and women in other businesses and professions.

Unlike many other unincorporated communities of coal miners in this region, Buxton was not a "camp," but

3. View to the north of downtown Buxton, probably taken from the water tower sometime prior to 1912. Lot 8, or 8 East Third Street, *foreground;* the two YMCA buildings, *extreme upper left;* and the power plant and the first company store, *left of center.* (Courtesy of the Iowa State Historical Department)

rather a town with a centralized business and commercial district (see Fig. 3), planned streets, and relatively commodious houses set out on numbered, quarter-acre lots in a well-established settlement pattern (see Fig. 4). Today

few obvious vestiges of the town remain. The houses and other buildings have been dismantled or moved away and the long-abandoned streets have been blurred by erosion and other natural agencies of time (see Fig. 5). Farm ponds and agricultural terraces have been built in this locality to make modern land uses more effective, and the site of the former town is now the scene of pastures and of fields for corn, soybeans, oats, and hay. Livestock now graze where miners once descended upon the train depot to ride out to the coal mines while their wives pursued

4. Plat map of Buxton, Iowa, dated 1919. The area included is Section 4, the main portion of town owned by the Consolidation Coal Company, and the northern portion of Section 9, showing some of the outlying settlements. (Reprinted from Geo. A. Ogle and Co. 1919:25)

5. Overview of the Buxton townsite, looking southeast from Mahaska County, 1980. (Courtesy of the ISU Archaeological Laboratory)

homemaking activities and business enterprises and their children strolled to school. Tractors now cultivate the land where horse-drawn buggies and, later, Model T Fords negotiated Buxton's ordered, but often mud-rutted, streets. Although a mere half century or so has passed since the demise of Buxton, the townsite is now an archaeological site as much as any such places of human activities that were abandoned and buried hundreds or even thousands of years ago.

Scientific questions still remain, however, as popular rumors run rampant about the life and times in Buxton. Was the population of the town four thousand—or was it six thousand, or nine thousand, or even twelve thousand? Was the population predominantly "colored," as one said in those days in place of the more currently-used terms "black" or "African-American"? These are questions to ponder. One man who was a coal miner in his youth at Buxton recently maintained

that "there was not any black and white trouble in Buxton and everybody was a person." A woman who spent her childhood in Buxton now recalls that Buxton "was a kind of heaven to me, in a way of speaking, 'cause the memories were so nice." Such philosophical statements are challenges to those interested in understanding the nature of race relations and utopian communities in the United States.

Still other questions assault the archaeologist standing in the middle of a patently featureless pasture, holding a panoramic view of Buxton as photographed about 1907 in one hand and in the other hand a town plat map drawn up in 1919. Where is Main Street? Were there indeed houses on each numbered, quarter-acre lot along East Third Street—wherever that might be, up the hillslope? Where did the former residents throw out their garbage? Could we find their trash dumps? Would the refuse tell us anything about ethnicity in the town or about the generally prosperous economic conditions that reportedly existed in Buxton?

The systematic exploration of these and other questions concerning the town of Buxton was initiated under the auspices of a federal grant from the Heritage Conservation and Recreation Service to Iowa State University. The project, undertaken in cooperation with members of the Buxton, Iowa Club Inc., was facilitated by the Iowa State Historical Department's Division of Historic Preservation. Three principal approaches were utilized in the project: archival studies, oral histories, and archaeological investigations. Principal academic disciplines represented in the project included history, sociology, and archaeology.

Among the general aims of the interdisciplinary project were goals to (1) reconstruct more fully the history of Buxton, Iowa—its peoples, cultures, and contributions; (2) establish programs giving black high school and college students an opportunity to learn about their cultural heritage; and (3) facilitate future recognition and protection of the townsite. In line with these interdisciplinary goals, specific objectives for the archaeological investigation of Buxton included (1) conducting field surveys and test excavations at the townsite, (2) instituting an archaeological internship training program, with recruitment of interns being targeted principally towards descendants of former Buxton residents, and (3) collecting and documenting material cultural data of sufficient quality and quantity such that the townsite might be nominated for inclusion on the National Register of Historic Places.

*   *   *

Archaeological investigations were conducted within the townsite formerly owned by the Consolidation Coal Company: Section 4, T 73 N, R 17 W, Bluff Creek Township, Monroe County, Iowa. These investigations involved historical archaeology, that is, the study of human behavior in the past primarily through the analysis of material remains as guided and assisted by the data known from written records and oral history. Among the primary sources for archaeological investigations are portable objects (such as tools, utensils, items of clothing), structural artifacts (such as building foundations, window glass, bricks and mortar, streets), and ecofacts (such as food remains or evidences of the past environments in which humans lived). These data collected by the archaeologists supplement written records, photographs, and the memories of informants in reconstructing the cultural patterns and lifeways which obtained in Buxton during the first quarter of the twentieth century.

This book reviews the archaeological field and laboratory investigations, describes the nature of the evidence encountered, and formulates some general, though preliminary, reconstructions concerning the human activities that occurred in Buxton, as reflected in the material residues of the past. It is hoped that the Buxton case study ultimately will join the nineteenth-century black urban community of Weeksville—situated in the Bedford-Stuyvesant section of Brooklyn, New York (Bridges and Salwen 1980)—in reawakening, if not kindling, an awareness and interest in preserving ethnic history and cultural resources at local and regional levels.

*   *   *

The following discussion is divided into seven sections:

1. Review of the scope and schedule of the archaeological investigations at Buxton.
2. Consideration of the geographical context of Buxton and its position in the economic geology of the region.
3. Summary of the information obtained from the archaeological reconnaissance survey of the Buxton townsite. The general procedures of the survey are discussed in addition to a review of the data discovered in individual site survey units within the larger reconnaissance units.
4. Discussion of the results of the archaeological test excavations in the former downtown area of Buxton. This summarizes our present knowledge of the structural evidence for such buildings as the company store and stone warehouse, the pay office, the YMCA buildings, the power house, the White House Hotel, and other business/commercial buildings. In addition, several domestic areas are described, including the area around a privately owned house southeast of the company store and an area between the former East Third and East Fourth streets where company-owned houses once stood.
5. Summary of information pertaining to portable artifacts collected at the Buxton townsite. Artifacts made of ceramics, glass, metal, celluloid, rubber, shell, bone, leather, hair, textiles, paper, stone, miscellaneous materials, and composite materials are included. Remains of plants and animals are also reviewed.
6. A look at the sociocultural system of Buxton from the standpoint of historical archaeology. This discussion integrates data pertaining to (a) business, commercial, and occupational enterprises, (b) household and domestic activities, (c) transportation and communal utilities and facilities, (d) recreational activities, and (e) religious and mortuary patterns.
7. Summary and general conclusions pertaining to the quality and extent of the Buxton townsite from the viewpoint of archaeology, and to the significance of the Buxton experience from an archaeological and larger anthropological perspective.

2: Scope and schedule

AN initial task of the archaeologists involved perusing published accounts of Buxton in various regional journals, issues of the *Iowa State Bystander*, and other newspapers. Equally important was the inspection of photographs from both private collections and the Iowa State Historical Department. As transcripts of the interviews being conducted by the historians and sociologists were completed, the archaeologists reviewed these records and compiled lists of items that might be represented by the portable artifacts, structural remains, and ecofacts at the Buxton townsite. All of these historical sources were studied primarily from the standpoint of deriving specific information pertaining to the material cultural patterns of Buxton: for example, the settlement plan of the town, the nature of company houses, the construction of privately-owned homes, the location and size of public buildings, the types of food and clothing being sold in the company store and other commercial establishments in the town, and the kinds of sanitation and transportation facilities available to the residents of this community.

In addition, the archaeologists engaged independently in informal discussions on selected topics with various informants, many of whom also were being interviewed by the historians and sociologists. Of great assistance, for example, was specific information provided by Archie Harris—who grew up and worked in Buxton and still lives within the section of land

8

comprising the abandoned townsite—and by Dorothy Neal Collier and Harvey Lewis, members of the Buxton, Iowa Club Inc., who formerly resided in the town. Many others, particularly Loren Blomgren, Mabel Blomgren, Jack Jones, and the families of Pete Keegel, Case Keegel, and Joe Keegel, shared photographs and other pertinent data with the archaeologists. These people and others in the Buxton locality were able to provide a good deal of information about locations of streets and buildings prior to the abandonment of the town and the agricultural modification of the land.

INITIAL VISIT TO THE BUXTON TOWNSITE

The archaeologists were introduced to the Buxton townsite during June of 1980 by William L. Collier, member of the Buxton, Iowa Club Inc. (see Fig. 6). William was born and reared in Des Moines, where he is now a professional for a steel manufacturing firm (see Fig. 7). William's mother is Dorothy Neal Collier, who was born and spent her childhood years in Buxton (see Fig. 8). Dorothy, one of the founders of the Buxton, Iowa Club Inc., has long been engaged in research on Buxton and has shared her information with others for many years. Dorothy's father was George Neal, who came to Buxton in its early days and worked as a tailor in a shop in Coopertown, a "suburb" in Mahaska County across the road from

6. Archaeologists' initial visit to the Buxton townsite in 1980, guided by William Collier, member of the Buxton, Iowa Club Inc. Artifacts were observed along the edge of Bluff Creek. (Courtesy of the ISU Archaeological Laboratory)

7. Photograph of Dorothy Neal Collier and her son, William Collier, taken in Des Moines in 1981. Dorothy Collier is one of the founders of the Buxton, Iowa Club Inc. (Courtesy of the ISU Archaeological Laboratory)

8. Portrait of the George Neal family in Buxton, circa 1910. *Left to right:* George Neal, Dorothy Neal (Collier), Harry Neal, and Alice Mobilia Snead Neal; the dog's name was Kid. (Courtesy of Dorothy Neal Collier)

the north end of the Buxton townsite (see Fig. 9). George Neal is also remembered as a notable member of the Buxton Wonders baseball team (see Fig. 10).

In guiding the archaeologists around the former business and commercial district of Buxton, William Collier pointed out the visible ruins of the company store. His mother, he said, had told him her memories of walking along the cinder road from George Neal's house on Gobbler's Nob to the company store. Many items in the company store had attracted the young girl's eye: candy, dolls, toys, and fruit produce kept fresh by an automatic sprinkling system. William also located a linear gully along the hillslope and, referring to the 1919 plat map, identified the present surface feature as the former alignment of Buxton's Main Street (see Fig. 11). Here he noted the steep slope that his mother refers to as Coal Chute Hill. Old photographs of Buxton show the mechanical system that conveyed coal from the railroad

9. Photograph taken in a tailor shop in Coopertown in 1914. George Neal is on the right; the man at left is unidentified. The calendar on the wall advertises B. F. Cooper's Drugstore and is turned to November 1914. (Courtesy of Dorothy Neal Collier)

10. Photograph of the Buxton Wonders baseball team, probably taken circa 1911. George Neal is second from the right in the front row; Ed Peterson, the coach, is in the middle of the second row. (Courtesy of Dorothy Neal Collier)

11. William Collier showing archaeologists the remains of Buxton's Main Street along Coal Chute Hill, 1980. (Courtesy of the ISU Archaeological Laboratory)

tracks to residential neighborhoods at the top of the hill (see Fig. 12). Dorothy Collier had recalled to William stories about how she and other Buxton "kids" used to sled down this hill in the winters of her childhood.

Other structural remains at the Buxton townsite were identified by William Collier on that initial visit. The ruins observed included portions of the Consolidation Coal Company's stone warehouse, a brick vault, the YMCA buildings, and some foundations said to be surviving portions of the White House Hotel. Identification of these extant features on the land surface provided a basis for analyzing the 1919 plat map of the town and for determin-

12. View of the coal conveyor along Buxton's Main Street at the top of Coal Chute Hill, probably taken circa 1908. Note water tower to left and mule team and wagon to right. (Photo credit attributed to Wilma Stewart)

ing the degree of association of streets and buildings shown on that document with the vestiges of the community revealed in aerial photographs taken of Section 4 in 1937 and 1977.

This initial field visit was not only instructive in previewing some of the physical characteristics of the site but also in comprehending the magnitude of attempting to understand a community that once extended over more than a square mile in space. Perhaps more importantly, the visit provided a dramatic linkage between objects and people. Chunks of concrete, scattered bricks, linear depressions in the ground, pieces of broken china, and soda pop bottles were not simply generalized and impersonal fragments of material culture from some bygone era. They were part of a specific past remembered individually by people who once lived in this space and now were scattered around Iowa and farther afield throughout the United States. Similarly, the meaning of the Buxton experience extended beyond the memories of specific individuals who once lived there to the lives of their children and *their* perceptions of family history and cultural heritage. The Buxton project did not just consist of an academic pursuit of esoteric knowledge and the objective combination of documentary studies, oral history, and archaeology. It was part of an ongoing process in which individuals and groups identify in the present by reference to their shared experiences of the past.

PRELIMINARY FIELD INVESTIGATIONS, 1980

During June and July of 1980, permission was obtained from several of the principal landowners of the Buxton townsite for the archaeologists to conduct a preliminary reconnaissance and surface survey. Charles Wever, president of the Monroe County Historical Society and retired Monroe County engineer, helped the archaeologists obtain the plat maps and aerial photographs used in maintaining spatial controls in the field. Limited baseline investigations were accomplished by four trained employees of the Iowa State University Archaeological Laboratory and four students enrolled in the ISU Archaeological Field School, Anthropology 429.

Four principal tasks were undertaken during July of 1980: (1) a general reconnaissance of the entire downtown, or business-commercial, district of Buxton; (2) an initial transit survey establishing a locational grid system along the alignment and perpendicular to the former First Street (see Figs. 13 and 14); (3) a visit to the cemetery for the purpose of recording information from the gravestones that could be found within the dense cover of shrubs, weeds, and other vegetation obscuring the ground surface; and (4) a controlled surface collection in an area of approximately 50 acres near the center of the section. The latter field, which was planted to beans in the summer of 1980, had been the location of several schools, at least one church, and a number of company-owned houses. In essence, these operations indicated the generally abundant quantity and relatively good quality of archaeological data at the townsite, along with the availability of material remains pertaining to several different aspects of Buxton's social and cultural system (domestic, mortuary, commercial/industrial, and recreational).

This preliminary information, along with the establishment of an initial lo-

13. [left] Archaeologists setting out the east-west baseline at the Buxton townsite, 1980. View is to the west. (Courtesy of the ISU Archaeological Laboratory)

14. [below] View looking east along East First Street from the corner of Main and First streets sometime prior to 1912. Note the telegraph office and first company store at middle left; the main YMCA building is at the extreme right. (Courtesy of the Iowa State Historical Department)

cational system at the site, provided the basis for considering the potential of the townsite for future field investigations. Following the procedures of the Smithsonian Trinomial System, the Buxton townsite was given the official archaeological designation 13MO10: "13" stipulating Iowa in a list of alphabetically arranged states, "MO" referring to Monroe County, and "10" indicating that the Buxton townsite is the tenth archaeological site to be officially designated in Monroe County.

PRELIMINARY LABORATORY ANALYSIS, 1980–1981

During the subsequent months artifacts collected in the field were cleaned and cataloged at the Iowa State University Archaeological Laboratory. The controlled surface survey, during which materials were collected in separate quadrats measuring 100 ft square, produced a variety of portable artifacts (including broken bottles, china, crocks, toys, buttons, and tools), evidences of previous structures (including window glass, nails, brick fragments, chunks of mortar, and door hinges), and some bones of butchered animals. The general provenience of these materials was plotted by quadrat on a horizontal plan in an attempt to find some correlation between the present distribution of surface materials and the previous location of buildings and streets. Plans were made to test hypotheses concerning the location and nature of buried structures suggested by the distribution of surface artifacts within the investigated quadrats.

PLANNING THE INTERNSHIP PROGRAM

One goal of the Buxton archaeological project was to recruit interns, particularly individuals from the black community, to participate in the 1981 field season. The purpose of this phase of the project was to introduce descendants of Buxton, and other interested persons, to the techniques of studying the past via archaeology in conjunction with documentary studies and oral history. Announcements of the internship program were mailed to all members of the Buxton, Iowa Club Inc., and an advertisement was placed in the *Iowa State Bystander*. Information also was distributed through other channels, including the ISU Office of Minority Student Affairs and the Admissions Office, the National Association for Interdisciplinary Ethnic Stud-

15. Martin Peterson and Dena Bergquist Peterson, residents of the Swedish community in the Buxton area. These portraits are thought to have been taken between 1915 and 1918. (Courtesy of Nancy Wallace)

ies, and several black studies programs throughout the country. Of the four individuals who completed applications for the internship program, three were accepted. Two enrolled and completed the internship program: J. Charles Lockett (a graduate student in Afro-American Studies at the University of Iowa and the grandson of James Congress Dixon, who lived and worked in Muchakinock, the Consolidation Coal Company town antecedent to Buxton), and Olivia Smith (then an employee at the Great Plains Black Museum in Omaha). A direct Buxton descendant, Nancy Wallace, already was enrolled as an anthropology major at Iowa State University, and she elected to register for credits in the summer archaeological field school rather than applying to the project as an intern. Nancy's grandparents, Martin Peterson and Dena Bergquist Peterson, here pictured in Fig. 15, lived in the Buxton area and were active in the Swedish community there prior to moving to Des Moines.

THE 1981 FIELD SEASON

During the spring of 1981 several short field trips were made to the townsite to further investigate the cemetery and to photograph and record surface features before they were again obscured by vegetation. A large field crew returned to Buxton for intensive fieldwork during the last two weeks of June and the first three weeks of July 1981. During this time the archaeological crew lived on the William Penn College campus in Oskaloosa and commuted each day to the field to engage in reconnaissance, survey, and test excavations at the townsite. Under our direction during the 1981 field season were eleven trained workers paid from project funds, eight students registered for academic credit in the ISU Archaeological Field School, and the aforementioned two interns.

Field investigations during 1981 involved four principal operations: (1) extending the surface survey begun in 1980, as much as possible, to the entire section of land comprising the townsite; (2) mapping the visible structural remains in the downtown district of Buxton; (3) conducting selected test excavations to elucidate general architectural details of buildings being mapped and to gather associated portable artifactual data; and (4) conducting subsurface probing and/or limited test excavations to discover evidence for buried structures and other features. The location and scope of the archaeological survey and excavation activities were governed by such factors as the willingness of landowners to grant access to the land, the relatively large size of the project area, and the finite resources of time, money, and personnel available for the 1981 field season. Ultimately landowners granted permission for the field party to conduct a reconnaissance survey of slightly more than three-fourths of Section 4. Subsurface investigations were concentrated in the northern and central portions of the townsite, given that (a) this area included the entire downtown area of Buxton as well as a principal residential neighborhood and (b) the landowners involved were extremely cooperative in allowing such explorations to be conducted. The results of the 1981 field investigations are summarized in subsequent sections of this discussion.

CONTINUING LABORATORY WORK, 1981–1983

The laboratory processing and analysis of data collected in the field during the summer of 1981 began in July of that year and continued into the spring of 1983. During this time archaeological laboratory personnel and research assistants collated archival and oral historical information with archaeological data. Several students pursued topics of special interest for academic credit. These research topics included aspects of the Swedish community in Buxton, the nature of the town's regional and national economic trade patterns, and the distribution of emollient containers at the townsite in relation to the possible differential use of skin conditioners by Buxton's former residents.

Archaeological laboratory work preliminary to a final synthesis requires the completion of a number of processing and analytical operations. These procedures include washing and cleaning artifacts, stabilizing fragile items such as leather and bone, gluing together pieces of broken ceramic and glass containers, numerically cataloging each item or group of items according to the provenience in which it was found, tabulating the distribution and frequencies of all artifacts from survey units and excavations, searching through written sources to identify products according to patents and manufacturers' marks, photographing and/or preparing line drawings of representative artifacts, analysis of horizontal profiles drawn in the field and the redrawing and reduction of these as floor plans of buildings or plan views of excavation units, analysis of vertical profiles drawn in the field and the redrawing of these as schematic cross sections displaying the stratigraphy at the site, preparing various overall maps of the site, selecting photographs of the town and its former occupants to document the historical archaeology of the townsite, and collating information from previous residents regarding the identity of former structures in the town and the function of individual artifacts discovered in the field.

These time-consuming and arduous tasks must be added to the popularly conceived "romance of archaeology" in the field before any final synthesis can be achieved. In this instance artifacts in excess of 25 thousand items are at hand, in addition to some one hundred field maps and profiles, stacks of colored slides, and dozens of field notebooks. Some aspects of the total archaeological inventory still merit further analysis. For the purposes of this discussion, however, a good many summary statements and conclusions can be made on the basis of the extensive laboratory processing and analysis of field data accomplished to date.

3: Buxton's setting: geography, economic geology, and town planning

LOCATED along Bluff Creek in northern Monroe County, Buxton was situated physiographically in the Southern Iowa Drift Plain landform region (Prior 1976:45–48). The topography of this region consists of steeply rolling hills with occasional level bottomland terraces and some areas of relatively level upland divides. Throughout this region tributaries of the Des Moines River have cut down into deposits of Upper Pleistocene loess, Kansan glacial till, and underlying Carboniferous bedrocks. One of these tributaries, Bluff Creek, was explored partially as early as 1846 by David D. Owen and mentioned in his *Geological Survey of Wisconsin, Iowa, and Minnesota,* published in 1852 (Beyer and Young 1903:357).

In many respects the dissected hills of the Buxton townsite – Section 4 of Bluff Creek Township – are typical of the general landforms of the Southern Iowa Drift Plain region. On its course to the Des Moines River, Bluff Creek flows through the northwest corner of the section. Bedrock deposits are exposed upstream along the creek and in several spots along two deeply incised drainageways that empty into Bluff Creek within Section 4. The general geomorphology of the townsite can be seen on aerial photographs taken in 1937 and 1977, here reproduced as Figures 16 and 17, respectively. The

valley along Bluff Creek is relatively narrow and the surrounding range of elevations is considerable – reflected not only by vestiges of the original dendritic drainage pattern but also by the farm ponds and contour terraces built to check the hillside erosion rampant throughout this region since it was opened up to modern agriculture.

The soils in Section 4 are expressive of not only the underlying geological strata but also the native vegetational assemblages. Published surveys of this locality (Orrben and Tharp 1931; Brown et al. 1936) describe the upland soils as Weller silt loam and Grundy silt loam, developed from loess deposits, and as Shelby silt loam and Lindley silt loam, developed from glacial till. These surveys show Dubuque silt loam, developed from residual bedrock, along the hillslopes and Wabash silt loam, derived from alluvium, on the bottomlands. More recent soil descriptions (Oschwald et al. 1965) and the soil survey presently being completed for Monroe County (USDA 1981) provide more precise detail. Predominant in the eastern half of Section 4 are upland soils mapped as Mahaska, Otley, and Taintor, which are derived from loess and reflect a native prairie vegetation. An upland prairie regime is also represented by a small area of Lamoni soil, developed from glacial till, in the

16. Aerial view, Section 4 of Bluff Creek Township, Monroe County, Iowa, taken in 1937. (Courtesy of the ISU Archaeological Laboratory)

northwest corner of the section. Upland divides in the northern and western parts of Section 4 are mapped as Ladoga and Pershing soils, which are derived from a parent material of loess under a native vegetation of mixed prairie and forest. On the upper hillslopes, developing from shale bedrock residuum, are soils mapped as Gosport and Bauer, which reflect, respectively, forest and prairie plant assemblages. The lower hillslopes and terraces in Section 4 consist of soils developed from alluvium: the Ely and Colo-Ely-Judson complex, which once consisted of prairie, and the Okah soil, which originally supported a forest cover. The bottomlands along Bluff Creek and the large tributary drainageways are mapped as Colo, Lawson, Koszia, and Vesser—soils developed from silty alluvium and reflecting a native prairie vegetation.

According to the map of Monroe County in the Andreas atlas, during the 1870s woods covered the northwestern two-thirds of Section 4 except for an "island" of upland prairie that extended into Section 5 (Andreas 1875:70). The Andreas map shows the southeastern one-third of Section 4 in prairie. In 1903 L. H. Pammel noted that most of the best timber in this area had been removed during the period of early Euro-American settlement, and that much of the second growth of trees had suffered from dry weather and over-grazing during the late nineteenth century (Pammel 1903:423). Previously, scattered groves of cottonwood and willow trees grew along the bottomlands and lower terraces of this region, while the hillslopes and some upland summits supported stands of walnut, hickory, basswood, maple, ash, wild cherry, plum, and some oak.

From the standpoint of economic geology if nothing else, Buxton owed its existence to the presence of coal in the underlying bedrocks of Monroe County and its environs. Below the deposits of loess and glacial till in this region are extensive Carboniferous strata (Beyer and Young 1903:363–77). Upper Carboniferous or Pennsylvanian formations of the Des Moines Stage include the Chariton conglomerate, the Appanoose limestone, and the Monroe beds of sandstone, shale, and coal. The latter beds were referred to as the "Coal Measures" and were the formation of primary economic importance. Below these strata were Lower Carboniferous or Mississippian limestone, sandstone, and shale formations of the St. Louis Stage.

17. Aerial view, Section 4 of Bluff Creek Township, Monroe County, Iowa, taken in 1977. (Courtesy of the ISU Archaeological Laboratory)

18. The outfitted Buxton mine rescue squad in front of their special rescue car, circa 1914. (Courtesy of Nancy Wallace)

The early history of coal mining in Iowa has been dealt with extensively elsewhere (Hinds 1909; Lees 1909; Olin 1965) and need not be handled in detail here. Several salient points, however, are relevant to understanding the town of Buxton and its relationship to the coal mining operations of the Consolidation Coal Company at the turn of the century. During the 1870s, the Consolidation Coal Company, under superintendent John E. Buxton, had established a company town called Muchakinock in Mahaska County south of Oskaloosa. During the 1890s the superintendency of the company passed from John E. Buxton to his son, Ben C. Buxton. By 1900, for a variety of economic reasons, the Consolidation Coal Company decided to extend its operations farther west in Mahaska and Monroe counties, and they moved their company town from Muchakinock to a new settlement, which they called Buxton. The coal mines worked by the colliers living in Buxton were some distance from the town but were primarily within Bluff Creek Township of Monroe County and Jefferson Township of Mahaska County (Beyer and Young 1903:394–98; Hinds 1909:232; Lees 1909:545–50 and 556–61). Alex Erickson, who lived in Buxton and worked as a coal miner there, recalled the location of ten mines operated by Consolidation Coal Company in Monroe and Mahaska counties while Buxton was in existence (Alex Erick-son, personal communication 1981). Former Buxton residents have vivid memories of the trains that transported the miners to and from the outlying mines each day; the trains and miners also appear in a number of photographs from that period (see Fig. 18).

The potential for coal mining in the Buxton locality, particularly along Bluff Creek, was discussed by Charles A. White (1870:267–68) in his early review of the geology of Iowa's "coal counties." Some coal for local wintertime use was extracted from openings along Bluff Creek as early as 1881 (Beyer and Young 1903:394). Almost 20 years passed, however, before the coal resources of the Bluff Creek Basin began to be exploited intensively. The events that followed resulted in an economic boom for Monroe County and the establishment of the settlement at Buxton. In the words of geologists S. W. Beyer and L. E. Young (1903: 394–95):

It was not until 1901 that the district became a real factor in the coal production of the county and in 1902 the basin became a most important mining community in the state. In 1900 and 1901 the Consolidation Coal Company founded the town of Buxton on the extension of the Muchakinock branch of the Chicago & Northwestern railway and opened mine number 10 about two miles south of the town. In 1901 and 1902 the company put down shaft No. 11, which is located about a mile south of number 10. Both shafts are in full operation at the present time, while shafts 12 and 13 are being sunk.

Stratigraphic sections reported for mines number 10 and 11 indicate that they contained up to seven coal seams ranging from six inches to over six feet in thickness. The impacts of Consolidation Coal Company operations in Monroe County were immediate and dramatic. According to Beyer and Young (1903:382), Monroe County coal production for 1901 exceeded that for 1900 by more than 25%—the unusual increase resulting from the Consolidation Coal Company mines in the Bluff Creek Basin. By 1901 Monroe County had surpassed Mahaska County in Iowa's bituminous coal industry, becoming the "banner county both in total output and the number of men employed"; and during the following year "Monroe more firmly established her supremacy as the ranking mining community in the state, mining being second only to agriculture" (Beyer and Young 1903:356–57).

A comparison of Monroe County plat maps for the years 1896, 1919, and 1937 shows the radical changes in land use that occurred in Section 4 of Bluff Creek Township in less than four decades (see Fig. 19). Section 4 originally comprised a small number of large tracts representing agricultural fields. Then it was transformed into an urban community subdivided into many small lots for houses and businesses (see also 1919 Buxton town plat map, Fig. 4). Finally, the section reverted into a small number of relatively large farm units. To anthropologists particularly interested in studying the nature of settlement patterns, the specific time

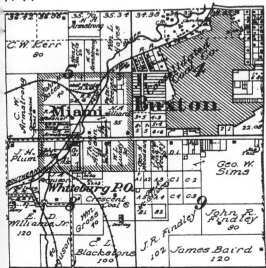

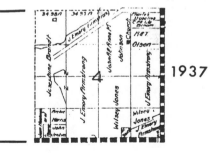

19. Sequence of plat map segments illustrating the fluctuation in settlement and land use within Section 4, Bluff Creek Township, from 1896 to 1937. (Adapted from maps published by Northwest Publishing Co. in 1896 and Geo. A. Ogle and Co. in 1919 and from the plat book for Monroe County of 1937)

framework and mechanics of setting up the new urban community at Buxton are especially intriguing. How large was the town's population? How fast did it grow? What were the factors determining the form of the settlement? What processes were involved in assembling a relatively large population at this location?

Just how quickly Buxton grew after it was established during the second half of the year 1900 is not clear. Nor is it entirely certain exactly how large the town ultimately became. We do know that at the time the 1900 federal census was taken, Consolidation Coal Company's base of operation was still at Muchakinock. Shortly thereafter the move to the Buxton townsite was launched. According to Rye's (1972:943) quotation of federal and state census figures, the population of Bluff Creek Township rose from 998 in the year 1900 to 4874 in 1905; and the population of Jefferson Township in Mahaska County rose from 969 in 1900 to 2164 in 1905.

At a national level the speed of Buxton's growth and the uniqueness of the town's population were noted in publications such as *The Southern Workman.* Writing in 1908, Richard R. Wright, Jr. (1908:494) commented, "Ten years ago, Buxton, Iowa was not on the map. To-day it is a thriving mining town of more than 5000 inhabitants, having perhaps a larger number of Negroes than any other town north of Missouri and west of the Mississippi." Furthermore, Wright observed that Buxton was established by B. C. Buxton, who "conceived the idea of building a Negro town, and doing, along with his business, some real philanthropic work among the Negroes." Thus we conclude that a considerably large population assembled with fair speed at Buxton under the benevolent

organization of the Consolidation Coal Company.

Although Consolidation Coal Company's town holdings were restricted to Section 4 of Bluff Creek Township in Monroe County, it should be noted that the population of Buxton extended across the county line into Jefferson Township of Mahaska County – particularly in "suburbs" such as Gainestown and Coopertown. Hedge (1906:78) observed in his history of Mahaska County that Buxton "lies mostly across the line in Monroe County, but has several hundred of its population in this county." Indeed, some county plat maps of Mahaska County even extend the southern limits of Jefferson Township into Monroe County so as to include the larger portion of Buxton. The manuscript *Census Register* for 1905, furthermore, includes members of a number of Buxton families who actually resided in Mahaska County – for example, the Baxter, Blomgren, Cooper, Cruickshank, Fields, Gaines, Harris, London, Schipper, Shelton, Thomas, and Williams families. These people and others were prominent in the history of Buxton, and many living descendants of these families served as informants during this study. Others are mentioned in published sources or referred to in the interviews conducted during the recent project. Suffice it to say that any estimate of Buxton's population must take into account those people living in Mahaska County as well as Monroe County. Other statistics from a secondary source support the general demographic configuration indicated above: *Polk's Iowa Gazetteer* listed the Buxton population as 2500 in its 1903–1904 edition and as 5000 in its 1905–1906 edition (R. L. Polk and Co. 1904:241; 1906:250).

Buxton's population appears to have grown after 1905 and may have peaked about 1910 or shortly thereafter, according to Rye's (1972:943) analysis of census data from Bluff Creek and Jefferson townships. Rye allowed for 1000 permanent residents in each township and then concluded that "this leaves slightly more than 5,500 people in the Buxton area. (The camp was spread out with several 'suburbs.') Further assuming that it would not be too difficult for the census takers to miss five hundred in such a mining camp atmosphere, this would place the total at 6,000." Although it cannot be considered as authoritative a source as the census records, *Polk's Iowa Gazetteer* lists Buxton's population as 6000 in its entries for 1913 and 1914 (R. L. Polk and Co. 1913:242; 1915:239). By 1915, however, the population of Bluff Creek and Jefferson townships had declined, and it continued to do so for the next ten years (Rye 1972:943). Buxton's decline may have been a slower process than its birth; by 1925, however, the townsite was virtually abandoned.

In addition to the relatively rapid population growth at Buxton, the establishment of the settlement appears to have been methodically planned. Included in Beyer and Young's (1903:394, Fig. 68) discussion of the geology of Monroe County is a photograph of Buxton taken from the west in 1902 or 1903. The photograph is not clear, but rows of uniform house structures can be seen in addition to what seem to be several large buildings in the downtown district. The form of the town at that time quite obviously corresponds to the essential pattern revealed in photographs taken a few years later (see Figs. 2 and 3) and to the orderly layout of the town as drawn on the 1919 plat map (see Fig. 4). Beyer and Young's (1903:395) observations in 1903 lend credence to this view:

> Buxton is an ideal mining town. It was laid out on a rolling hillside facing north and west. Houses are better built and larger than those usually provided in mining camps. They average one full story and a half and are well kept. The streets are regularly laid out and the town as a whole presents a thrifty appearance.

Indeed the settlement pattern appears to have been thought out well beforehand and then executed in a systematic manner.

The planned community provided a centralized business and commercial district with water and electrical utilities, cultural and recreational facilities – including two YMCA buildings, an artificial lake, a ball park, and a carnival ground – a regularized system of streets, space for schools and churches, large lots that could accommodate gardens and some livestock, relatively well-built houses for rent by company workers, and areas for the construction of privately owned homes.

Architectural drawings on file at the Iowa State Historical Department indicate that W. A. Wells and the Consolidation Coal Company secured the services of Frank E. Wetherell, a noted regional architect, in designing many of the buildings in Buxton. Wetherell's firm was based originally in Oskaloosa and later moved to Des Moines, where it operates today. Between 1901 and 1904 Frank Wetherell drew up plans for the African Methodist Episcopal Church, the Mount Zion Baptist Church, the high school, an "eight-holer" outhouse (presumably for the high school), and the model of the miners' houses, with associated cisterns. Wetherell may have been the architect for some of Buxton's other downtown buildings and might even have contributed ideas to the town's original plan. In this case, the architects and engineers who designed the physical layout of Buxton appear to have anticipated by several decades the application of scientific planning to the creation of company mining towns (cf. Lohmann 1915; Magnusson 1920:27–40 et passim).

To be sure, aspects of the settlement pattern related to the local topographic setting: (1) the railroad followed along low terraces above the right bank of Bluff Creek; (2) the business district was located within the valley on terraces and toeslopes adjacent to the railroad; (3) the residential area extended up the hillslopes, along the ravines, and on the uplands south and east of the business district; (4) two or three streets appear to have followed the alignment of ravines; and (5) the superintendent's house was situated above the left bank of Bluff Creek, figuratively as well as literally above and isolated from the townspeople within view across the valley.

Perhaps even more striking, however, is an apparent lack of concordance of the settlement pattern with specific topographic features of the site. The grid of numbered streets parallels the alignment of the railroad but does not seem to have much relationship to the contours of the hills and ravines. It is possible, though not probable, that the 1919 plat map was somewhat more idealized than accurate. Analysis of the map in the field, however, suggests to the archaeologists that this is not the case—except for the route of West Fourth Street, which is shown extending *over* or *through* the reservoir into West Swede Town! Otherwise, the plat map and available photographs indicate that the numbered streets and several unnamed per-

pendicular streets did indeed cross hill and dale, traversing "thick and thin" along lines presumably preconceived by the architects of the town.

In sum, the settlement pattern of Buxton reflects a template from the urban scene superimposed upon the rural countryside. In size, plan, and organization Buxton cannot really be referred to as a "camp," as it often has been called. Such a term fails to distinguish Buxton from the smaller, shorter-lived, and less complexly organized mining communities more typical of this region (Rutland 1956). On the other hand, the term "metropolis" appears to be a somewhat extravagant label for Buxton in a demographic sense if not in the sociological connotation many people may have of the former community (*Iowa State Bystander* 15 January 1909 and 24 October 1919; Rye 1972:247). But Buxton *was* certainly a sizeable and well-planned town by Iowa standards of both then and now. Furthermore, the settlement lasted for nearly a quarter of a century, had a black population of relative proportions never before or after paralleled in Iowa, and offered its residents a range of amenities and cultural facilities virtually unheard of in mining communities of that period and, for that matter, absent in many towns throughout the region today. Buxton was the product of rather specific circumstances stemming from its geographic and geological setting, the socioeconomic milieu of the coal mining and transportation industries at the turn of the century, and some farsighted efforts in urban community planning. In these respects as well as others, the Buxton settlement was unusual, if not unique.

4: Archaeological reconnaissance survey of the townsite

THE surface survey of the Buxton townsite followed procedures previously employed by ISU Archaeological Laboratory personnel in the Saylorville Reservoir project (Gradwohl and Osborn 1973:15–19) and the Ames Reservoir project (Gradwohl and Osborn 1972:20–27). The entire project area, in this instance Section 4 of Bluff Creek Township, was divided into primary target areas referred to as *reconnaissance units*. These reconnaissance units were delimited along the property lines of the present landowners. Within each reconnaissance unit, assuming the landowners granted permission for the field party to enter their property, the archaeologists conducted a surface inspection as appropriate to ground cover conditions and uses of the land.

Areas actually explored by surface reconnaissance procedures were designated *site survey units*. For the purposes of spatial control the boundaries of site survey units were often determined by fence lines or in some instances by topographic features separating pasturelands, fields supporting crops of hay or oats, or fields being cultivated for the growing of row crops. These differing and changing modern land uses, of course, greatly influence the quantity and quality of data that can be obtained during a surface recon-

naissance survey. Artifacts collected from each site survey unit were bagged separately for further processing and analysis. Oftentimes closer spatial control was maintained by designating specific collection areas within site survey units. During the surface survey the proveniences of these collection areas and of observed structural remains were marked on an enlarged copy of the 1977 aerial photograph. This, in essence, served as a base map.

The information derived from the surface survey provides a basis for a preliminary evaluation of the distribution of extant cultural resources within the townsite. These data also have furnished a baseline for planning future field investigations at Buxton and for considering the eligibility of the townsite for inclusion on the National Register of Historic Places.

In general the categories of information observed in the field and discussed below include the following: (1) some existing remains of buildings and associated features—foundation remnants, collapsed "caves" or storm cellars, abandoned cisterns and wells; (2) some evidence of transportation networks—the main railroad bed, sections of street alignments, bridges, and culverts; (3) portions of the centralized water control facilities and distribution system to the commerical/business district—the reservoir, the concrete spill-way, the breached earthen dam, and water pipes; (4) portions of the central-ized downtown heating and sanitation systems—rubble tentatively identified as ruins of the power plant, steam pipes, sewage conduits, and toilet facil-ities; (5) some vegetational evidence of former flower and vegetable gardens; (6) numerous localized garbage dumps; and (7) generalized scatters of refuse that may reflect sheet midden deposits, destruction debris, and/or materials distributed by plowing and other mod-ern land use activities.

The information available from each reconnaissance unit in the Buxton townsite is discussed in the following pages. For each site survey unit inves-tigated in the field, the following data are summarized: (1) general location within Section 4, (2) relationship to the corresponding area on the 1919 plat map, (3) present land use conditions, (4) nature of the surface reconnais-sance and information, where appropri-ate, from informants and old photo-graphs, (5) structural remains, if any, observed during the surface inspec-tion, and (6) portable artifactual and ecofactual remains collected or ob-served. Throughout the following dis-cussion, correspondences to the 1919 plat map can be checked by referring to Figure 4. Further spatial controls and associations with present land use conditions can be checked by referring to the 1937 aerial photograph of Sec-tion 4 (Fig. 16) and the 1977 aerial pho-tograph of the townsite (Fig. 17). Fig-ure 20 is a graphic representation of the site survey units, and Figures 21 and 22 present a tabular summary of general classes of portable artifacts and ecofacts collected within the site survey units.

RECONNAISSANCE UNIT B

Reconnaissance Unit B consists of the Blomgren property located in the northeast corner of Section 4. Various informants have stated that this por-tion of Buxton was known as East Swede Town, although that designation does not appear on the 1919 plat map. The plat map shows the easternmost part of this area (NE¼, NE¼, NE¼ of Section 4) divided into nine unnum-bered property units, each approxi-mately one acre in size. The plat also shows the location of a church and a single unnamed street, oriented north-south, in this portion of Buxton. The land directly to the west on the plat map (NW¼, NE¼, NE¼ of Section 4) is not divided except for several num-bered, quarter-acre lots at the east end of A Street and East First Street corre-sponding to the western edge of Re-connaissance Unit B.

As a part of the field survey of Re-connaissance Unit B, members of the field party talked to the present prop-erty owners, Loren and Mabel Blom-gren and their father, Emanuel Blom-gren. The Blomgrens not only allowed the field party to conduct a surface re-connaissance of their property, but they also provided a good deal of oral historical data about Buxton and gen-erously invited the inspection of some written documents, photographs, and other materials in their collection (Ma-bel, Loren, and Emanuel Blomgren; personal communications 1981). Emanuel Blomgren was born in Much-akinock, moved to Buxton with his family soon after the town was es-tablished, and went to work in the mines of the Consolidation Coal Com-pany when he was about fourteen years old. The Blomgrens have a por-tion of a record book, handwritten in

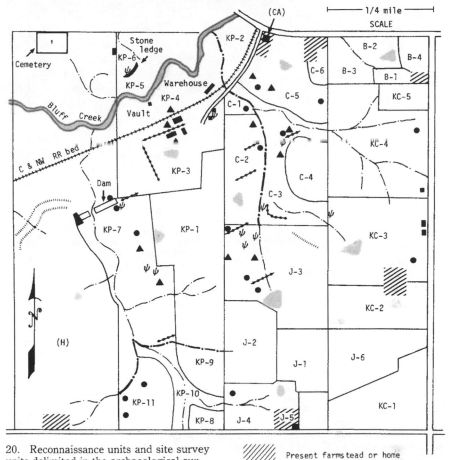

20. Reconnaissance units and site survey units delimited in the archaeological surface survey of Section 4, Bluff Creek Township. Surficial features pertinent to the occupation of the Buxton townsite are noted.

/////	Present farmstead or home
(grey shape)	Modern farm pond
ξ,,,	Modern terrace
—·—	Extant drainage or ravine
B-1	Site survey unit
■	Standing building or structural remains of former town
▲	Construction debris
●	Cistern or well
••••••	Linear feature (street)
ψ	Botanical evidence

Swedish, of the Swedish Lutheran Church from the 1890s when the congregation was still in Muchakinock. The church building was moved from Muchakinock to its location in Buxton (East Swede Town), where it stood until it burned down on 21 December 1954 (see Fig. 23). Mabel Blomgren re-

Site Survey Units	China tableware and containers or sherds	Stoneware containers or sherds	Miscellaneous ceramics	Transparent glass containers or fragments and closures	Milk glass containers and lid liners	Miscellaneous glass objects	Brick, mortar, and other construction materials*	Metal artifacts	Leather, cloth, and rubber artifacts	Miscellaneous wood, bone, stone, shell, etc.	Site Survey Unit Totals	Reconnaissance Unit Totals
B-1	47	5	...	18	9	2	1	6	...	1	89	
B-2	2	2	...	5	...	1	...	...	...	...	10	284
B-3	42	15	...	17	8	3	1	2	...	...	88	
B-4	45	13	...	34	5	...	...	...	...	...	97	
KC-1	5	3	...	31	1	...	...	2	...	2	44	
KC-2	6	1	...	4	2	...	...	...	...	1	14	
KC-3	18	1	1	44	3	...	1	4	...	...	72	260
KC-4	19	6	2	26	4	1	...	5	1	...	64	
KC-5	28	5	2	25	4	...	...	2	...	...	66	
J (general-donation)	1	...	2	4	1	...	...	11	...	...	19	
J-1	755	227	38	1088	125	5	...	15	1	4	2258	
J-2	505	61	18	431	75	5	...	12	1	...	1108	3808
J-3	60	24	...	125	8	3	...	13	10	3	246	
J-4	17	20	2	30	7	1	1	12	...	2	92	
J-5	...	...	...	...	...	...	...	...	...	...	0	
J-6	41	7	1	26	8	...	...	...	...	2	85	
C-1	14	...	1	16	...	...	...	...	...	...	31	
C-2	104	24	5	217	23	2	...	12	...	1	388	
C-3	160	102	2	255	42	...	...	25	51	3	640	1890
C-4	...	...	...	...	...	...	...	...	...	...	0	
C-5	123	25	2	114	14	...	...	5	1	1	285	
C-6	249	68	7	177	34	2	...	7	...	2	546	

GRAND TOTAL: 6242

21. Tabular summary of general categories of portable artifacts found in the eastern half of the Buxton townsite, 1980 and 1981. (*During the 1981 field season, only selected constructional materials were picked up during the reconnaissance survey; other materials were observed but were not collected.)

23. Swedish Lutheran Church formerly located in Buxton's East Swede Town. (Courtesy of Mabel Blomgren)

called that the church had stained glass windows colored blue, pink, and white. After the church burned down she found and saved a fragment of the blue stained glass. Mabel Blomgren has scrapbooks containing photographs of Buxton and of the Swedish Lutheran Church, which continued to be used long after the demise of the town.

At the time the field survey was conducted, this entire portion of the townsite was in pasture or under cultivation for the production of hay. Part of the

Site Survey Units	China tableware and containers or sherds	Stoneware containers or sherds	Miscellaneous ceramics	Transparent glass containers or fragments and closures	Milk glass containers and lid liners	Miscellaneous glass objects	Brick, mortar, and other construction materials*	Metal artifacts	Leather, cloth, and rubber artifacts	Miscellaneous wood, bone, stone, shell, etc.	Site Survey Unit Totals
KP-1, 1980 Controlled quadrat survey	1962	661	68	3178	394	33		165	7	100	6568
KP-2	...	...	...	1	...	...	...	...	...	...	1
KP-3	8	4	2	30	...	10	...	8	...	4	66
KP-4	23	10	17	39	16	30	1	171	108	37	452
KP-5	...	...	...	...	...	...	...	...	...	...	0
KP-6	...	...	...	1	...	...	...	...	...	...	1
KP-7	183	117	17	454	30	8	...	37	97	27	970
KP-8	6	3	...	3	...	...	...	...	...	...	12
KP-9	68	19	2	70	10	...	...	1	...	...	170
KP-10	43	41	4	227	14	11	...	22	36	6	404
KP-11	7	3	2	43	5	...	1	4	...	...	65

GRAND TOTAL: 8709

22. Tabular summary of general categories of portable artifacts found in the western half of the Buxton townsite, 1980 and 1981. (*During the 1980 controlled quadrat survey of SSU KP-1, transparent glass and milk glass artifacts were lumped together for the purposes of the distributional analysis. This procedure was changed for the reconnaissance survey conducted during the 1981 field season.)

land surface had been modified by the construction of a farm pond subsequent to the abandonment of the town. Reconnaissance Unit B was divided into four site survey units (SSUs).

A surface survey of *SSU B-1*, presently in pasture, failed to reveal any in situ remains of the Swedish Lutheran Church (see Fig. 24). Construction materials, including some chunks of limestone, pieces of brick, and fragments of mortar, were observed but not collected along Blomgren's south fence line. These materials may represent debris from the church foundation, but this fact cannot be demonstrated definitely at the present time. Artifacts collected in SSU B-1 include 47 china tableware and container fragments, 5 stoneware container fragments (including the lid of a snuff jar), 18 transparent glass container fragments, 9 milk

24. Archaeological reconnaissance crew inspecting the location of the former Swedish Lutheran Church in Site Survey Unit B-1, 1981. View is to the east. (Courtesy of the ISU Archaeological Laboratory)

glass fragments, 2 miscellaneous glass objects, a fragment of linoleum, 6 metal objects (including a hinge), and a whetstone.

SSU B-2 was also in pastureland and surrounded the recently constructed farm pond. Only 10 artifacts were collected from this site survey unit: 2 china tableware or container fragments, 2 stoneware container fragments, 5 transparent glass fragments, and 1 miscellaneous glass object.

SSU B-3, located to the southwest of a small ravine containing some relatively recent debris, was planted in alfalfa during the 1981 field season. This field was inspected immediately after the hay crop had been cut in early July. In spite of the relatively poor surface visibility in this site survey unit, 88 artifacts were collected. These included 42 china tableware or container fragments, 15 fragments of stoneware, 17 pieces of transparent glass containers, 8 milk glass fragments, 3 miscellaneous glass objects, a brick, and 2 metal artifacts.

SSU B-4 also was planted in alfalfa and was similarly investigated subsequent to the cutting of the hay crop. The surface of SSU B-4 yielded 97 artifacts: 45 china fragments, 13 stoneware pieces (including a small crock lid), 34 transparent glass fragments, and 5 milk glass specimens (including a small cosmetic jar). In sum, Reconnaissance Unit B did not reveal a large number of surface artifacts or definable concentrations of materials. This is not surprising given the extant land use and ground cover conditions. In addition, one might hypothesize from the 1919 plat map that this area of Buxton was less densely settled than the central portion of the town. Thus the fact that a significant number of artifacts showed up at all on the present ground

surface may indicate the potential for subsurface pits filled with debris from the occupation of East Swede Town.

RECONNAISSANCE UNIT KC

Reconnaissance Unit KC consisted of the property presently owned by the Case Keegel family along the eastern side of Section 4. According to the 1919 plat map, much of this area consisted of relatively large parcels of land owned by W. J. Jones, W. R. Jones, Susie Jones, C. R. Foster, and H. A. Armstrong. The name H. A. ("Hobe") Armstrong appears frequently in discussions of Buxton (cf. Swisher 1945:179; Rye 1972:941–42.) At one time he was referred to as the "richest colored man in Iowa" (*Iowa State Bystander,* 27 December 1912). Hobe Armstrong was a businessman in Muchakinock, a recruiter for the Consolidation Coal Company of black miners in the south, and the owner of a meat market and several properties in Buxton. Case Keegel (personal communication 1981) indicated that he had purchased some of his property from the Armstrong family.

The northern portion of Reconnaissance Unit KC corresponds to large, unnumbered lots in the area of Buxton referred to as East Swede Town. The plat map shows a building marked "school" in this area, directly southwest of the "church" (Swedish Lutheran Church) that once stood on the property presently owned by the Blomgren family. The plat map also shows numbered, quarter-acre lots along the eastern ends of streets between East Second and East Seventh streets. In addition there are some numbered, quarter-acre lots shown along two unnamed east-west streets leading into the central part of town from the section road east of Section 4. Today most of this portion of Section 4 is in pastureland and fields being cultivated for the growing of hay, oats, and row crops. Within the northern end of the property there are the upper reaches of the large, tree-filled ravine that runs westward onto the property presently owned by the Carter family. Toward the center of Reconnaissance Unit KC a farm pond has been constructed to prevent further headland erosion along the ravine and to provide water for livestock. For the purposes of this investigation, Reconnaissance Unit KC was divided into five site survey units.

SSU KC-1 is an irregularly shaped field at the southeast corner of Section 4 and was planted in corn during the summer of 1981. This area, essentially the southeast diagonal half of the SE¼ of the SE¼ of the section, shows up clearly on the 1919 plat map as an undivided property owned by H. A. Armstrong. Directly north of this property on the plat map are numbered, quarter-acre lots at the end of East Fourteenth Street, an area presently owned by the Jones family and here referred to as SSU J-6. The fence line now separating the C. Keegel and Jones properties appears to follow the alignment of East Fourteenth Street west from the section road; it then turns south and west, apparently along the back of the numbered lots formerly platted to the south of East Fourteenth Street. In spite of optimal reconnaissance survey conditions, relatively few artifacts were observed in this field. The paucity of materials is compatible with the likelihood that this area never did contain dwellings or other permanent structures. Of the 44 artifacts collected in SSU KC-1, there were 5 china tableware or container fragments, 3 stoneware sherds, 31 transparent glass container frag-

ments, 1 piece of milk glass, 2 metal artifacts (including a horse or mule shoe), and 2 pieces of slate or shale.

SSU KC-2, a field located directly south of the Case Keegel home, was planted in oats during the 1981 field season. On the 1919 plat map most of this area is not subdivided, the exception being a row of numbered lots north of an unnamed, east-west street extending west from the section road into the town along the line between the SE¼ and NE¼ of the SE¼ of Section 4. SSU KC-2 was inspected soon after the oats had been harvested and, although surface visibility was not optimal, some materials could be seen. In addition to scattered pieces of bricks and mortar, which were observed but not collected, the following 14 artifacts were obtained: 6 china fragments, 1 stoneware sherd, 4 transparent glass pieces, 2 milk glass fragments, and 1 piece of slate or shale.

SSU KC-3 is large pasture north of the Case Keegel home. The southern portion of this site survey unit corresponds to several relatively large parcels of land that, according to the 1919 plat map, were owned by W. R. Jones, W. J. Jones, Susie Jones, and C. R. Foster. The northern end of SSU KC-3 corresponds to an area on the 1919 plat map that includes (1) a large lot belonging to H. A. Armstrong along the section road at the eastern edge of Section 4, (2) an unnamed street extending west from the Armstrong lot into the town along an alignment north of the east-west center section line, (3) a row of numbered, quarter-acre lots directly south of the unnamed east-west street, and (4) numbered, quarter-acre lots on the north side of the end of East Seventh Street. Subsequent to the abandonment of Buxton, a farm pond was constructed in the west central portion of SSU KC-3 to check erosion at the end of a ravine running northwest into the property presently owned by the Carters. Along the upper reaches of that portion of the ravine can be seen debris that postdates the Buxton urban settlement.

The field reconnaissance of SSU KC-3 revealed evidence of several former structures: (1) ruins of a rectangular, flat-roofed root cellar, or "cave," of mortared brick and stone; (2) ruins of a rectangular, brick root cellar with a domed roof and square facade, shown here in Figure 25; (3) a small round depression, possibly marking the location of a previous well or cistern; and (4) a row of rose bushes, perhaps marking the edge of a previous lot or fence line. At least one of the two root cellar structures appears to have been associated with Hobe Armstrong's lot. Case Keegel (personal communication 1981) was of this opinion and remembered also a house structure that formerly stood near the "caves." He recalled that the Armstrongs moved that house from this location to another property owned by their family outside Section 4.

Although the ground cover in the pasture inhibited optimal surface visibility, cultural materials were observed in SSU KC-3, especially at spots where burrowing animals had disturbed the ground. In addition to some scattered cinders and pieces of brick, mortar, and window glass that were observed but not picked up, an inventory of 72 artifacts was collected in SSU KC-3: 18 china fragments, 1 stoneware sherd, 1 ceramic doorknob, 44 fragments of transparent glass containers, 3 milk glass fragments, 4 metal artifacts (including a horseshoe and a zinc jar lid fragment), and 1 brick marked "A. P. Green."

25. Ruins of a brick-walled "cave" or root cellar within Site Survey Unit KC-3, 1981. View is to the south. (Courtesy of the ISU Archaeological Laboratory)

SSU KC-4 is a large field covering the majority of the SE¼ of the NE¼ of Section 4 and part of the adjoining NE¼ of the NE¼ of the section. The 1919 plat map shows the eastern portion of this area divided into unnumbered property units of one or two acres in size along an unnamed, north-south aligned street that continues on through the area referred to by former Buxton residents as East Swede Town. The western part of SSU KC-4 corresponds to the eastern ends of streets between East Second and East Sixth streets on the town plat. Bordering these streets, except along the margins of the ravine, are quarter-acre lots, most of which are numbered.

During the 1981 field season SSU KC-4 was planted in alfalfa and was not yet mowed at the time the field reconnaissance crew was conducting the surface survey. Hence the ground surface could not be inspected effectively. Except for checking out two surface anomalies close to the section road, the reconnaissance of SSU KC-4 consisted of walking around the periphery of the field and searching exposures along the large ravine. Two structural features were observed: (1) the ruins of a brick root cellar, or "cave," and (2) a small, circular depression partially lined with bricks, probably representing an abandoned cistern or well. An inventory of 64 portable artifacts was collected in this site survey unit: 19 china tableware or container fragments, 6 stoneware pieces, 2 miscellaneous ceramic artifacts (a drawer pull and a doorknob with a locking mechanism), 26 fragments of transparent glass containers, a portion of a glass kerosene lamp chimney, 4 milk glass pieces, 5 metal artifacts (including an iron stove door, a buckle, and a hitch pin), and a portion of a leather boot or shoe.

SSU KC-5, a small field at the northeast corner of Reconnaissance Unit KC, consisted of a pasture and livestock lot at the time the archaeologists visited the site. This area, directly south of the former Swedish Lutheran Church, is within the part of Buxton referred to as East Swede Town. The 1919 plat map shows this area divided into unnumbered lots of approximately one acre in size. The aforementioned unnamed north-south street also bisects this unit of the town. At a location corresponding to the northwest corner of SSU KC-5, the plat map shows a building marked "school." Presumably this designates the school associated with the church and attended by children of the East Swede Town neighborhood, according to Archie Harris and Alex Erickson (personal communications 1981) and other former residents of Buxton.

The surface of SSU KC-5 yielded 66 artifacts. Given the mediocre surface visibility and the small size of SSU KC-5, this collection indicates a higher potential for cultural materials in East Swede Town than demonstrable from the present data available from the contiguous site survey units where the ground cover is even more dense. Included in the inventory of specimens from SSU KC-5 are 28 fragments of china tableware or containers, 5 stoneware sherds, 2 miscellaneous ceramic artifacts (a china doll fragment and an insulator), 25 transparent glass container fragments, 4 pieces of milk glass (including a small jar), and 2 metal artifacts (including a railroad spike).

RECONNAISSANCE UNIT J

Reconnaissance Unit J consists of the property presently owned by the Jack Jones family in the southeastern quarter of Section 4. On the 1919 Buxton town map, nearly all of this area appears platted as quarter-acre lots along streets between East Sixth and East Fourteenth streets. The map shows the southern end of Main Street cutting diagonally through the western end of the SW¼ of the SE¼ of Section 4. Quarter-acre lots are platted to the west along streets between West Tenth and West Fourteenth streets. A wide, unnamed street is shown running north-south along the center section line from the road at the south edge of Section 4 to the corner of Ninth and Main streets in Buxton. Several smaller unnamed and irregularly spaced streets, mostly running parallel to Main Street, are also indicated within this part of the plat map. A large, undivided lot owned by John Baxter is shown on the plat map at the south central edge of the property designated Reconnaissance Unit J. The Jones family's present home is situated on land corresponding to a portion of the Baxter lot on the old town plat.

Today most of the land within Reconnaissance Unit J is in pasture or fields being cultivated for the production of

row crops and hay. The heads of two
ravines exist in the southwestern and
north-central portions of the reconnaissance unit. To check erosion along
these ravines, two farm ponds were
constructed subsequent to the abandonment of the town. Still remaining at
the eastern edge of the Jones farmstead is an old, one-story frame house
that dates back to the time when Buxton was a town. At present Jack Jones
uses the house for the storage of tools
and household equipment. The Jones
family has a small collection of bottles
and other items they have found on
their property over the years. In addition to granting permission for the survey crew to conduct a surface reconnaissance of his property, Jack Jones
kindly contributed a number of artifacts to the project. These items included a small ceramic bowl with a
molded lion's head design, a porcelain
figurine, a "Frozen Charlotte" china
doll, several bottles (including a pop
bottle marked "Diamond Bottling
Works, Albia, Iowa"), a milk glass
Ponds cold cream jar, a brass buckle,
an iron step for a horse-drawn buggy,
several metal harness fittings, and a
mule shoe.

The field survey of Reconnaissance
Unit J, which was divided into six site
survey units, was productive in yield-
ing a large number of portable artifacts
and in revealing the potential for identifying some subsurface structural remains.

SSU J-1 corresponds to platted quarter-acre lots along streets between
East Eleventh and East Fourteenth
streets. This site survey unit was under cultivation for the growing of soybeans during the summer of 1981, and
the exposed ground surface provided a
large quantity of artifacts for collection
by the survey crew. An inventory of

2258 items includes 755 china tableware and container fragments, 227
stoneware container fragments, 38
miscellaneous ceramic objects (including door handles, insulators, a marble,
a "Frozen Charlotte" doll, and fragments of china doll heads and appendages), 1088 transparent glass container
and closure fragments, 125 milk glass
fragments (including small cosmetic
jars, preserve jar lid liners, and a fragment of a lamp shade), 5 miscellaneous
glass objects (including buttons and
marbles), 15 metal fragments, the upper portion of a leather shoe with metal
eyelets, and 4 pieces of bone and shell.

SSU J-2, an adjoining field, also was
under cultivation for the growing of
soybeans. In reference to the 1919 plat
map, this field corresponds to a series
of quarter-acre lots along streets between East Ninth and East Thirteenth
streets. The southern end of Main
Street also extended into this area.
Surface collecting in this unit yielded
1108 items: 505 china fragments (including portions of toy dishes), 61
stoneware sherds, 18 miscellaneous
ceramic objects (including doorknobs,
a drawer pull, doll fragments, marbles,
and a clay pipe stem), 431 transparent
glass fragments, 75 milk glass pieces,
5 miscellaneous glass objects (including buttons), 12 metal artifacts (including a button, a door handle, a spoon
bowl, a flatiron, and a hammerhead),
and a portion of a leather shoe or boot.

SSU J-3 comprises most of the NW¼
of the SE¼ of Section 4. According to
the 1919 plat map, it was entirely
divided into quarter-acre lots along
streets between East Sixth and East
Eleventh streets. Several smaller, intersecting, and unnumbered streets are
also shown in this area of the town's
plat. For example, one street is indicated paralleling the western side of a

north-south running ravine, the headlands of which can still be observed in SSU J-3. This portion of Buxton, according to the plat map, would be the district directly southeast of the Fifth Street school, the former high school, and the Mt. Zion Baptist Church. Today this entire area is in pasture except for trees and dense shrub cover along the ravine. A farm pond has been constructed at the south end of this drainageway to control erosion and provide a source of water for cattle.

Interestingly enough, given these modern land use conditions, a reconnaissance of this area revealed surface indications of a number of potential structural features and localized deposits of garbage and other debris associated with the occupation of the town. Two linear depressions oriented northeast-southwest were observed that appear to correspond with portions of East Sixth and East Eighth streets. Three small round depressions, one containing mortared bricks, are thought to be the remains of filled-in cisterns or wells. Two concentrations of stone, brick, and mortar were noted; these may represent the ruins of house foundations, chimneys, or other structures. A linear ridge oriented northwest-southeast was observed in the northeast corner of SSU J-3. This surface feature does not correspond to any street or other structure shown on the 1919 plat map and is presently interpreted as an agricultural terrace constructed at some time subsequent to the abandonment of Buxton.

In three distinct areas of the present pastureland, the field crew recorded concentrations of plants that appeared to be "out of context": irises, roses, strawberries, grapevines, asparagus, and mint. While certain of these might have been distributed by birds or planted following the abandonment of the town, the botanical assemblage appears to be evidence of some of Buxton's former flower and vegetable gardens. At least five concentrations of debris were noted in SSU J-3, either at points along the ravine or at spots throughout the pasture that had been dug up by burrowing animals. The latter concentrations probably reflect subsurface garbage pits and/or trash-filled cesspits. In addition to construction materials, broken bottles, dishes, and other artifacts, these concentrations contained notable amounts of cinder and ash.

The field crew collected 246 artifacts in SSU J-3: 60 china pieces, 24 stoneware sherds (including a Western Stoneware Company vessel fragment), 125 clear glass fragments (including medicine bottles and stoppers, soda and alcoholic beverage bottles, kerosene lamp chimney fragments, a vase, tumbler fragments, pitcher fragments, and a portion of a pressed glass pitcher or fruit stand with a gilded surface), 8 milk glass specimens (including a button and ointment jars), 3 miscellaneous glass objects, 13 metal artifacts (including a pair of scissors, several washtubs, and enameled-ware utensils), 10 leather fragments (including pieces of infants' shoes as well as adult footwear), a painted wooden stick, and 2 pieces of bone.

SSU J-4, located at the southwest corner of Reconnaissance Unit J, consists of pastureland around the upper reaches of a ravine that runs west across the north-south center section line of Section 4. The lower course of the waterway, located on property presently owned by the Keegel family, had been dammed to form a reservoir at the time Buxton was a flourishing town. The upper reaches of the drainage are shown on the 1919 plat map, and the area corresponding to SSU J-4 on the map is platted as numbered, quarter-acre lots east and west of Main Street on Twelfth, Thirteenth, and Fourteenth streets. Today erosion is partially checked by a farm pond constructed at the head of the ravine.

While inspecting the ground surface north of the ravine, members of the field crew noted a small round depression that may represent a filled-in cistern or well. Several large concrete slabs were noted along a modern field access road; these may have been moved in from elsewhere in the locality. During the summer of 1981, limestone blocks were hauled from the collapsed stone warehouse on the Keegel property in "downtown" Buxton to the ravine on the Jones property. Here they were used to riprap the culvert and prevent further erosion under the north-south fence along the center section line. This sort of "adaptive reuse" of materials, of course, has been going on throughout the years since Buxton ceased to exist as a town. Of the 92 artifacts collected from the surface of SSU J-4, there are 17 china fragments, 20 stoneware sherds, 2 miscellaneous ceramic objects (a toy duck and a door handle), 30 transparent glass container fragments, 7 milk glass pieces, a portion of a glass serving bowl, a mortar fragment, 12 metal artifacts (including a dishpan, a casserole stand, a large hinge, and a harness turret), a carbon rod, and a piece of hematite.

SSU J-5 consists of the Jones home and surrounding yard and was not treated as a unit for surface inspection as such. Of particular interest, however, is the old, one-story frame house that stands at the eastern edge of the property (see Fig. 26). The front porch

26. House structure still standing at the Buxton townsite within Site Survey Unit J-5, 1981. View is to the northeast. This house corresponds to one of the styles of privately owned houses in Buxton as pictured in early issues of the *Iowa State Bystander*. (Courtesy of the ISU Archaeological Laboratory)

of this house has settled considerably, but its roof is still supported by slender, lathe-turned columns and fancy, Victorian-style brackets. The one large front window has a stained glass upper panel. This house compares in style with some of the privately owned homes in Buxton as pictured in early issues of the *Iowa State Bystander*.

SSU J-6 is a triangular-shaped extension of the Jones property into the SE¼ of the SE¼ of Section 4. This area can be seen clearly on the 1919 plat map as a series of numbered, quarter-acre lots at the eastern ends of East Twelfth, East Thirteenth, and East Fourteenth streets. During the summer of 1981 alfalfa was being grown in this field. The reconnaissance crew walked over this field soon after the hay crop had been cut. Surface visibility was poor, but some scattered construction materials were observed in addition to the 85 artifacts collected: 41 china tableware and container fragments (including a vessel base marked "Made in Holland"), 7 stoneware sherds, a ceramic marble, 26 transparent glass fragments, 8 milk glass pieces, and 2 clam shells.

RECONNAISSANCE UNIT C

Reconnaissance Unit C comprises the property presently owned by the Raymond Carter family in the northeastern quarter of Section 4. Nearly all of Reconnaissance Unit C, according to the 1919 plat map, was divided into numbered, quarter-acre lots along streets extending from B Street and A Street at the north to East Seventh Street at the south. In addition to the parallel numbered streets, the plat map also indicates an unnamed, east-west aligned street that extended into Buxton from the Hobe Armstrong property at the eastern edge of the town. This street, located to the north of the center section line, is shown running just south of a tributary ravine and then turning north-south along the western edge of the main ravine between East Sixth and East Third streets. From this point two unnamed streets continue northwest perpendicularly across East Second Street to East First Street and the downtown district of Buxton.

Five individual buildings are indicated on the plat map corresponding to Reconnaissance Unit C. At the northwest edge of the unit are shown two churches and two undesignated buildings. The churches are apparently the First Methodist Church and the African Methodist Episcopal Church (see Fig. 27). The fifth specifically mapped structure is marked "school" and is located near the center of the section along East Fifth Street, corresponding to the southwest corner of Reconnaissance Unit C. This designation may refer to the high school or to what appears on photographs to have been a power plant or utility building ancillary to the high school. The high school, however, was not standing as of 1919. According to the *Iowa State Bystander* (18 October 1907), this building burned down in 1907. Former Buxton residents report that the structure was never rebuilt and that students subsequently attended public high schools in nearby towns or private schools outside the area.

Today the area within Reconnaissance Unit C consists of pastureland, hayfields, and fields being cultivated for the growing of corn and beans. The reconnaissance unit is transected by a large ravine and its side branches, along which grow trees of substantial size and shrubbery of considerable density. Several trash dumps can be observed along these ravines. Some of these represent refuse and construc-

27. View to the northeast of Methodist churches along the northern entrance road into Buxton. *Left,* the First Methodist Church; *right,* the African Methodist Episcopal Church, also referred to as St. John's. (Photo credit attributed to Wilma Stewart)

tion debris from Buxton, although much of the material postdates the settlement period of the town. One extant farm pond and one previous farm pond, now drained, are among the land modifications that have occurred subsequent to the demise of Buxton. In the process of working their land, Raymond and Laurina Carter have found various artifacts associated with the former town: bottles, jars, marbles, and other items. They kindly shared this information with the field reconnaissance crew in addition to granting access to their property for the purposes of the surface survey. The archaeological crew investigating Reconnaissance Unit C divided the area into six site survey units.

SSU C-1, located above the left bank of the ravine southeast of the present entrance road into the Buxton townsite, was in pasture during 1981. In this locality the 1919 plat map shows an undesignated building and portions of numbered, quarter-acre lots along East First Street. The present ground surface revealed no obvious structural remains except the location of a former well or cistern. The 31 portable artifacts collected in SSU C-1 included 14 china tableware or container fragments, a portion of a china doll, and 16 transparent glass container fragments.

SSU C-2, also in pasture during the summer of 1981, is a larger unit of investigation extending south along the left bank of the ravine to the center section line. According to the 1919 plat map this unit would correspond to numbered, quarter-acre lots along streets between East Second and East Sixth streets. At the location corresponding to the southwest corner of SSU C-2, the plat map shows a "school" thought to be the high school or its ancillary building. A north-south oriented

road formerly ran along the western bank of the ravine. No remains of the school building were discovered during the surface reconnaissance of SSU C-2, nor could the street be clearly defined. Vague, flattened surfaces above the left bank of the ravine suggested but did not clearly demonstrate the specific alignment of the former unnamed north-south street.

During the surface reconnaissance of SSU C-2, four indications of structural remains were observed: (1) a concentration of brick, limestone, mortar, and boards, probably representing debris from a house structure; (2) an abandoned cistern or well; (3) a linear erosional feature corresponding to the alignment of East Third Street; and (4) a linear erosional feature corresponding to the alignment of East Fourth Street. Artifacts were observed at several spots along the edge of the ravine, as well as more generally scattered on the surface of the pasture. Of the 388 portable artifacts collected in SSU C-2 were 104 china fragments, 24 stoneware sherds, 5 miscellaneous ceramic objects (including a portion of a china doll and several insulators), 217 transparent glass container fragments, 23 milk glass fragments (including a small deodorant jar and a portion of a lamp globe), a fragment of carnival glass, a glass button, 12 metal objects (including a railroad spike, a clamp, and a horseshoe), and a piece of molded carbon.

SSU C-3 is an irregularly shaped site survey unit that follows the ravine and its branches on the Carter property and includes the adjacent pastureland on the hillslopes generally east of the ravine. Dense timber and shrubbery abound along the fairly steep-sided ravine. At its southeastern end the ravine has been eroded down to bedrock. At the south end of SSU C-3 the bottom of the ravine is broad and marshy. The 1919 Buxton plat map shows this area essentially as numbered, quarter-acre lots along streets between East First and East Seventh streets. Also within this area is shown the unnamed east-west street leading into town north of the east-west center section line. Although ground cover conditions were not optimal for surface investigations, the reconnaissance revealed a number of indications of the previous urban settlement: (1) an abandoned cistern or well; (2) a concentration of mortared brick, probably representing a house foundation, a collapsed chimney, or a cistern; (3) scattered sandstone blocks and mortar, possibly associated with a previous building; (4) a rectangular area outlined by cedar trees, perhaps marking the boundaries of a former yard; (5) a patch of iris, apparently "out of context," suggesting a remnant of an old flower garden; (6) a linear, flat, and eroded surface appearing to be a portion of East Third Street; and (7) a linear, eroded depression located south of the ravine at the southern end of the survey unit and corresponding to the alignment of the east-west street entering the town from the former Hobe Armstrong property.

Several localized trash dumps along the ravine yielded a sizeable number of artifacts; other items were found scattered throughout the pasture. Of the 640 artifacts collected in SSU C-3 there are 160 china tableware and container fragments, 102 stoneware sherds, a ceramic drawer pull, a flowerpot fragment, 255 transparent glass specimens, 42 milk glass pieces (including three small jars and a lamp globe fragment), 25 metal objects (including a portion of a fire grate, a stove

handle, a wrench, a rake fragment, a coal scuttle, an oil can, kerosene lamp parts, and portions of a washtub), 51 leather shoe portions and harness fragments, a molded carbon rod, and 2 sawed bones.

SSU C-4 consists of an upland field between the branches of the previously discussed ravine referred to here as SSU C-3. During the summer of 1981 this field supported a narrow strip of alfalfa along its western edge, but the majority of the field was in soybeans that had been planted at close intervals by drilling. Thus the field could not be inspected without considerable damage to the crop, and at any rate the crop cover would have resulted in very poor ground visibility. In walking along the edge of the field, however, members of the field party could observe some pieces of china, stoneware, glass, and metal in areas of relatively sparse vegetation. This field would correspond to an area of numbered, quarter-acre lots along streets between East Third and East Sixth streets on the 1919 Buxton map.

This area is of particular interest given several conversations the archaeologists have held with Dorothy Neal Collier (personal communications 1981 and 1982). As discussed previously, Dorothy Collier's father, George Neal, was a tailor in Buxton and a notable member of the Buxton Wonders baseball team (see Figs. 8, 9, and 10). Dorothy Collier's collection of family photographs and memorabilia includes a postcard dated 1911 and addressed to her father at 34 East Fourth Street in Buxton. The location of Lot 34 on East Fourth Street, according to the 1919 plat map, would fall within the field designated SSU C-4 (see Fig. 4). This location is also supported by Dorothy Collier's interpretation of various photographic overviews of the town and her descriptions of how she walked from her house to the Fifth Street School, Coal Chute Hill (Main Street), and the company store. Dorothy Collier recalls that her parents' house was in the neighborhood of Buxton called Gobbler's Nob. If the street addresses correspond to lot numbers on the 1919 map, and if Dorothy Collier's recollections can indeed be linked to the geographic and topographic features as observed within Section 4 by the archaeologists, then we can conclude that the area designated SSU C-4 was that portion of Buxton formerly known as Gobbler's Nob. Previous publications (cf. Swisher 1945:182; Shiffer 1964:345) mention Gobbler's Nob but do not indicate its location within the former town.

SSU C-5 consists of a large field east and south of the Carter's home and north of the large ravine on their property. As mentioned above, the 1919 Buxton plat map shows the location of two churches and a smaller, undesignated building at the western edge of this property. Most of the remaining area north of the ravine is platted in numbered, quarter-acre lots along B and A streets, and East First, East Second, and East Third streets. During 1981 this field was being cultivated for the production of hay. The ground surface here was inspected immediately after the first hay crop had been harvested. Observed surface evidence for the existence of previous structures consisted of two abandoned cisterns or wells; a small, tree-filled depression with bricks and mortar; and a larger, shallow depression with scattered pieces of brick, fragments of mortar, and cinders. The position of the latter surface feature appears to correspond

closely with the location of the African Methodist Episcopal Church as shown on the Buxton plat map. Further investigation, however, would be necessary to demonstrate this correlation.

It should also be noted that large sections of concrete, bricks, and iron gutters were observed pushed into the ravine directly south of this locus. It is possible that these materials might be debris from the dismantling of the two church structures that once stood along the north entrance road into Buxton. Included in the inventory of 285 portable artifacts collected in SSU C-5 are 123 china pieces, 25 stoneware sherds, 2 china doll fragments, 114 transparent glass container fragments, 14 milk glass pieces, 5 metal artifacts (including a sadiron, a door lock mechanism, and a portion of a sewing machine stand), a piece of rubber webbed belting, and a fragment of molded carbon.

SSU C-6 is a small field located directly southeast of the Carter home and was being cultivated for the growing of corn and beans during the 1981 field season. The 1919 plat map indicates that this area was formerly the location of several numbered, quarter-acre lots along A Street and the end of East First Street. An unnamed street is also shown running perpendicularly from East First Street, across A Street, to the section road dividing Monroe and Mahaska counties. Judging from the density of surface artifacts, this area must once indeed have contained several dwelling units. An inventory of 546 items was collected in SSU C-6: 249 china fragments, 68 stoneware sherds, 7 miscellaneous ceramic objects (including insulators and doll fragments), 177 transparent glass container fragments, 34 milk glass pieces, 2 glass buttons, 7 metal artifacts (including a railroad spike and a horseshoe), and 2 sawed bone pieces.

CARLSON PROPERTY (CA)

Southeast of the intersection of the section road separating Monroe and Mahaska counties and the north entrance road into the Buxton townsite, there is a home and surrounding yard owned by the Art Carlson family. This property corresponds to the large lot owned, according to the 1919 Buxton plat map, by J. D. Thomas. Several residents of the area reported to the archaeologists that a drugstore once stood at this location (Mabel and Loren Blomgren, personal communication 1981; Joe Keegel, personal communication 1981). Given the present use of this property, the archaeological field crew did not seek permission to conduct a surface reconnaissance of this portion of the townsite. The Carlson house, however, appears to be of a style resembling that of several privately owned homes pictured in early issues of the *Iowa State Bystander*. Further investigations might well consider the architecture and history of this particular structure.

RECONNAISSANCE UNIT KP

Reconnaissance Unit KP is comprised of the property presently owned by the Keegel family and is under the management of Pete Keegel. This property includes all of the eastern half of the NW¼ and the entire eastern half of the SW¼ of Section 4. On the northeast the Keegel property juts out into a portion of the NW¼ of the NE¼ of Section 4; along its western border the property extends around the periphery of the former Buxton reservoir into parts of the NW¼ of the SW¼ and the

SW¼ of the NW¼ of Section 4. Literally and figuratively, Reconnaissance Unit KP is a cross section through the Buxton townsite. Reference to the 1919 plat map shows that Reconnaissance Unit KP includes most of the downtown, or business, district of Buxton south of Bluff Creek along the railroad, plus an extensive residential area extending from First Street on the north through Twelfth Street on the south.

Within the downtown district some 50 structural units are shown on the 1919 plat map. Of these indications on the map, only two are specifically identified – those being the two YMCA buildings. Various former Buxton town residents and others long familiar with this locality shared with the archaeologists their interpretations of the structures shown on the plat map as those related to buildings they remembered in the community (see Fig. 28). Of par-

28. Archaeological field school student discussing Buxton with two former residents of the town. Photo was taken at the ruins of the White House Hotel. *Left to right:* Archie Harris, Nancy Wallace, Alex Erickson. Nancy Wallace's grandparents, Martin Peterson and Dena Bergquist Peterson, are also former members of the Buxton community. (Courtesy of the ISU Archaeological Laboratory)

ticular assistance were Archie Harris and Dorothy Collier and many others, including Mabel Blomgren, Loren Blomgren, Alex Erickson, Jack Harris, Jack Jones, Case Keegel, Joe Keegel, Pete Keegel, Harvey Lewis, Martin Schipper, and Orville Schipper (personal communications 1980 and 1981). Not surprisingly, there was some disagreement on the identification of individual buildings shown on the map, and some of the platted structures could not be specifically identified. Various informants, however, identified the following structures on the plat map: the company store, a large company warehouse, the pay house, a telephone/telegraph office, a boiler house/power plant, a pump house, several machine shops and sheds, a mule barn, the railroad depot, several ice houses, several warehouses and lumber yards, a bandshell, a meat market, a bakery, and a building formerly housing the Perkins Hotel and post office.

South of the main business district of Buxton the 1919 plat map shows a residential area consisting of numbered, quarter-acre lots on numbered streets running perpendicular to Main Street. The lots are numbered sequentially in separate series extending east and west from Main Street; and the streets are designated "East" and "West" respective to their directional relationship to Main Street. The numbered streets actually are oriented northeast-southwest, roughly paralleling the railroad tracks. Main Street, aligned northwest-southeast, transects the numbered streets from First Street to Ninth Street at a point near the north-south center section line. From this point a wide, unnamed street continues on south following the north-south center section line to the county road at the south end of Section 4. While this

latter unnamed street segment was undoubtedly the main thoroughfare into town from the south, the division of numbered streets into "East" and "West" between Tenth Street and Fourteenth Street continues along the northwest-southeast alignment of Main Street. The latter street segment, however, does not intersect the county road at the south end of Section 4. Several short, unnamed streets, generally paralleling Main Street, are also shown on the 1919 plat map. In addition, within Reconnaissance Unit KP there is a major portion of a narrow, unnamed street which takes a zigzag southeasterly course from the front of the YMCA buildings, through East Second Street, to East Ninth Street. Within Reconnaissance Unit KP the 1919 plat map also shows a reservoir along the large tributary drainage that runs northwest into Bluff Creek in the western part of Section 4. The alignment of the dam is shown between West Third and West Fourth streets, and the reservoir extends southeast to West Eighth Street.

Three specific buildings are designated within the primarily residential area near the center of Section 4 along the eastern edge of Reconnaissance Unit KP: two "schools" on East Fifth Street and a "church" on East Sixth Street. On the basis of information from various former Buxton residents, these structures are identified as the elementary "Fifth Street School," the former high school, and the Mt. Zion Baptist Church. Two other specific buildings are shown at the corner of West Eleventh Street and the unnamed street that runs along the north-south center section line. These buildings are designated "school" and "church." The previous structure is recalled by various informants as the elementary

"Eleventh Street School." The denomination of the church on West Eleventh Street cannot be stated with certainty at the present time. The southern end of Reconnaissance Unit KP corresponds to a quarter-mile-long, undivided property, which the 1919 plat map indicates was owned by H. A. Armstrong. This property is bordered by the county section road between Sections 4 and 9. The adjacent portion of Section 9—outside the townsite controlled by the Consolidation Coal Company—shows as privately owned properties on the 1919 map. That area of Section 9 corresponds to a district referred to by many former Buxton residents as either Sharp End or Sharp's End.

Today the northern and western portions of Reconnaissance Unit KP are mostly in open pastureland. Certain areas now in pasture were cultivated for short periods of time in the past, according to Pete Keegel and Case Keegel (personal communications 1981). Trees and, in some instances, dense shrub vegetation can be seen along the banks of Bluff Creek and its tributary drainages as well as on the bottom and around the periphery of the reservoir that once existed in Buxton. After the townsite was abandoned two farm ponds were built on this property. Also constructed subsequent to the demise of Buxton were a silo, a concrete feedlot pad, a corral, and two grain bins, all of which are associated with the Keegels' farming operations. Within the former business district of Buxton a few vestiges of the previous urban settlement can still be seen. Most obvious are portions of the Consolidation Coal Company's stone warehouse and a brick vault, formerly part of the pay house. Also visible are ruins of the company store, some foundation remnants of the two YMCA buildings, portions of several house foundations and sidewalks, the old railroad bed, several culverts, the north end of Main Street (Coal Chute Hill), and the ruins of a building identified as the White House Hotel, which does not show up on the 1919 plat map. Some other structural remains are present but are not as immediately visible.

Several fields in the eastern part of Reconnaissance Unit KP currently are being cultivated for the production of crops. During the 1980 season these fields were planted in soybeans, and thus the ground visibility in the early summer months was optimal for investigation by surface reconnaissance. In 1981, however, these fields were planted in oats. Thus they could not be surveyed until after the crops had been harvested, and even then surface conditions were less than ideal. The modern land use conditions also limited the areas available for subsurface investigations. Test excavations, for example, were conducted in areas of the townsite presently in pasture rather than in fields being cultivated for the growing of crops. For the purposes of the surface survey, Reconnaissance Unit KP was divided up into eleven site survey units.

SSU KP-1 consists of a large field in the east central portion of Reconnaissance Unit KP. In reference to the 1919 plat map, this field corresponds to a primarily residential area of numbered, quarter-acre lots on streets between East Third Street on the north and West Tenth Street on the south. Main Street is shown running diagonally through the western portion of this site survey unit. Along the eastern edge of SSU KP-1, near the center of Section 4, the corresponding portion of the 1919 plat map shows the location of

29. [above] Photographic view to the northwest of a residential area of Buxton, taken sometime prior to 1908. The larger buildings on the horizon are, *left to right:* the Mount Zion Baptist Church, the elementary Fifth Street school, and the high school. (Courtesy of the Iowa State Historical Department)

30. [below] The 1980 archaeological crew conducting a reconnaissance of a former residential area. View is to the southwest. This field (Site Survey Unit KP-1) corresponds to the portion of Buxton shown in Figure 29. (Courtesy of the ISU Archaeological Laboratory)

two "schools" (the elementary Fifth Street School and the high school) and a "church" (the Mt. Zion Baptist Church). These structures are also shown on a photograph taken in Buxton prior to 1907 (see Fig. 29). During the 1980 field season SSU KP-1 was being cultivated for the growing of soybeans, and the visibility of the ground was excellent for the purposes of conducting an archaeological surface survey (see Fig. 30). Under such conditions the field crew could expect to find occupational debris if the area had indeed been settled and if the artifacts and structural remains had not been completely removed by modern plowing and erosion.

Assuming the settlement pattern of this area of Buxton was as dense as indicated on the 1919 plat map, the archaeologists predicted that they would find some material evidence of the former community in spite of the processes by which the town had been dismantled and in spite of the modification of the site by natural agencies and by recent farming activities. Permission to conduct a surface reconnaissance of this field was kindly granted by Pete Keegel. The archaeologists, suspecting that the artifactual materials would not be evenly distributed throughout the field, decided to conduct a surface survey by collecting items separately in 100-ft-square quadrats. This procedure, although quite time-consuming, would allow for a comparison of zones of light and heavy artifact density. Those varying zones, if apparent, could then be analyzed in an attempt to correlate the distributions with the settlement pattern indicated on the 1919 plat map. At the outset it was realized that a direct and clear correlation would be difficult because the present field and the rows of crops were oriented north-south, whereas the streets and numbered, quarter-acre lots in Buxton were oriented on a northeast-southwest (or, more closely, an east-northeast/west-southwest) alignment. The surface reconnaissance of this field, however, had to be conducted *between* the rows of soybeans on a north-south axis so as not to destroy any of the crop.

The surface survey of SSU KP-1 ultimately included the investigation of 130 quadrats. Some general observations can be made concerning the quantity and quality of artifacts obtained.

The first observation is that abundant materials are indeed present in this cultivated field, and they represent portable artifacts and structural remains associated with the previous urban settlement at Buxton. Second, as suspected, the artifacts are not evenly distributed throughout the field. Quadrats ranged in number of collected artifacts from 0 to 372 items. At the low end of the distribution, two quadrats contained no artifacts and 17 quadrats contained fewer than 10 items each. At the high end of the distribution, 16 quadrats contained between 101 and 200 artifacts each, and two quadrats contained over 200 artifacts each.

The distribution of artifacts within the quadrats, displayed by units in increments of 50 items, is shown in Fig. 31. In this distributional display, two quadrats had no artifacts, 85 quadrats

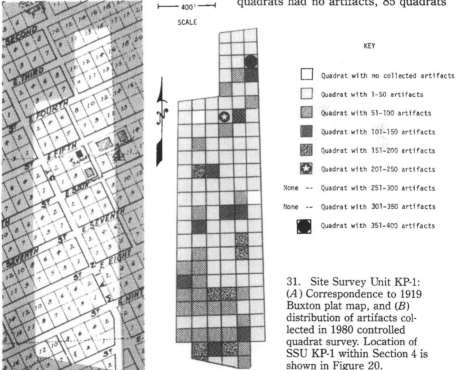

SCALE

|— 400' —|

KEY

☐ Quadrat with no collected artifacts

☐ Quadrat with 1-50 artifacts

▨ Quadrat with 51-100 artifacts

■ Quadrat with 101-150 artifacts

▨ Quadrat with 151-200 artifacts

⊠ Quadrat with 201-250 artifacts

None -- Quadrat with 251-300 artifacts

None -- Quadrat with 301-350 artifacts

◉ Quadrat with 351-400 artifacts

31. Site Survey Unit KP-1: (*A*) Correspondence to 1919 Buxton plat map, and (*B*) distribution of artifacts collected in 1980 controlled quadrat survey. Location of SSU KP-1 within Section 4 is shown in Figure 20.

A

B

contained between 1 and 50 items, 25 quadrats had between 51 and 100 items, nine quadrats had between 101 and 150 items, seven quadrats had between 151 and 200 items, one quadrat had between 201 and 250 items, no quadrat had between 251 and 300 or 301 and 350 items, and one quadrat had between 351 and 400 items. A third general observation thus arises from a rough correlation of these data with the 1919 plat map. For the most part, especially in the northern portion of SSU KP-1, higher densities of artifacts were collected in quadrats corresponding to the location of the backs of former lots, while lower densities of artifacts were collected in quadrats corresponding to previous streets and the fronts of lots. This apparent correlation is less clear in the data from the southwestern portion of SSU KP-1.

Following the 1980 field season it was hoped that excavations could be conducted in SSU KP-1 during 1981. These were to have tested some of the hypotheses concerning the possible correlation of the surface distribution of artifacts with the settlement pattern indicated on the 1919 plat map. During 1981, however, the field comprising SSU KP-1 was planted in oats. Although the landowner therefore was not anxious for excavations to be conducted in this field, he was willing to permit excavations in adjacent areas of pastureland. In that regard the surface survey data collected in SSU KP-1 in 1980 were important in designing excavation units in SSU KP-3 during the 1981 field season.

Qualitatively the artifacts collected in the quadrat survey of SSU KP-1 indicate something of the domestic, economic, occupational, and other sociocultural spheres of the former residents of Buxton. Within the inventory of 6568 items collected during the 1980 field season, there are 1962 fragments of "china" tableware and containers. Vessel forms include plates, serving dishes or platters, saucers, cups, mugs, bowls, condiment shakers, and miniature toy dishes. Larger sherds probably represent containers associated with hygiene: shaving mugs, washing bowl and pitcher sets, and "slop jars." Both porcelain and ironstone tableware varieties are present in both decorated and plain white forms. Decorations include raised molded motifs, luster band wares, gold edging, colored transfers, cobalt blue designs, and multicolored, hand-painted designs. Manufacturers' marks indicate some imported European items as well as wares produced at potteries in the eastern United States.

Represented by the 661 stoneware sherds collected in SSU KP-1 quadrats are food preservation, storage, and preparation vessels: large and small storage crocks and lids, mixing bowls, milk pans, jugs, and butter churns. Most of the stonewares are mold-made and exhibit glazes typical of twentieth-century manufacturing processes: Bristol glazes, white glazes, light blue glazes, and other colored glazes. Some wheel-turned wares with salt glazes and Albany slips are more typical of nineteenth-century ceramics, although those products were also produced in Iowa and the Midwest during the early twentieth century. Included in the 68 miscellaneous ceramic artifacts are portions of china dolls' heads and appendages, marbles, smoking pipes, flowerpots, doorknobs, drawer knobs, and insulators.

Glass containers and their closures are represented by 3178 specimens collected in the quadrat survey of SSU KP-1. This inventory includes items of clear transparent glass, colored glass (brown, blue, light purple, green), and milk glass. Vessel forms represented are canning jars, condiment bottles and jars, medicine bottles, soda pop bottles, beer bottles, and cosmetic and ointment jars. Medicine bottle stoppers, glass lids, and liners for zinc preserve jar lids also are present. Within the category of 394 miscellaneous glass artifacts are fragments of windowpanes, marbles, buttons, insulators, kerosene lamp chimneys, lamp bases, vases, figurines, pitchers, drinking tumblers, and cut or pressed glass dishes and bowls.

A good many of the 165 metal artifacts cannot be identified yet, but represented in this inventory are nails, nuts, bolts, wire, files, wrenches, pliers, axes, picks, scale weights, railroad spikes, horseshoes, stove parts, and eating utensils. Shoes and perhaps harness fragments are represented by seven pieces of leather and rubber. Within the collection of 100 miscellaneous objects are pieces of unworked bone, sawed bone fragments, shell buttons, unworked shells, clinkers, pieces of coal, a possible whetstone, and one prehistoric chert tool. Construction materials were observed throughout the field but were not systematically collected except for a small representative sample. Included in that sample are 33 specimens of bricks, mortar, plaster, concrete, and tile. Chunks of limestone were also observed in SSU KP-1, especially along the eastern edge of the field. These might represent displaced remnants of foundations from large structures such as the school buildings and the Mt. Zion Baptist Church (see Fig. 29). That association, however, cannot be demonstrated at the present time.

SSU KP-2 is a small portion of pasture at the north-central end of Section 4 and is bounded by Bluff Creek, a tributary ravine, the north entrance road leading into the townsite, and the county section road that bends north into Mahaska County. Except for the curving track of the Iowa Southern/ Chicago & North Western Railroad, no structures or designated properties are indicated on the corresponding portion of the 1919 plat map. According to Joe Keegel (personal communication 1981) a blacksmith shop once stood in this locality near Bluff Creek. Directly north across the county road in Mahaska County on land presently owned by the Orville Schipper family were several ancillary business and residential "suburbs" of Buxton. These settlements are referred to as Coopertown and Gainestown in previous publications (Swisher 1945:182; Shiffer 1964:345) as well as by former Buxton residents and others familiar with the area (Dorothy Collier, Archie Harris, Joe Keegel, Martin and Orville Schipper; personal communications 1980 and 1981). Coopertown was named after B. F. Cooper, a prominent druggist in the Buxton community. Gainestown designated the area of business establishments run by the father of the late Reuben Gaines. Site Survey Unit KP-2 was in pasture during the 1981 field season and the dense grass vegetation masked the ground surface. The former railroad bed could still be observed, but only one portable artifact was found: the base of a glass container marked B. B. W., probably a Buxton Bottling Works soda pop bottle.

SSU KP-3, presently in pastureland containing a farm pond, corresponds to a major portion of "downtown" Buxton as shown on the 1919 plat map. Within this site survey unit, arbitrarily designated as the area south of the former railroad bed, once stood the company store, the telephone/telegraph office, two YMCA buildings, and the White House Hotel, in addition to buildings that various informants referred to on the map as a meat market, an ice house, a bandshell, warehouses, a lumber yard, a railroad depot, and the structure housing the Perkins Hotel and the post office. The plat map also shows numbered, quarter-acre lots along streets between First and Third streets, the northern end of Main Street, a narrow, unnamed street that begins in front of the YMCA buildings and runs on a zigzag southeasterly alignment (see Fig. 3), and another short, unnamed street near the north-south center section line of Section 4. When the archaeologists first visited Buxton during the summer of 1980, William Collier—their guide around the townsite—identified the railroad bed, a concrete culvert over which the railroad passed, and the ruins of the company store, the YMCA buildings, and the White House Hotel. He also pointed out the north end of Main Street, indicated today by an eroding gully along the hillslope that many former Buxton residents called Coal Chute Hill. It was along this slope that William Collier further impressed the archaeologists by finding a complete soda pop bottle marked "Nevins Bottling Works, Buxton, Ia."

Subsequent surface reconnaissance of SSU KP-3 in 1980 and 1981 revealed other structural remains: surface indications of portions of First Street and Third Street, ruins of several house structures, a root cellar, sidewalks, and a steel culvert under the entrance road from the north. Certain of these structures were further investigated by test excavations (see Chap. 5 discussion of

Structures 2, 4–15, and 18–21). Beyond these materials, 66 portable artifacts were collected in SSU KP-3: 8 china tableware fragments, 4 stoneware sherds, 2 miscellaneous ceramic objects (an insulator and a "Frozen Charlotte" doll), 30 specimens representing clear glass containers (including a complete medicine bottle and the Nevins Bottling Works soda pop bottle), 10 miscellaneous glass fragments (including portions of kerosene lamp chimneys), 8 metal artifacts (including a Hutchinson lightning bottle closure and a 1900 dime), and 4 miscellaneous items (including pieces of slate). Probing with a solid steel rod suggested the presence of subsurface structural remains in the northwestern part of SSU KP-3 (see Fig. 32). These remains may represent the foundations of the railroad depot and/or the Perkins Hotel (see Fig. 33), but such correlations cannot be demonstrated at the present time.

SSU KP-4 is a portion of the Keegels' pasture between the abandoned railroad bed on the south and Bluff Creek on the north. As one drives into the townsite from the north, one can observe two of the most visible remains of former Buxton buildings: the Consolidation Coal Company's stone warehouse with a red tile roof, and a red brick vault that was once part of the company office and pay house. According to the 1919 plat map, many other buildings once stood in this part of Buxton. The buildings, as identified on the map by various informants, included machine shops and sheds, a mule barn, a boiler house/power plant, an ice house, a pump house, and a bakery. The plat map does not show any streets north of the railroad tracks. Surface reconnaissance of this area resulted in the designation of one struc-

32. Archaeological survey crew conducting solid steel probe tests in Site Survey Unit KP-4, 1981. View is to the south. This general area corresponds to the locations of the former railroad depot, the post office, the headquarters of the *Buxton Gazette,* and the Perkins Hotel. (Courtesy of the ISU Archaeological Laboratory)

33. The Buxton railroad depot and tracks of the Chicago and North Western Railroad. The building at left at one time housed the post office and the offices of the *Buxton Gazette.* View is to the west. (Photo credit attributed to Wilma Stewart)

ture (Structure 17) north of the company store. These ruins are thought to be remnants of the boiler house/power plant building. Also identified, on the basis of information from Archie Harris (personal communication 1981), was the end of a large sewer—designated Structure 26—that empties out into Bluff Creek north of the stone warehouse. Some structural debris and surface anomalies were observed and designated (Structure 16) southwest of the stone warehouse; these remains, however, were not further investigated or identified. Several other surface anomalies were noted in SSU KP-4. They were, however, rather vague and time did not permit designation or further investigation during the 1981 field season.

Some portable artifacts were found along the banks of Bluff Creek and many items were obtained from an unusual concentration north of the warehouse near the creek. The latter concentration was a veritable breccia of metal objects, leather fragments, pieces of cloth, slag, and other items cemented together by iron rust. This waste dump is tentatively interpreted as debris from a blacksmith shop. Within the inventory of 452 artifacts collected in SSU KP-4 are 23 china tableware fragments, 10 stoneware sherds, 17 miscellaneous ceramic objects (including a portion of a religious figurine representing the Madonna and Child), 39 transparent glass container fragments, 16 milk glass fragments, 30 miscellaneous glass pieces (including light bulb fragments), 171 metal artifacts (including nuts, bolts, wire fragments, nails, washers, files, a drill, chain links, segments of springs, and a pulley bracket), 1 brick marked "Century Crown," 108 fragments of leather and cloth (pieces of shoes and gloves, harness fragments, scraps of asbestos and burlap), and 37 miscellaneous items (including sheets of mica, newspaper fragments, seeds, and slag).

SSU KP-5, presently in pasture, consists of the bottomlands and low hillslopes north of Bluff Creek. The corresponding portion of the 1919 plat map does not show any buildings, streets, or lots in this location. A surface reconnaissance of this area failed to reveal any structural remains or portable artifacts.

SSU KP-6, located in the northwest corner of Reconnaissance Unit KP, is also above the left bank of Bluff Creek in an area where no structures or designated properties appear on the 1919 town plat map. Within this pasture, however, a large stone retaining wall is readily visible from Bluff Creek and from vantage points in the townsite to the south. This limestone revetment, which local residents call "the stone ledge," was designated Structure 22. Along this wall can be seen barberry bushes, trumpet vines, and trees that appear to be remnants of intentional landscape plantings. Several local residents (Archie Harris, Loren Blomgren,

Mabel Blomgren, and Joe Keegel; personal communications 1980 and 1981), recalled that the hilltop surface above the stone wall was the location of a large house. This was the residence of Ben Buxton's family and of subsequent superintendents of the Consolidation Coal Company. The location, it should be noted, affords an extensive panoramic view over the Bluff Creek Valley, the former downtown portion of Buxton, and a good deal of the northern residential areas of the town.

The Buxtons' house and ancillary buildings show on two photographs in the collection of Ada Baysoar Morgan, daughter of E. M. Baysoar, who was a superintendent at Buxton during the second decade of the town's existence. As discussed elsewhere, subsurface archaeological investigations verified the location of this house and an associated cistern (Structures 23 and 24). Several other buildings shown in the old photographs are identified as barns, a probable garage, and a water tower. Foundations of those buildings (designated Structural Complex 25) can be seen immediately west of the Keegels' north-south fence line on property presently owned by the Jack Harris family. Because of the ground cover conditions in SSU KP-6, few surface materials were observed. Only one artifact was collected on the surface here: a complete glass bottle marked "Rubifoam, For the Teeth, Put Up by E. W. Hoyt & Co., Lowell, Mass." Other artifacts obtained in test excavations at the site of the superintendents' house are described in Chapter 5.

SSU KP-7 consists of a tree-lined stream bed and an adjacent pasture corresponding to the area of the former Buxton reservoir and the adjoining numbered, quarter-acre residential lots between West Third and West Tenth

34. Remains of the dam that once impounded the Buxton reservoir, 1901. View is to the southwest. (Courtesy of the ISU Archaeological Laboratory)

streets as shown on the 1919 plat map of the town. In spite of the thick vegetational ground cover in this site survey unit during the summer of 1981, a number of vestiges of the former urban settlement could be seen. Particularly prominent are embankments of the breached earthen dam (see Fig. 34), a portion of the concrete spillway and gate, and two cistern-like water control structures near the eastern end of the dam. Also observed were two concentrations of constructional debris, probably representing previous buildings; two linear erosional features along the alignments of West Third and West Ninth streets; a small, round depression, possibly evidencing a filled-in cistern or well; and three patches of iris, apparently marking the locations of former flower gardens.

Several concentrations of cultural debris were found, particularly along ravines adjacent to the borders of the former reservoir. Within the inventory of materials collected from SSU KP-7 are 183 fragments of china tableware and containers, 117 stoneware specimens (including fragments of butter churns, several sherds marked "Western Stoneware Co.," and a complete mold-made jug), 17 miscellaneous

ceramic objects (including doll fragments, door handles, and marbles), 454 transparent glass containers and fragments (including a perfume bottle, marked medicine bottles – "Dr. D. Jayne's Expectorant" and "Dr. Pierce's Anuric Tablets for Kidneys and Backaches" – and marked beverage bottles – "Albia Bottling Works," "Diamond Bottling Works, Albia, Ia.," "Hamm, St. Paul," and "Imperial Brewing Co., Kansas City, Mo."), 30 milk glass container fragments, 8 miscellaneous glass objects (including jelly glasses, a tumbler, and a marble), 37 metal objects (including pan fragments, an enameled pot, a spoon, portions of washtubs, a barrel hoop, an ice skate, kerosene lamp parts, and a door key), 97 leather and cloth fragments (including pieces of shoes, boots, and harnesses), and 27 miscellaneous objects (including a bone toothbrush handle, a worked bone disc, sawed bone fragments, and a prehistoric chert biface).

SSU KP-8, a small field at the southeast end of Reconnaissance Unit KP, was planted in oats during the 1981 field season. The corresponding area on the 1919 plat map is shown as a portion of a large property owned by H. A. Armstrong. The surface of SSU KP-8 was inspected soon after the oats had been harvested. No structural remains were observed and portable artifacts were scarce, evidence for the supposition that this portion of Buxton was not densely settled. Only 12 artifacts were collected in SSU KP-8: 6 china fragments, 3 stoneware sherds, and 3 pieces of glass.

SSU KP-9 corresponds to an area of numbered, quarter-acre lots on streets between West Tenth and West Twelfth streets on the 1919 plat map. This field was also planted in oats during the 1981 field season and was similarly subjected to a surface reconnaissance soon after the crop had been harvested. Although no structural remains were observed, portable artifacts were found scattered throughout the field. Of the 170 items collected in SSU KP-9, there are 68 china tableware and container fragments (including a portion of a toy teapot), 19 stoneware sherds, 2 miscellaneous ceramic objects, 70 transparent glass container pieces, 10 milk glass fragments (including a Mum deodorant jar), and 1 metal artifact.

SSU KP-10 consists of a Y-shaped wooded ravine located in the SE¼ of the SW¼ of Section 4. Water flowing down from the headlands of this ravine system was impounded to create the former Buxton reservoir to the north. Subsequent to the abandonment of the town, the dam was breached, allowing the water to flow along this drainage system directly into Bluff Creek in the NW¼ of Section 4. The 1919 plat map shows West Tenth, West Eleventh, and West Twelfth streets cutting across this area. However, most of the quarter-acre lots bordering the drainage are not numbered on the map, a fact that suggests they may not have contained houses. Today cultural debris is found along the course of the ravine, al-

though some of the materials apparently postdate the urban settlement at Buxton. Of the 404 items collected in SSU KP-10, there are 43 china tableware fragments, 41 stoneware sherds, 4 miscellaneous ceramic objects, 227 transparent glass containers and fragments (including a medicine bottle marked "Scott's Emulsion Cod Liver Oil With Lime and Soda"), 14 milk glass fragments (including a lamp globe), 11 miscellaneous glass objects, 22 metal artifacts (including stove parts, a pan, a hay fork, a hinge, and kerosene lamp parts), 36 leather and rubber shoe fragments, and 6 miscellaneous artifacts.

SSU KP-11 is a pasture located in the southwest portion of Reconnaissance Unit KP. Relative to the 1919 Buxton plat map this field corresponds to quarter-acre lots between West Tenth and West Twelfth streets, as well as to most of the undivided property unit owned by H. A. Armstrong. During the surface survey of SSU KP-11, the reconnaissance crew observed a brick-lined cistern or well sealed with a steel cover. Two circular surface depressions, perhaps representing filled-in cisterns or wells, also were noted. Although surface visibility was not optimal, 65 portable artifacts were collected: 7 china fragments, 3 stoneware sherds, 2 miscellaneous ceramic objects, 43 transparent glass container fragments, 5 milk glass objects, 1 marked brick, and 4 metal artifacts.

BUXTON CEMETERY

Although no cemetery is indicated on the 1919 plat map, Buxton did indeed have a graveyard for burying deceased members of the community. The cemetery is located along the county section line in the NW¼ of the NW¼ of Sec-

35. The Buxton cemetery as it appeared during the summer of 1980. View is to the southeast. (Courtesy of the ISU Archaeological Laboratory)

tion 4 and was owned by the Jack Harris family at the time of this study. In July of 1980 the archaeologists were guided to the cemetery by Jack Harris and Gerald Chamberlain. At that time most of the area was overgrown by trees, shrubs, and weeds, including large patches of poison ivy (see Fig. 35). Nevertheless several gravestones were observed, as was a plot marked off by a fence made from iron pipe set in concrete. Although no grave markers are present within the fenced-off plot, this location was reported to be the place where Reuben Gaines' parents were buried (Jack Harris and Gerald Chamberlain; personal communications 1980). Another grave plot was enclosed by a small, decorative iron fence. At this time it was also noted that many unmarked grave depressions were present in the cemetery. Furthermore, some of the extant gravestones had fallen over and still others apparently had been moved from their original plots. Several patches of day lilies were observed. These probably represent intentional flower plantings.

With the permission of the landowners, the archaeologists returned to investigate the cemetery in March of 1981, at which time vegetation obscured much less of the graveyard (see Fig. 36). During that visit additional gravestones were recorded and many unmarked grave depressions were observed. Assisting in the task of recording information from the gravestones were Dr. Charles Irby (professor and former chair of the Ethnic Studies Department at California Polytechnic State University in Pomona) and Dr. Gretchen Bataille (professor of English at Iowa State University and former chair of the Iowa Civil Rights Commission).

At present, 37 stone monuments, representing 41 individuals, have been observed. The many additional surface depressions, of course, indicate more individuals were actually buried in the cemetery. The possibility exists that additional stone monuments are presently masked by vegetation and recent soil accumulation. No attempt was made to search for gravestones that might be located below the present ground surface. Concerning data from the gravestones, some general statements can be made:

1. Interment dates observed on the

36. Recording information from a gravestone in the Buxton cemetery, spring 1981. View is to the southeast. (Courtesy of the ISU Archaeological Laboratory)

stones range from 1902 to 1923.

2. Individuals identified include 18 males and 21 females; gender of individuals marked by two stones cannot yet be determined.

3. Age of individuals at death ranges from one day to 74 years; males range from less than one year to 74 years, with an average of approximately 34 years; females range from less than one year to 68 years, with an average of approximately 39 years.

4. Sodalities and other group affiliations indicated on gravestones include United Mine Workers of America, Masons, Eastern Star, International Order of Odd Fellows, and Fifth United States Army Colored Infantry (see Figs. 37, 38, and 39). In this regard it is interesting to note that fraternal lodges and voluntary associations were mentioned frequently in issues of the *Iowa State Bystander* and have been considered significant in subsequent publications (cf. Rye 1972:949). The material evidence from the gravestones reflects the significance of these associations in the lives of those who have "passed."

5. The monument styles include tablets, gabled obelisks, and blocks; these seem to correspond well with gravestone styles for this time period in Iowa as reported by Coleen Nutty (1978) in her study entitled *Cemetery Symbolism of Prairie Pioneers.*

6. Most of the gravestones observed contain only names and vital statistical data, although epitaphs are included on eight monuments. These range from short statements ("At Rest") to several longer ones ("A precious one from us has gone/A

Selected gravestones in the Buxton cemetery.

Fig. 37.   Fig. 38.   Fig. 39.

Fig. 37.   J. H. Henderson, United Mine Workers of America.
Fig. 38.   W. Anderson Perkins and Martha Perkins Stewart.
Fig. 39.   Andrew Jackson, Co. K, Fifth U.S. Colored Infantry.

(Courtesy of the ISU Archaeological Laboratory)

voice we loved is stilled/A place is vacant in our home/Which never can be filled"). These data support the observation that epitaphs are present on early twentieth-century gravestones but are not as abundant and elaborate as those seen on nineteenth-century monuments.

7. Decorative motifs are present on approximately half of the monuments.

8. A prevailing impression people today seem to have is that the Buxton cemetery was exclusively for black people. This fact cannot be totally demonstrated from the present information available in the cemetery. Attempts have been made to identify individuals commemorated on gravestones in reference to available census data and information from former Buxton residents. So far the few individuals thus verified are all identified as black. All of these data are further significant when compared to the study of American colonial cemeteries (Dethlefsen and Deetz 1966; Dethlefsen and Jensen 1977) as well as to the specific regional model devised by Coleen Nutty (1978) for mortuary patterns in central Iowa.

HARRIS PROPERTY (H)

Most of the western quarter of Section 4 was owned until recently by Archie Harris, who was born in Coopertown, schooled in East Swede Town, and employed in the Consolidation Coal Company mines (Archie Harris, personal communication 1980). The property is presently owned by his son, Jack Harris, and Jack's family. As previously discussed, the Buxton cemetery is situated in the NW¼ of the NW¼ of Section 4 at the northern end

of the Harris property, although nothing is shown in that location on the 1919 plat map. According to Archie Harris (personal communication 1980), the land directly to the north of Bluff Creek was used as an area for circuses and carnivals at the time Buxton was a thriving town, while the area immediately south of the creek once contained a baseball park and tennis courts. The latter area was also the site for reunions held by former Buxton residents for a number of years after the town had been abandoned (Archie Harris, personal communication 1980). Harris furthermore indicated that the Nevins Bottling Works was situated at some location above the right bank of Bluff Creek near a bridge shown on the 1919 plat map.

Farther south in the SW¼ of the NW¼ of Section 4, the 1919 plat map shows the location of West Swede Town between the railroad tracks on the northwest and the dam for the reservoir on the southeast. West Swede Town is platted out in large, unnumbered lots and contains several unnamed streets. Two church buildings are shown on the 1919 plat map. In reference to the map, Alex Erickson (personal communication 1981) identified these structures as the Swedish Methodist Church and the Slavic Lutheran Church. An undesignated building is shown directly below the dam on the 1919 plat map. According to Archie Harris (personal communication 1980), this building was an icehouse. Along the eastern fence line of the Harris property, the 1919 plat map shows some numbered, quarter-acre lots along streets between West First and West Third streets.

To the west of the reservoir, corresponding to the NW¼ of the SW¼ of Section 4, the plat map shows a series of numbered and unnumbered long, narrow properties. This area is bisected by a single unnamed street running due south from West Swede Town. According to Alex Erickson (personal communication 1981) this area of Buxton was formerly referred to as Wells' Hill, after an official in the company store who had a large house in this vicinity. W. A. Wells is identified by Swisher (1945:186) as the operator of the company store and a brother-in-law of Ben Buxton. The 1919 plat map shows the SE¼ of the SE¼ of Section 4 as large property holdings owned by Maggie Burkett, Howard Ashby, George H. Woodson, John and Irene Jenkins, and Minnie B. London. George Woodson, an attorney, and Minnie London, a schoolteacher, are mentioned by Swisher (1945:181, 192) as being prominent among the blacks of Buxton.

Reference to the 1977 aerial photographs shows that the Harris property has been modified by the construction of a farm pond and several agricultural terraces since the abandonment of the urban settlement at Buxton. During the 1980 and 1981 field seasons, most of this property was being cultivated for the production of row crops and hay.

During July of 1980 Jack Harris escorted the archaeologists on a visit to the breached dam. While walking through fields corresponding to a portion of West Swede Town and to some of the quarter-acre lots shown between West First and West Third streets on the plat map, the group noted but did not retain some scattered pieces of broken china, stoneware, and glass. Some scattered artifacts also were observed on the surface of the field between Bluff Creek and the cemetery while Harris guided the archaeologists to the cemetery. When the archaeologists returned to investigate the cemetery in March of 1981, they walked west to the graveyard from SSU KP-6 on the Keegel property. In so doing, they observed and photographed along the north-south fence line the aforementioned foundations of the outbuildings associated with the house of Ben Buxton and subsequent superintendents of Consolidation Coal Company. Some scattered pieces of ceramics and glass, in addition to bits of construction materials, were observed but not collected in the cultivated field between the fence line and cemetery. According to Archie Harris (personal communication 1980), within this field there once stood a house that may have been the home of the caretaker for the Buxton residence. The artifactual material observed in this field might be associated with that previous structure. Beyond those investigations the remainder of the Harris property was not systematically surveyed by surface reconnaissance because permission to do so was not granted during the 1981 summer field season.

5: Test excavations and investigation of former buildings

SUBSURFACE archaeological investigations were concentrated in three loci in the north-central portion of the Buxton townsite. First was the former downtown, or main business-commercial district (see Fig. 40). Although informants mention stores and other businesses such as Foster's Store (near the Cinder Road?) and Larson's Store (in East Swede Town), most of the business, commercial, and large community buildings were located on the toeslopes and terraces above Bluff Creek along the Chicago and North Western Railroad tracks (see backgrounds in Figs. 3 and 41). Second, archaeological test squares were set out on the hill summit south of the downtown district. This area, corresponding to a location between the former East Third and East Fourth streets as shown on the 1919 plat map (see Fig. 40), was previously the site of several company-owned houses set on quarter-acre lots (see foregrounds in Figs. 3 and 41). The third locality investigated by subsurface methods was the hill surface near the stone ledge north of Bluff Creek. That locus, affording a splendid view over the townsite, was reported to be the place where once stood the residence of Ben Buxton and subsequent mine superintendents of the Consolidation Coal Company. Interestingly enough, no structures were indicated at this place on the 1919 Buxton plat map.

The north-central portion of the townsite was selected for subsurface testing during the 1981 field season for several reasons. First, it appears as if the size and range of public, or communal, buildings at Buxton was unique, or nearly so, for early twentieth-century mining communities in Iowa, if not elsewhere in the prairies and plains. Second, this portion of the townsite still included some aboveground structural remains that could be mapped and documented expediently. In several cases, however, these structural remains were observed to be rapidly deteriorating. Thus it seemed prudent to record these structures before the evidence was further destroyed. Third, the north-central portion of the townsite previously included residential structures as well as business and commercial establishments. There were the potentials for discovering the location of company-owned houses, as well as privately owned homes, and for investigating possible socioeconomic and/or ethnic factors as might be reflected in the associated portable artifactual remains. Fourth, this area of the townsite was entirely in pasture. The landowner thus was willing to let the archaeologists excavate on this portion of his

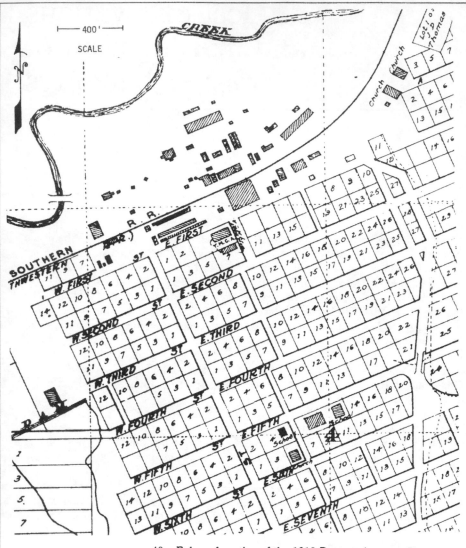

40. Enlarged portion of the 1919 Buxton plat map. Shown are the main business/commercial district, the adjacent residential area, and the lower portion of the reservoir.

41. View to the north of downtown Buxton, probably taken from the water tower sometime after 1911. *Foreground,* Lot 7 on East Fourth Street and Lots 8 and 10 on East Third Street; *left center,* the two YMCA buildings and the Consolidation Coal Company office, containing the pay vault; *left,* on the hill above Bluff Creek, the residence and associated buildings of the mine superintendent; *center,* the White House Hotel, the second company store, and the power plant; *extreme right,* the African Methodist Episcopal Church and the Buxton Hotel (?) in Gainestown/Coopertown. (Photo credit attributed to Wilma Stewart)

property as opposed to a field directly south that had been sown to oats for the 1981 growing season.

It was the latter field, Site Survey Unit KP-1, that was investigated by a controlled quadrat surface survey during the summer of 1980, at which time the field was plowed for the cultivation of beans. Therefore the archaeologists had to abandon their previous plans to investigate that portion of the townsite roughly corresponding to the area between East Fourth and East Seventh streets on the 1919 plat map. The surface materials collected in that field during 1980, however, were very useful in extrapolating presumed settlement pattern configurations into the pastured property available for test excavations during the 1981 field season.

Although the time available for field investigations was not sufficient for the complete documentation of any one building, an attempt was made to map the locations and to record the primary architectural plans for all readily visible structural remains in the downtown district (see Fig. 42). Field numbers were assigned arbitrarily to each apparent structural unit since in some cases the buildings could not be specifically identified on the basis of available documentary sources. Identifiable structures that were mapped and/or partially explored by test excavations include the company warehouse; the second company store, or "Monroe Mercantile Company"; the company pay office, including the brick vault; the main YMCA building; the small YMCA building; and the White House

59

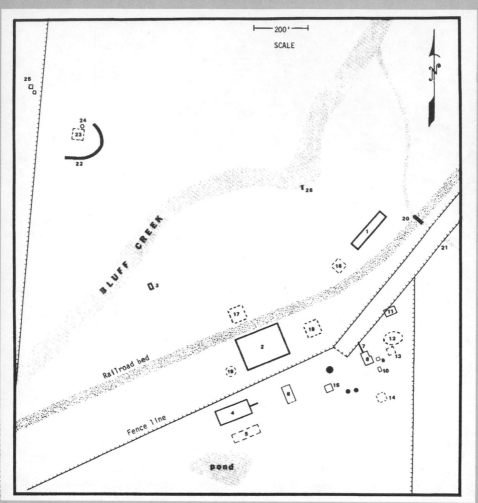

42. Locational map of designated structures within the Buxton townsite. Solid lines indicate extant, visible structures or foundations, while dashed lines delimit building depressions or buried foundation remnants. Solid dots indicate the locations of a present-day silo and two smaller grain storage bins.

LIST OF STRUCTURES

1 – The Stone Warehouse
2 – The Company Store
3 – The Company Business Office Vault
4 – The Main YMCA
5 – The Boys' YMCA
6 – The White House Hotel
7 – Sidewalk & Steps to Structure 8
8 – Residential Building Foundations
9 – Segmented Concrete Slab
10 – "Cave" or Root Cellar
11 – Residential Building Foundations
12 – Structure Depression
13 – Wall and Rubble

14 – Structure Depression
15 – Limestone & Concrete Floor
16 – Structure Depression
17 – The Power Plant
18 – Armstrong's Meat Market (?)
19 – Telegraph Office (?)
20 – The Concrete Viaduct
21 – The Steel Culvert
22 – The Stone Revetment
23 – The Mine Superintendent's Residence
24 – Cistern near Structure 23
25 – Outbuildings & Water Tower Associated with Structure 23
26 – The Sewer Pipe

Hotel (designated, respectively, Structures 1 through 6). The location of the White House Hotel, it should be noted, does not appear on the 1919 plat map, although photographs show that this building was under construction at the time the second company store was being built—i.e., 1911–1912. Other ruins or surface indications presumed to be business/commercial enterprises include those designated as Structures 16 through 19. These remains may correspond, respectively, to the location of maintenance shops, the boiler house/power plant, a meat market or icehouse, and a telegraph office as variously referred to by several former Buxton residents who visited the site while the archaeologists were working there. These identifications, however, are not yet fully demonstrated.

A domestic complex is represented by Structures 7 through 10. Included in this complex are the remains of at least one house (possibly rebuilt or enlarged over time), several sidewalks (both concrete and brick), concrete steps, a "cave" or storm cellar, a cistern, and a concrete platform for a shed. A privately owned house stood at this location, according to members of the Joe Keegel family who lived in the home into the 1950s, after which the structure was torn down. In earlier times, according to several informants, that building may have been associated with Dr. E. A. Carter, a prominent black physician in Buxton. Structure 11 represents the foundation of another presumably privately owned home. Structures 12 through 15 may represent former domestic structures, although this hypothesis cannot be substantiated at present.

A complex of structures, designated Structures 22 through 24, is located on the hill to the north of Bluff Creek.

These remains are presently identified, respectively, as a stone block revetment (called locally "the stone ledge"), the subsurface foundations of a large structure presumed to be the residence of the mine superintendent, and an associated buried cistern. Located along a fence line directly to the west are some concrete foundations designated Structure 25. This complex may represent outbuildings associated with the mine superintendent's home. Historic photographs of the superintendent's residential area show barns, a probable garage, and a water tower in this approximate locality. As mentioned previously, no structures appear in this location on the 1919 Buxton plat map, although a contemporary map at a smaller scale (Fig. 19) does show the generalized location of buildings north of Bluff Creek.

In addition to these structures in the north-central portion of the townsite, several others were designated and mapped in the field: Structures 20, 21, and 26, which are, respectively, a concrete viaduct over which lies the Chicago and North Western Railroad bed, a steel culvert under the main access road into the present townsite area, and a large sewer conduit located along Bluff Creek north of the stone warehouse. Other structural remains were tentatively identified below the present ground surface west of the former corner of Main and First streets (see Figs. 32 and 33). These remains, generally indicated with assistance of a solid steel probe, may correspond to the locations of the former railroad depot and the structure or structures that at one time housed the Perkins Hotel, the post office, and the newspaper office of the *Buxton Gazette* (*Iowa State Bystander*, 18 September 1903, 2 November 1906, and 6 December 1907).

In an attempt to locate the position of former company-owned houses and associated artifacts, an excavation unit was set out at the south end of the pasture upslope from the two YMCA buildings. Extensive cultural deposits were discovered immediately below the ground surface and extending down approximately one foot to relatively sterile soil. Continuing deeper into the ground, however, were two buried structural features tentatively identified as a rectanglar, wood-lined, trash-filled cesspit, and a large, irregularly shaped garbage pit. The latter included a large number of bottles, preserve jars, storage crocks and jugs, china dishes and bowls, pieces of shoes and other clothing, toy fragments, tools, nails, window glass, and other items. These materials provide a valuable insight into a domestic inventory from Buxton. The position of these features, along with some associated postholes, is presently thought to correspond to the back of properties between East Third and East Fourth streets as shown on the 1919 plat map and photographs of this portion of the town (see Figs. 40 and 41). More specifically, it is probable that these remains of outbuildings and perhaps of fences are situated on ground formerly occupied by Lots 7 and 8 or Lots 9 and 10.

EXCAVATION METHODS AND PROCEDURES

The general procedures of archaeological excavation have been discussed extensively in other publications (Atkinson 1953; Clark 1960; Hester et al. 1975; and Joukowsky 1980), as have the theoretical and methodological axioms of historical archaeology (Deetz 1977; Noel Hume 1969 and 1974;

Schuyler 1978; South 1977; and Weitzman 1976). These matters will not be dealt with in detail here, except for several points relevant to the archaeological investigations at the Buxton townsite.

At any archaeological site some sort of system or systems of spatial control must be maintained so that the locational relationships of structures and other objects to each other can be recorded. A system of reconnaissance units and site survey units was used for the purpose of recording at least the general location of portable artifacts and structural remains discovered during the reconnaissance survey of Section 4 of Bluff Creek Township. Within each site survey unit more specific proveniences could be fixed by assigning numbers to individual "find spots" marked on the aerial photograph map of the section. In Site Survey Unit KP-1 the provenience of portable artifacts was recorded in reference to numbered quadrats, each measuring 100 ft square.

For the purpose of recording the spatial relationships of structures and subsurface excavation units in downtown Buxton, a grid system was established with the use of a transit instrument. In essence, this grid consists of a network of lines intersecting at right angles. The grid system can be extended to any part of the site so that the precise location of structures, excavation units, and other features can be marked on a base map. The grid system serves, then, as a large piece of graph paper upon which data can be plotted in horizontal plan. Most often archaeological grids are oriented on axes aligned on either true north or magnetic north. In the midwestern United States, especially, such grid systems are useful in reference to county roads, section and half-section line fences, etc.

In the case of the Buxton townsite, however, the archaeological grid system was aligned according to the historically known orientation of the street system and principal buildings of the town. This concordance of the grid system with the principal settlement pattern, it was felt, would enable speedy documentation of the data in the field; thus, the locational system used for mapping building remains at the townsite actually was aligned on a point 23° west of true north. However, to simplify description and recording in the field, the terms for the cardinal directions—north, south, east, and west—were used in a more general sense. The directional indicators later were converted to reflect bearings on true north when the final copies of maps and profiles were finished in the laboratory.

In this instance, the southwest foundation corner of the company store was used as a datum point. A north-south line was established paralleling the western wall of the company store. The north-south baseline extends up the alignment of the unnamed street, shown on the 1919 plat map, between the main YMCA building and the White House Hotel. That baseline runs parallel, therefore, to the alignment of Main Street as it is shown on the plat map extending from First Street to Thirteenth Street. Perpendicular to it is the east-west baseline, which runs along the former East First Street and thus parallels all the numbered streets shown on the 1919 plat map of Buxton.

A "grid origin," or main transit station, was set at the intersection of the main north-south and east-west baselines. This transit station is located 25 ft south of the southwest foundation

corner of the company store. That point was arbitrarily assigned the number North 5000/West 5000 (N5000/W5000) so that all places within Section 4 could be measured with reference to the northwest quadrant of an imaginary grid, the origin of which would be 0/0. Coordinates within this northwest quadrant are recorded in terms of the number of feet north and the number of feet west that any given point is located from the imaginary origin. This procedure, as indicated, is absolutely arbitrary but is a matter of convenience, making it unnecessary for crew members to figure out four sets of coordinates as they move around the square-mile section of land recording the locations of archaeological data. Reference to the field map would immediately indicate, for example, that a provenience of N5035/W4985 would be within the ruins of the company store, while N6000/W5200 would be situated across Bluff Creek and atop the hill where Ben Buxton once sat out on his front porch enjoying the view of his town. Finally, the field map would show that the provenience of N4231/W5122 is located in "Feature 1," which was discovered below the present ground surface in an excavation unit up the hill from the YMCA. Here, according to archaeological evidence, people whose names may not be known sat—perhaps reading the Sears and Roebuck catalog—in an outhouse on a lot between East Third and East Fourth streets.

The general goals in investigating the ruins and other visible structural remains in downtown Buxton were to verify locations on the archaeological base map (see Fig. 42), to map the overall dimensions of the buildings, to record certain observable architectural features, and to obtain small collections of associated artifacts that might relate to the time period and/or functions of the structures. Since there were neither funds nor time to completely investigate any single building during the contract period, a decision was made to gather extensive, though limited, data on as many buildings as possible. Within that data base, then, future investigations could be considered for the purpose of gathering more intensive data on individual buildings. In most instances, small test pits or test trenches were excavated in an attempt to answer specific questions relating to the location of walls, the manner in which walls were constructed, and the relationships of buildings to other features of the town.

Test pits and test trenches, for example, were necessary to determine the dimensions of the small YMCA building and the probable location of the swimming pool reported to have once existed within that structure. Test trenches at the main YMCA building showed that the foundation walls and interior support piers were set into narrow bedding trenches and pits rather than surrounding a finished basement. Furthermore, the ground surfaces to the north and south of the main YMCA building had been raised by the piling up of fill dirt along the foundation walls. The ground surface upon which the mine superintendent's residence was built was similarly contoured artificially by the piling up of fill dirt held in place by a large stone revetment. Finally, test excavations at the company store revealed constructional details of that building and the presence of a wide concrete sidewalk, along which large iron lampposts once stood.

At the southern end of Site Survey Unit KP-3, a series of test squares was set out in an attempt to locate the structures that once stood on lots between East Third and East Fourth streets. Today there are no surface indications of these structures that show up on various photographs taken when Buxton was a thriving town. In this case, the excavation units were designated and labelled according to the site grid system. Whatever evidence would be found, then, could be plotted on the base maps even though there were no surface structures as points of reference.

Throughout the subsurface test excavations at Buxton, data collecting procedures more-or-less standard in archaeological investigations were employed. The bulk of the plow zone, extending down to approximately 0.6 ft below the extant ground surface, was removed by shovel and the soil was sifted through half-inch or quarter-inch wire mesh screen to recover any artifacts from the fill. The technique of horizontal shovel skimming was employed to ascertain the contact with that portion near the former ground surface that had not been disturbed by modern cultivation. It was critical to inspect that contact zone carefully, since it offered the first opportunity to discover buried structural remains or artifacts that have not been moved by the plow from their "original" provenience. If buried features or artifacts were found, then, these were further explored by using smaller, more precise excavating tools: masons' trowels, dental picks, bamboo splints, whisk brooms, and paintbrushes.

Artifacts from each level and each test square or pit were bagged separately in paper sacks on which were recorded the site number, the horizontal and vertical proveniences of the material, the day the artifacts were excavated, and the names of the individuals who collected the items. All students kept journal notebooks recording daily where they worked and what they found. The field assistants or field supervisor kept a daily "progress sheet" for each structure and/or excavation unit. Drawn in the field were horizontal plans and vertical profiles recording structural evidence and stratigraphic data. Excavation units and some artifacts were photographed, using color slides, for the purposes of field documentation as well as for subsequent public presentations and publications. Each day the artifacts were transported from the townsite to our field headquarters at William Penn College in Oskaloosa. They were subsequently hauled back to the archaeological laboratory on the ISU campus to be cleaned and further processed.

THE STONE WAREHOUSE (STRUCTURE 1)

Structure 1 is the designation given to the one-story stone warehouse used in conjunction with the first, and possibly also the second, company store in Buxton. The building was constructed in 1905—"A mammoth stone warehouse 162 feet long . . . now nearing completion" (*Iowa State Bystander*, 17

November 1905). A later news item described the building further:

One warehouse 40 × 175 is of stone, steel frame, tile roof, in five separate fireproof compartments. The oil houses are of same construction. All oils, coal oil, miners' oil, turpentine, boiled oil, raw oil and gasoline are pumped into the building, as they are sold, by means of Bowser long distance self-measuring oil pumps. This fact greatly eliminates danger of fire and is the only systematic method of handling oil. That portion of the store, usually dirty, is as clean as any other (*Iowa State Bystander*, 6 December 1907).

The warehouse, situated to the northeast across the railroad tracks from the company store's location, is one of the buildings shown on the 1919 plat map (Fig. 4). In 1980 this building was the most complete structure remaining in its original position within the Buxton townsite, although part of the southwestward end had begun to fall in (Fig. 43). Since 1980, however, both ends of the structure have collapsed (Fig. 44), and some of the resulting limestone rubble has been carried off and utilized elsewhere in Section 4.

Field documentation of Structure 1 included drafting a map of the structure in horizontal plan and taking measured drawings of several of the

43. View to the south of the Consolidation Coal Company's stone warehouse in 1980 with end wall still standing. (Courtesy of the ISU Archaeological Laboratory)

44. View to the south of the Consolidation Coal Company's stone warehouse as it appeared in 1981, after the end wall had collapsed during the winter. (Courtesy of the ISU Archaeological Laboratory)

building's structural elements, including the support trusses and the loading doors (see Figs. 45–46). The building is rectangular and measures 160 ft by 32.5 ft—dimensions that vary somewhat from those reported in 1907. It may be that the "oil houses" referred to were added to the length of the warehouse and the additional width included loading docks along one or both sides of the building. The walls of the warehouse are made up entirely of concrete-mortared, semidressed limestone block. The hipped roof extends the full

length of the warehouse and is composed entirely of interlocking, unglazed red ceramic roofing tiles. The manfacturer's stamp indicates that these tiles were produced by Ludowici of Chicago, Patent No. 983126. A series of angle-iron trusses bolted together with metal plates spans the width of the structure to support the weight of the roof. Across these main supports, lateral bands of angle iron had been affixed to carry each row of roofing tiles. The tiles had been fastened down to the lateral support rods

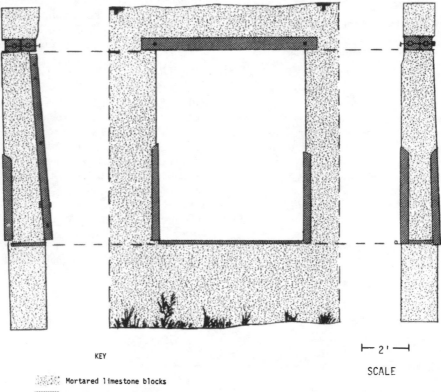

KEY

░░░ Mortared limestone blocks

███ Iron fixtures & fittings

⊢ 2' ⊣

SCALE

45. Exterior and side vertical plan views of one of the loading doors into the stone warehouse.

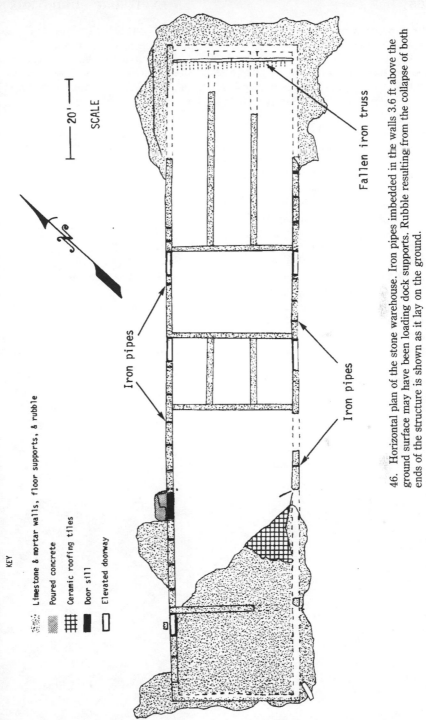

KEY

▓ Limestone & mortar walls, floor supports, & rubble

▒ Poured concrete

⊞ Ceramic roofing tiles

■ Door sill

☐ Elevated doorway

N

SCALE

├─ 20' ─┤

Iron pipes

Iron pipes

Fallen iron truss

46. Horizontal plan of the stone warehouse. Iron pipes imbedded in the walls 3.6 ft above the ground surface may have been loading dock supports. Rubble resulting from the collapse of both ends of the structure is shown as it lay on the ground.

by short lengths of wire strung through a hole molded into each tile.

On the basis of the height of interior stone floor supports and the height of the sills of the loading doors (see Fig. 45), the northeastward portion of the building had had an elevated floor approximately 4 ft above the ground surface. This presumably would have facilitated the unloading of goods from railroad cars and horse-drawn or motorized delivery wagons. The sills of the extant doorways in the southwest end of the building are, respectively, 0.9 ft and 1.7 ft above the ground surface, suggesting that the floors in the two large rooms at this end of the building were much lower. Across the interior of each loading door opening had hung a heavy, metal-plated door 6 ft across. At least one of these doors still remains in place. Each door had been suspended on two heavy iron pulleys that rolled on an iron track above the doorway, allowing the door to slide laterally open or closed. The lower portions of the jambs of the loading doors were clad with iron brace pieces to strengthen and protect them through heavy use. Based on the placement of these doorways, loading and unloading of goods probably took place from both long sides of the warehouse.

Artifactual remains recovered from the rubble of the stone warehouse are limited. These include samples of the limestone block and roofing tiles, a scrap of angle iron from a roof support, copper wire used to attach the tiles to the lateral roof supports, a portion of the metal track from above one of the loading doors, a porcelain fuse plate, and a porcelain light socket.

THE COMPANY STORE (STRUCTURE 2)

Structure 2 is the designation assigned to the remains of the second company store, constructed in 1911 in the center of Buxton's commercial district along First Street (see Fig. 40) and operated by the Monroe Mercantile Company. This structure was built over the location of the first company store, which had been erected in 1901 and was destroyed by fire on 21 February 1911 (*Monroe County News,* 23 February 1911). Projected plans for the

47. Photograph of the opening of the second company store (Monroe Mercantile Company) in Buxton. View is to the northwest. This photo was probably taken in late October or early November of 1911. The White House Hotel is under construction in the foreground; the Buxton Band is playing in the middle of East First Street; chimney stacks of the power plant may be seen behind the company store; and the residence of the mine superintendent is visible on the hill north of Bluff Creek in between the stacks of the power plant. (Courtesy of Dorothy Neal Collier)

48. Front of the Buxton Savings Bank, located in the southeast corner of the second company store building. View is to the northwest. Note the iron lamppost on the sidewalk facing out onto East First Street. (Photo credit attributed to Wilma Stewart)

store to replace that which had burned were discussed in the *Iowa State Bystander* of 10 March 1911:

The blueprint for the new fire proof company store building is already in the hands of manager, McRae, and the building will begin as soon as things can be gotten in readiness. The dimensions are 162 × 120, giving them a great deal more room than they had in the old building. There will be steel sliding doors between each of the departments with plenty of sky light thus enabling them to check a fire in any one of the building's departments without serious damage to the others. The building will only be one story and basement, with a great deal more basement room than they had before, which will do away with the stone ware house standing back of the store. When

completed the building will not only be the best and most substantial in Buxton, but one that would do credit to a large city.

To open the new structure upon its completion a formal celebration, including music by the Buxton Band, was held in late October or early November of 1911 (*Iowa State Bystander*, 10 November 1911; see Fig. 47). Other photographs of the period show the presence of the basement beneath the western portion of the store, the concrete sidewalk that spanned the entire store frontage along First Street, and the Buxton Savings Bank, located in the southeast corner of the store building (Fig. 48). Since the building had

been built on a slope descending to the Chicago and North Western Railroad tracks, entry into the basement for the unloading of goods could be made at track level on the north and west sides of the store, while customers would enter the first floor at street level from First Street on the south.

When the archaeological survey was undertaken in 1980 and 1981, the only visible structural elements of the company store remaining were segments of the foundation and bases of some of the interior support walls; a distinct depression where the basement had been; the concrete retaining wall along the north side, which had faced the railroad tracks; and brick buttresses that evidently had been added along the east wall sometime after the building's construction to provide additional support (Fig. 49). Brick and concrete rubble also lay scattered about within and just outside the limits of the structure's aboveground foundation.

Archaeological documentation of the structure was begun by mapping in horizontal profile all visible structural elements (Fig. 50), and vertical profile transects through the structure were measured and mapped with the aid of a transit theodolite along its length and breadth. A third vertical cross section was mapped across the length of the east half of the building along a line projected to have corresponded with that forming the back, or northward, interior wall of the bank. To facilitate the mapping process, the entire eastern one-third of the structure within the foundation limits, plus part of the concrete sidewalk immediately outside and to the south of the foundation, was shovel skimmed to remove the overlying vegetation and much of the accumulated soil cover. Shovel skimming was conducted within the basement portion of the structure only to expose the laid-brick door sill in the west wall. Probing with a steel rod throughout the basement interior revealed two isolated areas of broken concrete flooring still in place (see Fig. 50). The foundations of a concrete-walled enclosure nearly 7 ft square along the northern wall of the basement near the north door may represent the shaft of a small freight elevator.

To further investigate the nature of the interior subflooring, the exterior

49. Ruins of the second company store, 1981. This view to the southeast shows the remnants of the northern wall, which faced out onto the Chicago and North Western Railroad tracks. (Courtesy of the ISU Archaeological Laboratory)

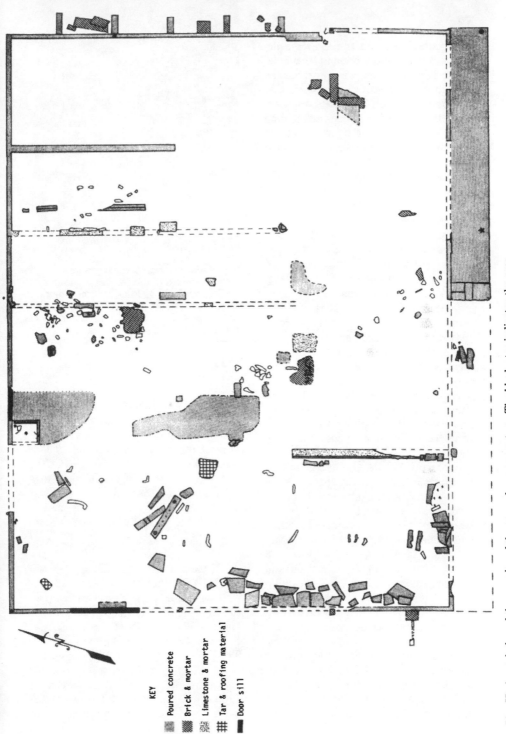

KEY

▨ Poured concrete

▧ Brick & mortar

▨ Limestone & mortar

Tar & roofing material

■ Door sill

50. Horizontal plan of the remains of the second company store. The black star indicates the area in the sidewalk bordering East First Street where sets of inscribed initials were discovered.

wall foundation, and the interface between that foundation and the sidewalk, two test pits were established around the corner of the structure that had been occupied by the Buxton Savings Bank (Fig. 51). Inside the building these tests revealed a poured concrete subfloor inset with wooden two-by-fours that apparently had served as nailers for a wooden floor (Fig. 52). Outside the building, located 3 ft away from the southeast corner within the concrete sidewalk was found the iron footing of a lamppost (Figs. 51 and 52). This same street lamp appears in one of the historic photographs taken of the bank front sometime after 1911 (Fig. 48). A third test pit was dug on either side of one of the interior wall foundations within the portion of the store to the north of the bank, and there it was found that slabs of cement flooring were in direct contact with the wall support. Within the concrete of the sidewalk segments exposed in front of the company store remain several sets of initials that probably date from the time the building was constructed in 1911.

Artifactual remains recovered during the investigation of Structure 2, both within and immediately outside of the extant foundations, include a limited amount of porcelain, ironstone china, and stoneware tableware; ceramic insulators; miscellaneous window and bottle glass fragments; cast iron and sheet metal items; battery parts; and a spark plug. Construction materials thought to be directly associated with the structure include iron pipe segments and pipe fittings, iron nails found imbedded in the rotted wooden nailers; porcelain toilet bowl and/or lavatory fixture segments, translucent textured glass of the variety used in rest rooms to provide both privacy and

51. Archaeological test excavations exposing remains of the southeast corner of the Buxton Savings Bank and the sidewalk facing out on East First Street. Note base of lamppost in the foreground. (Courtesy of the ISU Archaeological Laboratory)

natural lighting, sheet metal flashing, a large mass of tar paper and tar roofing material, and clay bricks carrying the various manufacturers' stamps of OSKALOOSA, BOONE B. T. & P. CO., BOONE CO., or IBCO. Of particular interest among the materials retrieved are a glazed ceramic marble and a nickel dated 1910.

THE COMPANY OFFICE (STRUCTURE 3)

Structure 3 is the designation given to the remains of the business office and associated vault of the Consolidation Coal Company at Buxton (Fig. 53). The brick vault was all that was visible of this building complex when archaeological reconnaissance was begun in 1980. The company office was apparently erected sometime in 1901 on

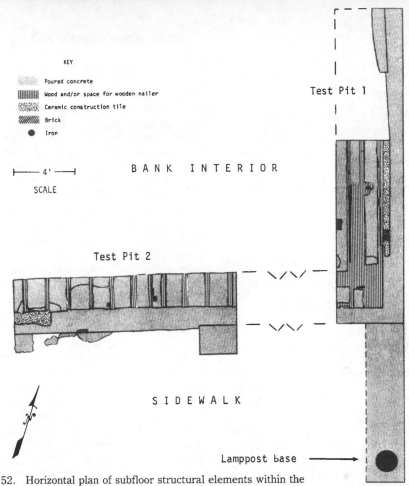

KEY

▨ Poured concrete

▥ Wood and/or space for wooden nailer

▨ Ceramic construction tile

▨ Brick

● Iron

├── 4' ──┤

SCALE

Test Pit 1

B A N K   I N T E R I O R

Test Pit 2

S I D E W A L K

Lamppost base ──→

52. Horizontal plan of subfloor structural elements within the Buxton Savings Bank and a portion of the sidewalk facing out onto East First Street.

53. Photograph of the office of the Consolidation Coal Company in Buxton. Attached to this building was a brick-walled vault. The mine superintendent's house shows to the right on a hilltop north of Bluff Creek. (Photo credit attributed to Wilma Stewart)

the basis of an account printed in the *Iowa State Bystander* of 18 September 1903:

The coal company moved its general offices from Muchakinock to Buxton August 26, 1901, and has an office building in Buxton. It was built especially for the purpose, is isolated from the rest of the buildings, has electric lights and a fine large brick vault for the safe keeping of the records and papers of the company. The office rooms, four in number, are neatly and comfortably furnished.

Steam for heating the coal company's office . . . [comes] from a power house. . . . The electric currents for lighting are also transmitted from this power house.

. . .The men are paid regularly twice a month in cash over the counter and not by check or envelope. Their statements are previously prepared and delivered to them and they draw their money on presenting the statement at the cashier's desk.

In 1981, documentation was made of the vault structure, which apparently had extended toward Bluff Creek from the back of the business office and therefore was not visible in any of the available photographs from the period (see Fig. 53). The vault is 13 ft by 20 ft and rises approximately 16 ft above the present ground surface. The foundation exterior is composed of semi-dressed, mortared limestone block; the foundation interior is apparently a filling of limestone slabs and chunks. The mortared brick walls, 1.5 ft thick, commence 3 to 4 ft above the present ground level. The wall thickness is made up variously of two courses of brick with an intervening hollow wall core or three solid courses of brick. The roof is also of mortared brick with an exterior coat of concrete forming a barrel vault or arch from front to back. On the vault structure's interior, patches of plaster may be noted on all four walls, and the floor retains some of its mortared surface. Wooden pegs

or plugs observed in the walls probably served as nailing inserts; two wooden boards remain on the south wall near the doorway. At the interior roof/wall juncture eight parallel 1-inch square iron rods span the width of the structure. From a board suspended from these is a broken bar-type insulator, to which is attached a cloth-covered wire, presumed evidence for electrical wiring within the structure. There are no windows, so some means of artificial lighting would have been necessary.

The historic photograph taken sometime after 1907 of the front of the office building (Fig. 53) shows it to have been a generally rectangular wooden frame structure with a stone block foundation. The exterior was sided with horizontal wooden clapboards and the hipped roof appears to have been wood shingled. Collectively, six windows and three doors are visible on the two sides of the structure shown. Along the peak of the roof three separate insulator-installed boards served as attachments for electrical lines. A bush or small tree may be noted to one side of the main entry door. Another photograph published in the 6 December 1907 issue of the *Iowa State Bystander* shows miners lined up in front of the business office

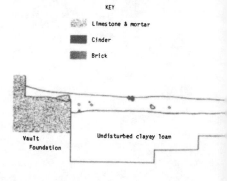

KEY

Limestone & mortar

Cinder

Brick

Vault Foundation   Undisturbed clayey loam

to receive their pay; the same bush is present although it had not yet attained the size seen in the later photograph.

When field investigations were begun near the brick vault in 1981, the office building's foundations were not visible. Therefore a series of shallow, hand-dug exploratory trenches was established extending out from each of the vault's foundation walls in the hope of locating subsurface structural evidence of the associated building (see Figs. 54 and 55). According to the landowner/farmer, the area around the vault had been plowed prior to its con-

54. Archaeological crew establishing test trenches to find the foundations of the Consolidation Coal Company office building, 1981. View is to the northeast. (Courtesy of the ISU Archaeological Laboratory)

version to pasture, and this upper-level disturbance was borne out in the vertical profiles exposed in the archaeologists' trenches. However, a portion of a mortared limestone block foundation was found to be partially intact just below the plow zone contact within Trench 1 (see Fig. 55). A lens of crushed cinder lay just above this foundation.

On the basis of this information, a steel probe was used in an attempt to follow the extension of the foundation outward from this point, and several test pits were established along the general alignment to document the nature of the remaining building foundation. Limestone pieces were found, although discontinuously, in some of the test pits (Fig. 56). Even though many foundation stones were missing, in several instances the outline of the trench in which the block had been laid could be discerned easily by soil texture and color changes. By these means, and by later correlating this information with the general building form seen in the historic photograph (Fig. 53), the dimensions of the company office building are postulated to have been roughly 72 ft by 25 ft; however, the last 15-ft section of the wall on the southeast corner appears to

55. Vertical profile of the east wall of Trench 1 at the company office building. Note the limestone foundation at the base of the vault, which probably served as the footing for the back wall of the office building.

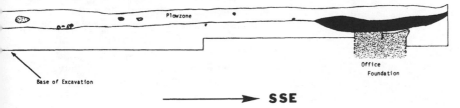

56. Archaeological intern discovering a portion of the stone foundation for the former coal company office building, 1981. (Courtesy of the ISU Archaeological Laboratory)

have been inset by about 5 ft (refer to Fig. 57). Within the foundation limits at least one mortared limestone pier or subfloor support was located. Outside the foundation line, a metal pipe 4 inches in diameter and surrounded by wooden boards was uncovered within Trench 2, and a smaller metal pipe was located sticking up out of the ground approximately 24 ft east of the vault (see Fig. 57).

Artifactual remains collected during the investigation of the company business office include a milk glass button, carbon battery posts, porcelain insulator fragments, window glass and miscellaneous pieces of bottle glass, iron nails and other metal objects, and a stoneware drain tile fragment. Additional structural evidence collected includes wood from around the pipe in Trench 2 and a piece of concrete that had fallen from the vault roof.

THE MAIN YMCA (STRUCTURE 4)

Structure 4 is the designation assigned to the remains of the large YMCA building in Buxton, a three-story structure located southwest and across First Street from the company store (see Figs. 40–42). Erection of the building was begun late in 1903, and it was formally dedicated on the Fourth of July in 1904 (*Iowa State Bystander*, 20 November 1903 and 15 July 1904). The cost of its construction was set at the princely sum of twenty thousand dollars. As a social, cultural, and recreational center, the YMCA served as a major gathering point for the largely black community:

One of the best Christianizing and civilizing is the YMCA. . . . It has a membership second to the largest of any colored YMCA in the United States. It is managed by that brilliant young Christian gentleman, Lewis E. Johnson. . . . He has night schools, a class in physical culture, bookkeeping, Bible study, shorthand and gymnastics. (*Iowa State Bystander*, 20 October 1905)

The facilities available there included an auditorium, a gymnasium, and a reading room (*Iowa State Bystander*, 6 December 1907). Former Buxton residents recall that the Lyceum Bureau brought in road shows to perform at the "Y" (Clayborne Carter in a manuscript to Hubert L. Olin, Febru-

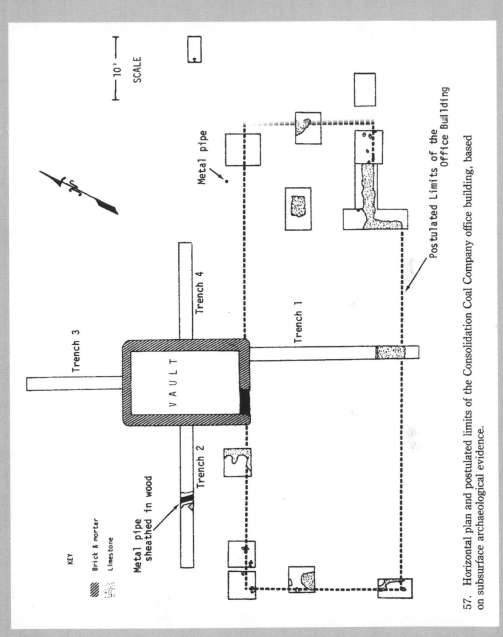

KEY

▨ Brick & mortar

▧ Limestone

Metal pipe
sheathed in wood

Trench 3

Trench 4

VAULT

Trench 2

Trench 1

Metal pipe

SCALE

─── 10'

Postulated Limits of the
Office Building

57. Horizontal plan and postulated limits of the Consolidation Coal Company office building, based on subsurface archaeological evidence.

ary 1963) and that movies were shown regularly in the auditorium (Naomi Ambey, Marjorie Brown, Dorothy Collier, John Pernot; 1980 interviews). Church services also were sometimes held there (Sister Marene Sofranco, interview 1981). Photographs record that Buxton had a basketball team that played its games at the "Y" (*Iowa State Bystander,* 6 December 1907) and the building also contained a pool hall (Towson 1915:266). Space was provided for lodge and union meetings, and the Buxton Band used the YMCA as its meeting hall. It was used during emergencies; the structure served as temporary quarters for school classes when the high school burned in 1907, and the auditorium was used for a time by the Monroe Mercantile Company when the company store burned in 1911 (*Iowa State Bystander,* 18 October 1907 and 3 March 1911).

A photograph taken around 1907 shows the northern and eastern sides of the YMCA and documents some of the building's external structural details (Fig. 58). An iron fire escape or exterior stair angles up the northern face of the structure to the third floor,

and in front of the building a fenced yard area and a walkway, probably of wood, can be discerned. Another photograph of the period reveals that the south exterior wall also carried an open iron stairway to the second and third floors.

In 1980, when archaeological survey and documentation was begun at Buxton, all that could be seen of Structure 4 were a few indications of a limestone block foundation surrounding an elongated depression, within which several large honey locust trees were growing. Cows often gathered there in the cool shade. A segment of a poured concrete sidewalk extending from the eastern end of the depression was also partially exposed; this is probably the "granitoid walk" reported to have been laid in front of the YMCA in 1911 (*Iowa State Bystander,* 10 November 1911).

Prior to mapping the structure in horizontal profile (the result of which is shown in Fig. 59), test pits were established to define the nature of the buried north and south foundation walls and of some interior supports (Test Pits 1 and 3), to ascertain the limits of the two eastern corners of the

58. View of the fronts of the YMCA buildings as seen from East First Street looking southwest. Photograph was taken in the latter part of 1906 or in 1907. Note the iron staircase along the northern wall of the main YMCA and the sidewalks in front of both buildings. (From the *Iowa State Bystander,* 6 December 1907)

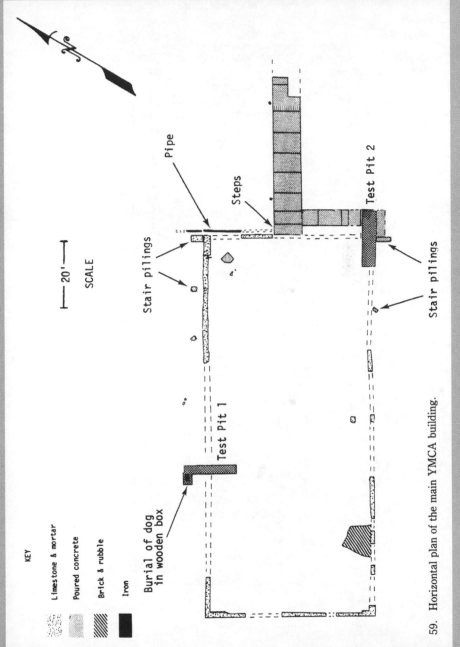

KEY

Limestone & mortar

Poured concrete

Brick & rubble

Iron

⊢———⊣ 20'

SCALE

Pipe

Steps

Stair pilings

Test Pit 2

Stair pilings

Test Pit 1

Burial of dog in wooden box

59. Horizontal plan of the main YMCA building.

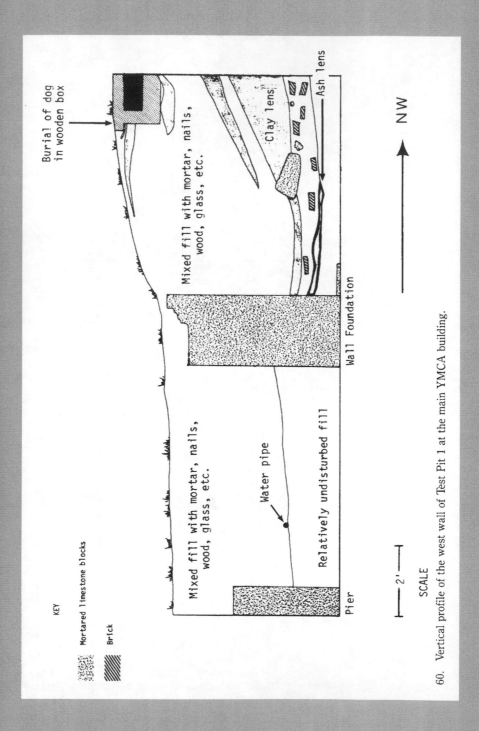

KEY

▨ Mortared limestone blocks

▨ Brick

Burial of dog in wooden box →

Mixed fill with mortar, nails, wood, glass, etc.

Clay lens

Ash lens

Wall Foundation

Mixed fill with mortar, nails, wood, glass, etc.

Water pipe

Relatively undisturbed fill

Pier

NW

⊢— 2' —⊣

SCALE

60. Vertical profile of the west wall of Test Pit 1 at the main YMCA building.

61. Archaeological crew members excavating Test Pit 1 at the main YMCA building, 1981. (Courtesy of the ISU Archaeological Laboratory)

62. Discovery of a dog buried in a wooden box alongside the main YMCA building, 1981. (Courtesy of the ISU Archaeological Laboratory)

63. The Buxton basketball team of 1907 with canine mascot. (From the *Iowa State Bystander*, 6 December 1907)

structure (Test Pits 2 and 4), and to explore the presumed footing for the outside metal stair on the north wall (Test Pit 5). Free-standing mortared limestone piers apparently had served as supports for the floor of the structure, a construction characteristic also noted at Structure 3. Two such floor supports were isolated within Test Pits 1 and 3 at Structure 4. Outside the foundation walls within these two test units, and to a lesser degree within the structure itself just below the floor level, was uncovered the construction debris and soil layering that had occurred at the time the YMCA was built. Also exposed was an accumulation of materials and mixed fill laid down since the building had been dismantled (refer to the vertical profile of Test Pit 1 in Fig. 60). A shallow grave of a medium-sized dog, interred in a wooden box and located beyond the northern foundation limit of Structure 4 (see Figs. 60–62), also was discovered. One might speculate that this was a team mascot such as the dog shown with the Buxton basketball team of 1907 (see Fig. 63).

The foundation corners of the front, or east wall, of the building were encountered within Test Pits 2 and 4 below 0.5 to 1.5 ft of modern slope wash and structural debris (see Fig. 64). Adjacent to the outside of each corner was found a piling or footing for the exterior metal stairways that had been attached to the north and south walls of Structure 4. The pilings on the north side of the building are of mortared limestone, while those on the south are of formed concrete. A poured concrete sidewalk, leading from the area of the front door around to the base of the metal stair on the building's south side, was traced by the use of a metal probe in conjunction with the controlled exposure of a segment of the walkway

64. Archaeological crew members unearthing and mapping the southeast corner of the main YMCA building, 1981. (Courtesy of the ISU Archaeological Laboratory)

(see Fig. 65). At least two sets of initials, dating from the time the sidewalk was laid, were found scratched into this segment of the sidewalk.

Cultural materials recovered from just within and immediately outside the foundations of Structure 4 include a large amount of structural debris such as chunks of concrete and limestone, bricks, drain tile, mortar, plaster, nails, window glass, shingling materials, metal hinges and a door plate, and metal pipe. Materials of a more domestic nature, also present in relative abundance, include several glass soda pop bottles and bottle segments (products of the Coca-Cola Bottling Company and local bottlers and datable to the occupation of Buxton), other clear or brown glass bottle fragments, metal crown bottle caps, glass lamp parts, a brass electric lamp fixture, light bulb bases, cathodes from an arc-light projector, porcelain and glass insulators, ceramic and metal fuses, iron pulleys, an iron barrel hoop, an unspent luger cartridge, a segment of a rubber tire from a Model T Ford, fragments of ironstone china table service and stone-

ware storage vessels, a metal spoon bowl, shell buttons, and ceramic marbles. Portions of an ornate wrought-iron baluster and a cast-iron stair tread or riser, both thought to have come from one of the exterior stairways, also were recovered. Collectively these items allude to the broad range of activities that took place within or near the Buxton YMCA.

THE BOYS' YMCA (STRUCTURE 5)

Structure 5 is the designation given to the remains of the smaller, or boys', YMCA, which was located immediately to the south of the main YMCA building (see Figs. 40–42). This long, wood-frame structure was erected late in 1906, almost three years after the first YMCA was established, at a reported cost of five thousand dollars (*Iowa State Bystander*, 2 November 1906, 23 November 1906, and 27 December 1912). The claim was made that the building constituted the only boys' department of a YMCA in the United States to be housed in its own

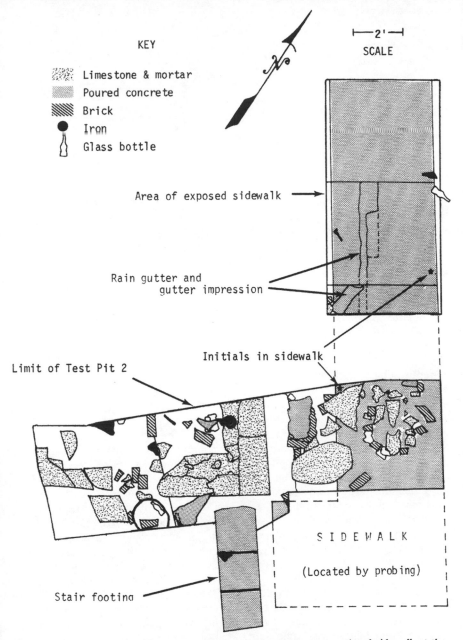

KEY

▓ Limestone & mortar
▒ Poured concrete
▨ Brick
● Iron
⬭ Glass bottle

N

⊢ 2' ⊣
SCALE

Area of exposed sidewalk →

Rain gutter and
   gutter impression →

Initials in sidewalk →

Limit of Test Pit 2 →

SIDEWALK

(Located by probing)

Stair footing →

65. Horizontal plan of Test Pit 2 and associated sidewalk at the main YMCA building. The southeast cornerstone of the foundation was exposed in this excavation unit.

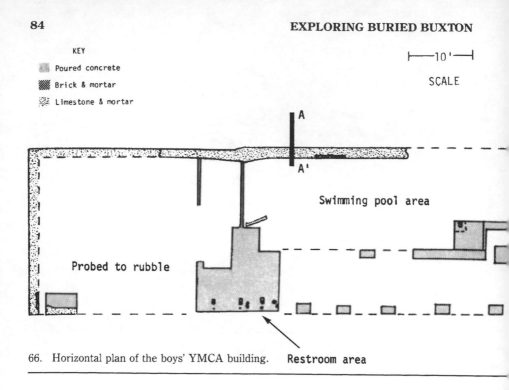

66. Horizontal plan of the boys' YMCA building.

separate structure (*Iowa State By-stander*, 4 November 1911). "Several hundred boys," it was reported, would spend their evenings there in study and gymnastics (*Iowa State Bystander*, 4 November 1910). According to oral history interviews of former Buxton residents who frequented the building, the ground-level floor had contained a swimming pool and restroom, while the upper floor was used as a dance hall, among other activities (Mike Onper, interview 1981; Harold Reasby, interview 1980).

A photograph taken around 1907 (Fig. 58) shows the building stood one and one-half stories high, faced east, was painted white, and exhibited a high, squared, false front. Main entry into the structure was evidently gained by way of a wooden stair leading to the upper floor. Windows are visible at both the upper-floor level and the near-ground level.

When archaeological reconnaissance of the townsite was begun in 1980, little of the foundation of Structure 5 could be seen above the pasture vegetation; however, faint foundation outlines could be followed along the western end of the structure's location on the basis of distinct variations in plant growth there. Silt redeposited downslope by erosion, associated with cultivation prior to construction of a nearby farm pond, was found to have buried the eastern foundation wall under as much as 2 to 3 ft of soil. Therefore, in order to map the structure in horizontal plan (see Fig. 66) a series of test pits was established at various points along the projected perimeter of Structure 5 to verify its presence and to document the manner of construc-

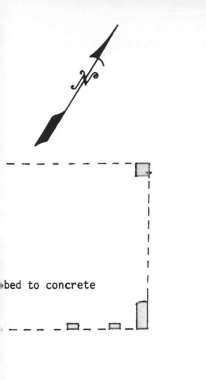

bed to concrete

tion and the types of construction materials used. Much of the foundation was found to be of mortared limestone, although along the south-facing wall this material was no longer extant. The general flooring material used on the lower level of the structure appears to have been concrete. A vertical profile taken through the northern foundation wall showed that it extends down 7 ft below the present ground surface. This depth was necessary to support the wall of the swimming pool, evidence for which occurs as a facing of smoothed concrete on the foundation interior and a smoothed concrete floor abutting the wall at a depth of 5.8 to 6.0 ft below the top of the foundation (see Fig. 67). By probing at regular intervals throughout the structure inte-

67. Vertical profile cross section through the north wall of the boys' YMCA building. Presumed interior of the swimming pool is to the left of the foundation wall; construction trench is to the right. Refer to Figure 66 for general location of profile.

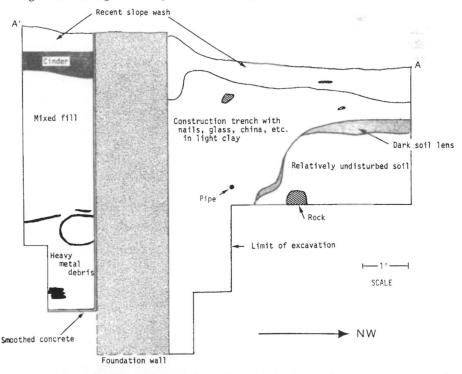

rior as well as by making a limited excavation along what was apparently the eastward corner of the pool, it appears the pool was probably 30 ft long and 14 ft wide, with an extension 8 ft long and 10 ft wide at the east end (see Fig. 66).

A controlled excavation of a portion of the structure along the south wall exposed the area in which the restroom facilities had been located. The seatings for three toilets were uncovered along with the lower sections of the water intake pipes, a sewer vent pipe, and a drain cleanout with intact plug. Impressions of the stool bases could be discerned in the concrete slab floor and holes in the floor 1 inch in diameter marked where the fronts of the toilet stalls had been attached. Artifactual remains recovered from the limited investigations at Structure 5 include a surprisingly large inventory of domestic debris in comparison to the amount of such structural materials as broken cement (some of which has lath impressions), brick, mortar, plaster, wood, nails, and window glass. Glass bottles and bottle fragments and parts make up the largest single category of the domestic items. These include soda bottles (one of which is from the "Buxton Bottling Works"), crown bottle caps, medicine bottles, glass stoppers, preserve jars, milk glass lid liners, and milk glass jars. Other glass items include a lid and pieces of colored glass and pressed glass. Other kitchen items include porcelain and ironstone china table service, stoneware milk bowl and storage container fragments, and portions of a cast-iron stove, including part of the cooking top and the shaker grate. Food materials were reflected in the presence of saw-cut bone. Miscellaneous materials include light bulb fragments, porcelain toilet bowl segments, porcelain insulators, stoneware drain tile, a chunk of lead, strap copper and copper wire, a coil of metal cable, a shell button, a ceramic marble, and a 1905 Liberty Head half dollar.

EVIDENCE FOR THE STREET FRONTING THE YMCA

The 1919 plat map of Buxton shows an unnamed street that began at East First Street and took a zigzag, southeasterly course generally parallelling Main Street (see Figs. 4 and 40). This street ran in front of the two YMCA buildings to East Second Street, jogged west slightly, then continued on to East Fourth Street, where it jogged west again and extended straight past the elementary Fifth Street School and Mount Zion Baptist Church to East Eighth Street. The street then jogged east and terminated at East Ninth Street. Portions of this unnamed street show up on photographs of the town taken before and after 1911, when the second company store was constructed (see Figs. 3 and 41).

While the topography of the ground surface between the YMCA buildings and the White House Hotel is suggestive of a portion of a street, the extant evidence for this feature is more subtle than are the surficial remains of East First Street and Main Street observed in the reconnaissance survey of SSU KP-3. To ascertain the location and nature of this unnamed street, a strategy of subsurface testing was employed on an alignment between the main YMCA building and the White House Hotel. Fourteen test holes were excavated with a posthole digger at 5-ft intervals along a line extending from the sidewalk in front of the YMCA to the raised ground surface along the western wall of the White House Hotel.

These test holes were excavated to depths of 2.0 to 2.6 ft below the present ground surface, and the fill from each test was carefully examined. The stratigraphy in the central test holes generally indicated an upper zone of mixed organic matter, then a zone with high concentrations of cinders, and finally a relatively sterile, light-colored soil of high clay content. The soil zone with cinders ranged from approximately 0.7 to 1.9 ft in thickness. Cinders were notably less prevalent towards the White House Hotel.

The band of cinder-concentrated soil appeared from these tests to be about 40 ft wide, corresponding roughly to the width of streets shown on the 1919 plat map. Various former residents of Buxton refer to a street they call the "Cinder Road." In analyzing their description, however, we do not believe that the street between the YMCA and the White House Hotel is that specifically referred to as the "Cinder Road." It is more likely that cinders were employed throughout the downtown area of Buxton to at least partially improve the condition of the unpaved roads. In any case, judging from the comments of many previous residents of the community, all of Buxton's streets were passable in dry weather but rather risky to travel in the rain.

THE WHITE HOUSE HOTEL (STRUCTURE 6)

Structure 6 is the designation assigned to the concrete foundation and associated stone rubble that are the only portions remaining of the White House Hotel, located directly south across First Street from the company store and east of the large YMCA (see Figs. 41 and 42). The hotel can be seen in its first stages of construction in an historic photograph documenting the grand opening of the company store late in 1911 (Fig. 47). It seems likely that the building would have been ready for occupancy by the beginning

68.   View of the White House Hotel, looking southeast from East First Street. An iron fence surrounds the front yard of the hotel. (Photo credit attributed to Wilma Stewart)

of 1912 because a notice run in the *Iowa State Bystander* for 8 December 1911 stated that "the new 17 room hotel that is to be operated by the M. M. Co. is nearly completed." Presumably the "M. M. Co." here refers to the Monroe Mercantile Company, which operated the company store in Buxton. According to *Polk's Iowa Gazetteer,* for at least the years between 1914 and 1923 the company controlled a hotel, as well as the company store, the bank, and a bakery.

Other than the brief reference to the number of rooms contained within the new hotel in the 1911 newspaper article, not much more architectural

description of this public house is available. A photograph made of the hotel as it would have been viewed from First Street sometime during or after 1912 is the most complete contemporary record yet discovered to document the structure (see Fig. 68).

When archaeological reconnaissance was begun at Buxton in 1980, the foundations of the hotel were largely masked by vegetation (Fig. 69). To record the remains of the hotel in the summer of 1981, this vegetation was removed by hand and the structure's foundations were mapped in horizontal plan (Figs. 70 and 71). While the northern half of the foundation had re-

69. Ruins of the White House Hotel, 1980. View is to the southwest. (Courtesy of the ISU Archaeological Laboratory)

70. Archaeological crew mapping the ruins of the White House Hotel, 1981. View is to the west. (Courtesy of the ISU Archaeological Laboratory)

71. Archaeological crew looking for the porch foundations and steps of the White House Hotel, 1981. View is to the southwest. (Courtesy of the ISU Archaeological Laboratory)

mained fairly well intact, the south end was found to have been reduced to a mass of concrete, limestone, and sandstone rubble (see Fig. 72). This circumstance made the structure's former length dimension somewhat difficult to ascertain; however, it appears that the hotel had probably been 34 ft wide and

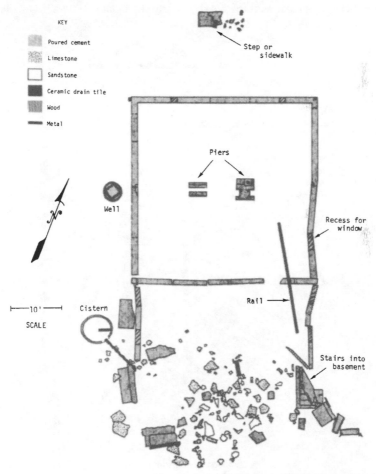

72. Horizontal plan of the White House Hotel ruins.

between 60 and 65 ft in length. Vertical profiles across the length and width of the structure also were measured and mapped (see Fig. 73). Features mapped outside the hotel's foundations near the west wall include a concrete-covered well and a somewhat larger, bell-shaped, concrete cistern. A ceramic tile pipe was found to extend underground from the interior of the cistern to the hotel foundation (see Fig. 72). Unlike the company store and the two YMCAs, which apparently received their water supply from a large central source, it appears that the hotel

had to rely on a well and cistern to provide the water needed for cooking, bathing, and doing the laundry for its guests.

To test for the presence of a basement floor and to document some of the construction techniques utilized, three test pits were dug within the foundations of the hotel. Test Pits 1 and 2 were placed on either side of a concrete support wall running the width of the structure and occurring about midway along its length. An apparent door or passageway opening is present along this wall. On the south

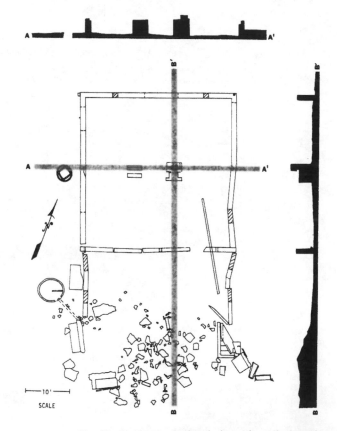

73.   Vertical cross-sectional views through the ruins of the White House Hotel.

side of the wall in Test Pit 2, a poured concrete floor was encountered at 6.8 ft below the top of the foundation walls. At this same depth in Test Pit 1, on the other side of the wall, no flooring material was encountered but two buried metal pipes were found. Within this northern basement "room" Test Pit 3 was placed adjacent to one of the support piers, and again evidence for a floor or subfloor was lacking. Probes made with a steel rod throughout the rest of the area confirmed that flooring was nowhere present there.

It may be assumed, then, that access into the hotel's basement was from the outside via concrete steps found in the rubble (see Fig. 72). These led into the southernmost concrete-floored room, the dimensions of which would have been approximately 22 ft by 34 ft. Natural lighting would have been available to this room through at least four short windows. Use of the larger room to the north was probably more restricted because of its dirt floor and the presence of only one small window on the east near the doorway. A small recess in each of the east and west foundation walls, both of which are in line with the central piers in this northern room, were noted and probably served to secure a primary support beam across the width of this section of the two-and-one-half-story structure. A fourth test pit was established outside and beyond the northward foundation wall of the building to test for any structural remains in the front yard associated with the porch seen in the historic photograph (Fig. 68). Test Pit 4 (see Fig. 71) revealed a broken concrete slab and concrete rubble that marked the position of either the lowest step and/or a sidewalk at the front of the hotel facing First Street and the company store.

Erosion downslope, resulting from cultivation in this general area subsequent to Buxton's demise, had created accumulations of silt up to 3 ft in depth within the foundation walls of the hotel. This recent slope wash had buried a fair amount of cultural debris that had been dumped into the basement of the building. A large amount of material from the dirt-floored area to the north included rotted wood and nails and some carved wood fragments (possibly segments of furniture), as well as plaster, a piece of shoe leather, a glass milk bottle, glass preserve jar fragments and milk glass lid liners, assorted bottle glass and decorative glass, ironstone china table service and stoneware jug fragments, ceramic and glass insulators, enameled metal pan segments and a metal bucket, a chrome-plated brass plumbing ring, and other assorted metal. Of particular interest is a milk glass butter dish lid stamped "Aug 6, 1889." From the area of the concrete-floored room to the south were collected several soda bottles and bottle fragments—including one marked "Buxton Bottling Works, Buxton, Iowa" and others manufactured by the Coca-Cola Bottling Co.—glass preserve jar segments, stoneware sherds, ironstone china fragments, glass and porcelain insulators, window glass, assorted metal, and leather. From around the sidewalk or step uncovered near the front of the hotel came ironstone china fragments, a glass bottle neck and other fragments, and nails. It seems quite probable that some of this material, particularly that from the dirt-floored area, had begun to accumulate while the hotel was still occupied; this suggests that the storage of preserved foodstuffs was one of the uses made of this basement area.

A RESIDENCE
AND OUTBUILDINGS
(THE STRUCTURE
7–10 COMPLEX)

Structure designations 7 through 10 were given to various structural remains associated with a former large, noncompany, residential-style dwelling located in the eastern portion of Buxton's downtown area (see Figs. 40 and 42). Structure 7 is the concrete sidewalk and steps that extend from the present entry lane (formerly First Street) up to the dwelling. The actual remains of the house, the attached porch, and the sidewalks associated with the side and back of the house are labelled Structure 8. Structure 9 consists of a concrete slab floor located east of the back portion of the house, and Structure 10 is a cave or root cellar located back of and slightly upslope from the house. A low, limestone block retaining wall also is present behind the house and near the cave. The presence of plantings of lilac bushes, gooseberry bushes, and catalpa trees in the area of the house and outbuildings can undoubtedly be attributed to the occupation of this structure.

Some information about the most recent occupation of this structural complex is available because the Joe Keegel family, which still resides within a few miles of the Buxton townsite, lived in the house for eight years in the 1950s. They said they made no modifications in the structure while they lived there. Sometime after the Keegels left the house was photographed (Fig. 74), and later it was torn down. The Keegels recalled having been told that a white doctor who later moved to Eddyville had lived in the house in the late 1920s and/or early 1930s. They had furthermore been told that prior to that time the house had been occupied by a black doctor (Joe and Nettie Keegel, personal communication July 1981). They thought, but were not sure, that the structure had once been the home and/or office of Dr. E. A. Carter.

Edward Albert Carter was a prominent black physician who spent his boyhood in Muchakinock, acquired a medical degree at the State University of Iowa, and returned to Buxton to practice medicine for the Consolidation Coal Company. His nephew and daugh-

74. Photograph of the house structure thought to be "Structure 8" in the archaeological listing. This photo was probably taken in the very late 1950s or early 1960s. (Courtesy of the Iowa State Historical Department)

ter both remember Carter's doctor's office and identify the structure in the photograph (Fig. 74) as the same building. They recall that patients entering the front door would walk into a waiting room on the right; a drug room was located to the left. Beyond these rooms, toward the back of the building, were located the doctor's office and operating rooms (Marion and Lawrence Carter, personal communication 1983). The Carter family left Buxton in 1919 and settled in Detroit (Marion Carter, personal communication 1981).

Archaeological documentation of the remains of this structural complex was begun in the spring of 1981, when the visible subunits were assigned structure designations (Fig. 75), and was later continued into the summer of that year. Most easily identified was the series of concrete steps and sidewalks, Structure 7, which had led up to the front door of the house from the entry road. A portion of wrought-iron fencing, probably readapted from some other location in the Buxton townsite, now bars cattle from crossing through the fence at this point to the access road. Several sets of initials could be

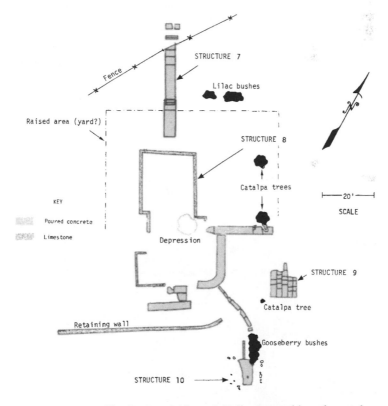

75. Surface evidence initially observed in and around a residential complex designated at Structures 7-10.

read in segments of this sidewalk, and additional initials, as well as the pawprints of at least one dog, could be discerned in the concrete sidewalk that lies along the east side of the house depression.

The house itself, Structure 8, was manifested as a slight, generally rectangular depression oriented northwest/southeast (Figs. 75 and 76). Within the foundation outline of limestone block was a smaller, localized depression that turned out to be a cistern. The Keegels noted that in spring, when the nearby catalpa trees were in flower, the fallen blossoms would give the water in this cistern a bitter taste (Joe and Nettie Keegel, personal communication 1981). To their knowledge the house had never had running water. From the Keegels' description and by studying a few of their family photographs, as well as the historic photograph reproduced in Figure 74, it is known that Structure 8 had been a two-story, wooden frame house without a basement. An open wooden L-shaped porch with turned wooden columns or posts to support the roof had spanned the front (northwest) and eastward sides of the structure. Limestone piers

had served to hold the porch footings up off the ground; these limestone supports were discovered by the archaeologists after some of the vegetation and accumulated silt had been cleared away.

According to the Keegels, the first-floor interior had included one long room across the front of the house. Beyond this room were two more rooms, one of which could be entered from the front room through a set of double doors. Another set of double doors in this second room led into the third room, within which was an open, L-shaped staircase that went up to the second floor. A fourth room could be entered from the third, and in this room a "back stair," also ascending to the second floor, was located. Via this fourth room the kitchen, at the back of the house, could be reached. A separate pantry and the back door were located in the kitchen area. The back door opened out into an enclosed back porch where the cistern was located. The roof of this porch was at the same level as the roof of the L-shaped porch along the front and side. From the back porch there had been a concrete sidewalk, still visible, that curved around

76. Partial unearthing of back sidewalk and side porch supports for Structure 8, 1981. View is to the southeast. (Courtesy of the ISU Archaeological Laboratory)

77. Archaeological crew mapping and exploring the east wall of Structure 8, 1981. View is to the north-west. (Courtesy of the ISU Archaeological Laboratory)

the house to the west and led to an out-house and toward the barn. The floor plan of the second floor of the house consisted of a walk space at the top of the staircase and two large rooms.

Beyond the southeast corner of the house was the segmented concrete slab designated Structure 9 (see Fig. 75). The Keegels said no structure existed there during their residence in the nearby house, but they had been told a coal shed once had stood at that location. A cave, or root cellar, dug into the hillslope behind the house was designated Structure 10 (see Fig. 75). Gooseberry bushes planted near the entrance now obscured its visibility, and only the top of the cemented vault and part of the stairway down into the mouth of the cave could be discerned. A path of broken concrete chunks led from the concrete sidewalk behind the house to the cave entrance.

In order to map this structural complex in horizontal plan, the archaeologists systematically removed vegetation from the area within and just beyond the house foundations. Selected areas around the back and sides of the house then were tested by shovelling and trowelling. After a concentration of cinders was encountered within one of the test trenches placed to the west of the house, an extended area was systematically probed with a steel rod to isolate a cinder path or

small road there. The location of a presumed outhouse pit also was detected by this method. A narrow test trench was excavated to the east of the house beyond the extension of the concrete sidewalk, and there another band of cinders, possibly indicating another cindered lane or road, was exposed.

As subsurface structural features were uncovered, these were added to the horizontal plan of the structural complex (Fig. 77). Perhaps most interesting among these features was the discovery of an earlier sidewalk of un-mortared brick beneath the concrete walk (Fig. 78). By following the extent of this buried walkway, it was found to have branched to the north along the

78. Exposed section along the east side of Structure 8 showing the concrete sidewalk superimposed over an earlier brick sidewalk, 1981. View is to the southwest. (Courtesy of the ISU Archaeological Laboratory)

east side of the house near the ter-
minus of the open porch. It also paralleled the house limits around the back
of the structure before curving off to
the west (see Fig. 79).

Small test trenches were dug on
three sides of the exterior of the cave,
or root cellar, to determine the shape of
the vault, and measured drawings of
the cave's interior walls were made.
The roof forms a simple barrel vault
and the walls are of smoothed concrete

plaster over brick; the floor is of
packed dirt. Wooden shelves were
noted only on the end wall of the structure. A 5-ft-square test pit was dug between the root cellar and the
segmented concrete slab as a control,
but no subsurface features or artifacts
were uncovered there.

Although most of the artifactual remains collected from this structural
complex were found buried about the
sidewalks and foundations of the

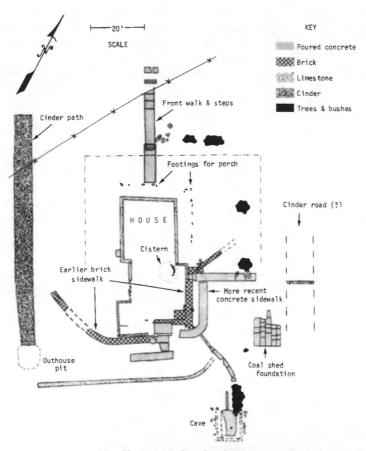

79. Horizontal plan showing interpretation of subsurface structural evidence discovered during 1981 within the area of Structures 7–10.

house, one iron singletree was collected from beside the concrete steps, a metal stake was found just below the ground surface at the segmented concrete slab, and three pieces of ironstone china and some green bottle glass were recovered from one of the test trenches at the cave. Of the 930 items found associated with the house, most can be classified as domestic debris. These objects include decorated porcelain tableware, vases, and/or figurine fragments; decorated and/or white ironstone china tableware items; glazed stoneware and earthenware lid and vessel segments; earthenware flowerpot fragments; bottle glass in clear, blue, brown, amber, and green tints; milk glass jars and decorative table items; a glass tumbler base impressed with the head of a military figure; a faceted glass bauble; glass lamp chimney fragments; a small glass ampule; glass preserve jars and jelly glasses; milk glass preserve jar lid liners and zinc preserve jar lids; a plated table fork stamped "Wm. Rogers and Company"; metal dish and pan fragments; a metal sprinkler bottle head; a metal shaving powder can, a razor handle, and a rusted razor blade; metal pocket watch parts; a brass harmonica plate; a brass lamp reflector; iron stove parts; metal bedspring segments; and a two-hole shell button.

Children's toys include several glazed (blue, blue and white, or brown) and unglazed clay marbles, as well as two glass marbles. A saw-cut cow bone indicates one former food source. Items of a more constructional nature include porcelain insulators, bars, and a light fixture; a glazed earthenware doorknob with metal shank; a ceramic drain tile fragment; window glass; dried paint chips and painted plaster; linoleum scraps; slate; paving bricks,

some of which are marked "Oskaloosa"; asphalt roofing shingles; and metal of all kinds, including iron spikes, nails, fencing staples, bearings, pipes, and the like. An ironshoe for a work-horse and an iron cowbell reflect farming activities that once took place here. An attempt was made not to collect any patently recent materials that might have become mixed with the earlier debris.

RESIDENTIAL BUILDING (STRUCTURE 11)

Structure 11 is the designation given to the remains of an apparent residential dwelling located due south from the stone warehouse and separated from that structure by the roadbed of the Chicago and North Western Railroad and the entry road into Buxton (see Fig. 42). Specific historic information regarding the appearance of the structure's exterior or any of its former occupants has yet to be discovered. The concrete foundations of Structure 11 are very near the present-day farm lane into the area, and a wire fence bordering the lane passes through a corner of the structure.

Archaeological documentation of the remains of this structure in 1981 consisted of mapping the visible foundations and associated structural elements in horizontal plan (see Fig. 80). The only portion of the foundation not exposed lay between the fence line and the lane; however, the presence of a buried foundation wall there was confirmed by the use of a steel rod as a probe. The dimensions of the dwelling measured roughly 42 ft by 28 ft. An underground basement or cellar had been present under the eastern portion of the structure; this basement had consisted of two rooms, each of which

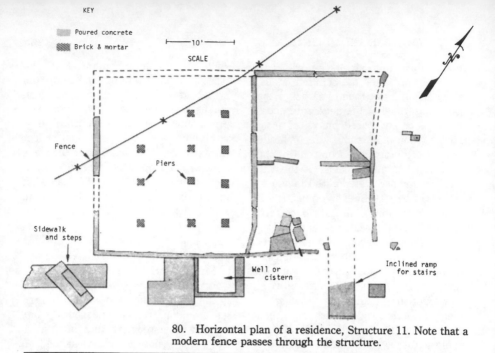

Fence

Piers

Sidewalk
and steps

Well or
cistern

Inclined ramp
for stairs

80. Horizontal plan of a residence, Structure 11. Note that a modern fence passes through the structure.

was approximately 17 ft by 14 ft, connected by a centrally placed doorway through the concrete dividing wall. Entry into the basement was from the outside at the back of the structure. An inclined ramp of concrete 4 ft wide leading down into the basement is thought to have formed the support for wooden stairs. The portion of the house under which there was no basement was supported by 12 mortared-brick piers, 11 of which are still visible. Several remnants of a poured concrete sidewalk and some displaced concrete steps were mapped at the back of the structure, and a concrete, squared-top well or cistern was situated immediately adjacent to the back foundation wall outside the house. No test pits were established within or near the structure because most of the foundations were already exposed, and no artifacts thought to be directly associated with the occupation of the structure were located or collected.

SURFACE INDICATIONS OF UNIDENTIFIED BUILDINGS (STRUCTURES 12–16)

Structure designations 12 and 13 were assigned to two flat or depressed areas to the east of Structure 8 (see Fig. 42). Some structural remnants, such as a segment of brick and stone wall, a few limestone blocks, and concrete rubble, were the only above-surface evidence that buildings once may have stood at these two locations. Metal pipes, ranging from 1 inch to 5 inches in diameter, could be seen to extend upwards or horizontally from the ground surface at various locations outside the structures. Structure 12, the larger of the two, is a slightly depressed oval area 60 to 65 ft long and 30 ft wide. The long downslope side of this area had been built up to form a low revetment. More recently this rim of earth was breached to promote drainage (Joe Keegel, personal communication 1981).

Just slightly upslope from this large depression stands a wall section of mortared brick, limestone, and concrete, and an adjacent concentration of rubble, an area referred to here as Structure 13. Extensive probing was conducted here with a steel rod and contact with scattered, buried, structural remains was made. On this basis it appears the foundations delimit a building roughly 25 ft square. Joe Keegel reported that in the 1950s a hexagon-shaped outbuilding was situated on this location. However, that building simply rested on the foundations of a former structure and did not conform to the outline of the visible foundations (Joe Keegel, personal communication 1981).

Archaeological documentation of these two structures included the drafting of horizontal profiles of both and the mapping of a vertical cross section through the general area. Two test pits, one just outside and another within the depressed oval, were excavated at Structure 12. Test Pit 1 revealed a lens of reddish cinders 0.3 ft thick just outside the low artificial embankment — possible evidence for the edge of a cinder-covered roadway or path running parallel to the alignment of the embankment. A much smaller lens of the same cinder was found within Test Pit 2 inside the depression. Also within this test pit was found a 5-inch-diameter metal pipe laid at the bottom of a 2.5-ft-wide trench. This pipe runs obliquely to the alignment of the embankment and falls in line with a pipe of the same diameter that is exposed on the surface outside of the structure.

The question remains as to the functions these two structures served during the occupation of Buxton and whether there is a direct connection between the two in terms of their use.

Joe Keegel remembered that when his family occupied the nearby house in the 1950s a "road" ran between the house and the location of Structures 12 and 13 (Joe Keegel, personal communication 1981), and it seems plausible that this was a remnant of one of the former north/south-trending streets in the town. If so, then it is likely that Structures 12 and 13 were located on a town lot separate from that on which Structure 8 is situated.

Artifactual remains collected from the test units in Structure 12 include several rim, base, and body fragments of white ironstone china; a few pieces of clear glass; a porcelain heating coil insulator; and an iron nail. From the surface of Structure 13 were recovered a heavy cast-iron plate and a chrome-plated metal cover, possibly from an electric iron and probably of recent vintage.

The Structure 14 designation was given to a distinct, roughly circular depression located well upslope from Structure 8 in an area thought to have been near East Second Street (see Fig. 42). Several brick and concrete foundation elements, including what is apparently a window well, are exposed within this depression, which now measures 32 ft by 27 ft. Also exposed is a length of heavy metal pipe, 5 inches in diameter, which lies in a horizontal position near the bottom of the depression. A small tree has become established near the center of the structure. A sharpened metal rod was used as an exploratory tool in an attempt to locate additional subsurface structural evidence. Probing was done at regular 2-ft intervals both within and immediately outside of the depression, and contact was made with solid material at depths ranging from 0.5 ft to 1.9 ft below the surface only within the limits of the depression. To document the structure, the visible above-ground elements were mapped in horizontal profile, and two cross-sectional profiles were measured and recorded.

Close examination of the ground surface surrounding Structure 14 revealed two small concrete rings 0.8 to 1.0 ft across and spaced 8 ft apart in an area nearly 27 ft northeast of the structure depression. Further scrutiny by clearing away the vegetation showed that these are concrete-lined post molds. A small test pit was established within 8 ft to the west of and in line with the two post molds, thereby uncovering a third concrete-lined post impression and some scattered limestone. This evidence suggests that a rather substantial fence had once stood to the north of Structure 14. The limited artifactual remains retrieved from this quick test along the presumed fence line include a decorated porcelain plate base, one fragment of clear glass, a small iron railroad spike, and some concrete mortar.

Structure 15 designation was given to a badly broken concrete slab and limestone block floor located immediately south of the present silo and cattle-feeding installation in Buxton's downtown area (see Fig. 42). The dimensions of these structural remains are roughly 15 ft by 20 ft. Members of the Keegel family recalled tearing down a barn at this location sometime after 1950 (Jim Keegel, personal communication 1981). Portions of the wooden superstructure were deposited at that time in the small ravine corresponding to Main Street (see Fig. 11). It is quite possible that Structure 15 represents a barn erected after the commercial center of the town was abandoned and built by a resident farmer strictly for the purpose of housing livestock and storing hay.

A faint depression and a diffuse scatter of concrete and limestone rubble was noted in Buxton's downtown district to the north of the former railroad bed and 50 to 75 ft south-southwest of the stone warehouse. This evidence is recorded as Structure 16 (see Fig. 42), although little more detail can be extrapolated about the structure that stood here on the basis of surficial remains alone.

THE POWER PLANT (STRUCTURE 17)

Structure 17 is the designation given to a concentration of concrete and limestone footings, mortared brick segments, heavy iron pipes and pipe fittings, and a collapsed iron tank located north across the railroad grade from the company store (see Fig. 42). This collection of structural elements is undoubtedly the remains of the power plant that once provided heat and electricity to most, if not all, of the business and commercial buildings in downtown Buxton, and that ultimately supplied electrical service to the residential district as well. The power plant apparently was erected sometime between 1900 and 1903, since a brief reference to the "power house" that supplied heat and light to the company office occurs in the *Bystander* of 18 September 1903. Two tall smokestacks are all that can be discerned of the structure in the photographs available (for instance, Figs. 3 and 41).

The fuel utilized was unquestionably coal, and the power generated produced steam for heating as well as electricity for lighting purposes. Mention is made in the 9 November 1906 *Iowa State Bystander* that in Buxton there were "new electric lights distributed

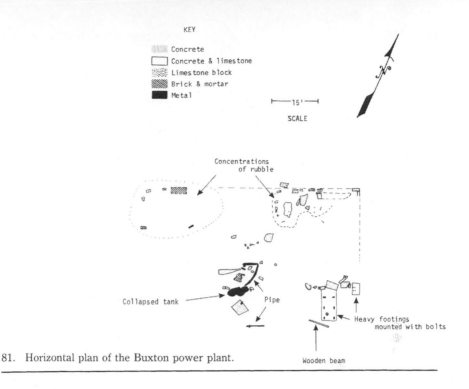

Concentrations
of rubble

Collapsed tank   Pipe

Heavy footings
mounted with bolts

81. Horizontal plan of the Buxton power plant.

Wooden beam

over the city," and poles to carry electrical lines are visible in views of the business area and some residential areas in many of the historic photographs available. By 1911, dependence upon the electrical current supplied by the power plant was fairly crucial to the town because a news item in the "Buxton Briefs" column of the *Iowa State Bystander* of 6 January 1911 states, "Our city has been in darkness for the past four or five days on account of the boilers at the power house needing repairs." Further evidence for some use of electricity in Buxton is present in the form of glass and ceramic insulators and light bulb fragments, which have been found at several loci throughout the townsite. However, many of the former residents of Buxton recalled that their homes did not have electricity, and lighting was provided totally by kerosene lamps (for example, Jeannette Adams, interview 1980; Lester Beaman, interview 1980).

In order to archaeologically document the power plant, vegetation obscuring the rubble was cut so that a measured horizontal plan could be drawn (see Figs. 81 and 82). In addi-

82. Archaeological crew mapping the visible ruins of the Buxton power plant, 1981. View is to the west with the brick vault in the background. (Courtesy of the ISU Archaeological Laboratory)

83. Scene along northern entry road into Buxton, showing Armstrong's Meat Market in the foreground. Other identified buildings include, *center,* a livery, and *background,* the First Methodist Church and the African Methodist Episcopal Church. View is to the north northeast. (Courtesy of Donald Gaines)

tion, some limited shovel skimming was done to expose a northeastward corner and to attempt to follow the projected walls from that exposed corner-stone. A fair amount of rubble, particularly in two concentrations, was encountered just below the ground surface. A limited number of artifacts associated with the structure was recovered, including miscellaneous metal fragments such as a small railroad spike, some clear glass, a porcelain insulator, a porcelain fuse holder, and a portion of a glass insulator marked "Petticoat."

POSSIBLE REMAINS OF ARMSTRONG'S MEAT MARKET (STRUCTURE 18)

On top of the small ridge immediately east of the foundations of the company store was noted a faint depression that was recorded as Structure 18. The position of this depression is directly across First Street (now an access lane) from the location of the present-day silo (see Fig. 42). The limits of this presumed structural depression are indistinct, and no further documentation was attempted at the time of the archaeological survey. On the 1919 plat map (Fig. 40) a few unidentified buildings are indicated in this general area, and several former residents of Buxton have related that Hobe Armstrong's meat market, a barn to shelter delivery wagons, a bandstand, and possibly other buildings were all located directly east from the company store (Naomi Ambey, interview 1981; Dorothy Collier, interview 1980; Archie Harris, personal communication 1980; Bessie Lewis, interview 1981; and Mike Onper, interview 1981). This information corresponds with buildings visible in the foreground of the photograph reproduced in Figure 83.

POSSIBLE RUINS OF THE TELEGRAPH OFFICE (STRUCTURE 19)

The designation of Structure 19 was given to a collection of concrete, mortared brick, and mortared limestone rubble that lay about the base of a large cottonwood tree 35 to 40 ft west of the company store (see Fig. 42). It is in this general vicinity that Buxton's telegraph office is reported to have once stood (Archie Harris, personal communication 1981), and the small building visible next to the first company store in a photograph taken sometime prior to 1911 (Fig. 14) may be this structure.

To document the structure a horizontal plan sketch of the rubble as it lay about the tree was made and the subsurface around the tree was probed with a steel rod. The probe made contact with solid material within an 8-ft-wide area both to the east and to the west of the tree, suggesting that hidden foundations, flooring, and/or more rubble may be present at this locus. The growth of the tree, however, has undoubtedly disturbed the original positions of the structural elements, if these are present.

CONCRETE VIADUCT AND STEEL CULVERT (STRUCTURES 20 AND 21)

The designation of Structure 20 was assigned to the concrete railroad viaduct lying beneath the Chicago and North Western track bed northeast of

84. Concrete viaduct over which the Chicago and North Western Railroad tracks passed at Buxton. The year 1918 is impressed into the upper part of the structure. (Courtesy of Charles Irby)

the stone warehouse (see Figs. 42 and 84). This structure was built to allow the flow of an unnamed tributary to Bluff Creek beneath the railroad tracks. The date 1918 has been molded into the eastward face of the viaduct, and on the side facing the warehouse various initials have been engraved into the concrete surface, along with the hand-inscribed date of 1919. It is assumed that this structure was built around the time of these dates to supplant an earlier, less permanent viaduct.

Several feet southeast of the railroad viaduct, a large, riveted steel culvert lies under the entrance road into the Buxton townsite. This culvert is referred to here as Structure 21 (see Fig. 42). It also serves to channel the flow of the small creek that empties to the north into Bluff Creek and probably dates from the time that Buxton was in its heyday.

THE MINE SUPERINTENDENT'S HOUSE (STRUCTURES 22–24)

Across Bluff Creek, to the north and west of Buxton's commercial/business

85.   Ben C. Buxton, first mine superintendent for the Consolidation Coal Company at Buxton. Buxton was 25 years of age when he came to the position in 1900. (Courtesy of the Iowa State Historical Department)

district, can be seen a revetment on the hillside that is known locally as the "stone ledge." This man-made surface feature, constructed to contain an artificially filled and levelled piece of ground upon which mine superintendent Ben Buxton (Fig. 85) could build his residence, has been designated Structure 22. The remains of the residence per se will be referred to here as Structure 23. Succeeding mine superintendents at Buxton also made this residence their home. The site provided a full and lofty view of the town to the south, and persons walking from the downtown Buxton area to the superintendent's house first had to cross Bluff Creek, via a bridge that continued as a raised walkway over the lower terrace, and to climb a wooden stairway placed at one point along the stone wall in order to reach the house (Ada

Baysoar Morgan, interview 1981). The stone wall, walkway, wooden stairs, residence, and associated outbuildings show clearly in an historic photograph taken between 1909 and 1913 when E. M. Baysoar was the mine superintendent (Fig. 86).

The wall obviously was impressive. One informant, Marvin Franzen, whose father was caretaker for Ben Buxton and subsequent superintendent, described it thusly:

That house had a big high . . . wall made out of quarry limestone rock. It . . . went all around the front yard. . . .That wall was as high as this ceiling; you couldn't climb up over it. You couldn't get over it. You had to come up that stairway. . . .
That was a hillside they built on and they probably had to fill it in, I reckon, and [the wall] was put there to hold the dirt up 'cause the house sat way up high. That house was high, way up high. (Interview 1981)

Although segments of the stone revetment have been allowed to crumble since the last mine superintendent left in the 1920s, it continues to present an impressive feature on the landscape (see Fig. 87). Relics of garden plantings still growing along the revetment include a lilac bush, trumpet vines, and barberry bushes.

The house itself was a large, two-and-one-half-story, white frame structure with dormered attic windows and an enclosed porch spanning the south and east exterior walls (see Fig. 86). Ada Baysoar Morgan, daughter of Superintendent Baysoar, and Marvin Franzen both recall that the house was supplied with electricity, a telephone, and hot and cold running water. Franzen's father had installed plumbing pipes of lead, and possibly some of copper, in the house. The first floor consisted of a small office, a front room with a view to the south and an open ascending staircase with "a big, fancy railing," a dining room, a kitchen, and a bathroom. The second floor, he remembers, had three or four bedrooms and a second, larger bathroom. There was a full attic, which he had never

seen, and a basement where the coal-fired furnace was located. The floors were of hardwood covered by throw rugs and/or runners, except in the kitchen where the floor was covered with linoleum; the woodwork was "real

86. Photograph of the residence and associated buildings of the Consolidation Coal Company mine superintendent at Buxton, taken sometime between 1909 and 1913. View is to the north. Note the stone revetment over which extends a wooden stairway. These steps and a wooden pedestrian bridge led across Bluff Creek to the company office building. To the left show the water tower and barns or garages. (Courtesy of Ada Baysoar Morgan)

87. Stone revetment at the mine superintendent's residence, as it appeared during the spring of 1981. This stone ledge was designated Structure 22. View is to the north. (Courtesy of the ISU Archaeological Laboratory)

light colored" (Marvin Franzen, interview 1981). The house is said to have stood empty after the mid-1920s until it was dismantled sometime in the 1930s (Archie Harris, personal communication 1980; Joe Keegal, personal communication 1981). Although the superintendent's house and attendant outbuildings are visible in several photographs taken during Buxton's height (such as Figs. 2, 41, 47, and 53), none of these structures was included on the plat map of the town drawn up in 1919 (Fig. 4).

Since no above-surface remains of the superintendent's house were visible for documentation by the archaeologists in 1981, a series of three long probing transects oriented north-south with the site grid were made with a sharpened, solid-steel rod (see Fig. 89). In areas in which solid subsurface contact was made, small test pits were established to investigate the nature of the material below. Through these it became evident that most of the house foundations probably lay to the east of the position of the probing transects, because some suspected foundation material was found within the easternmost probing alignment. Therefore,

88. Remains of the stone foundation of the mine superintendent's residence, as discovered in an archaeological test pit in 1981. The residence was designated Structure 23. View is to the northwest. (Courtesy of the ISU Archaeological Laboratory)

additional test pits were established in that area (see Fig. 89). Within four of these pits were found isolated segments of mortared limestone foundation block, including one that is undoubtedly the southeast cornerstone of the house (see Figs. 88 and 90). Limestone blocks found lying outside the established house foundation line are thought to have been footings on which supports for the enclosed porch rested. It was noted that the fill around the foundation units was considerably mixed, probably as a result of the levelling and landscaping of the area prior to construction of the house.

Within the fill around the foundations and below the porch floor of the structure, most of the artifactual remains recovered are constructional in nature. These consist of cut and wire nails, window glass, fragments of wood, ceramic drain tile fragments, and pieces of asbestos and plaster. Of a more domestic nature are a light bulb base; stoneware vessel fragments; two pieces of ironstone china; a small, opaque glass bead; and several clear glass bottle segments, one of which is a bottle base with a molded fisherman and fish design virtually identical to that on a complete bottle, collected in SSU KP-10, marked "Scott's Emulsion Cod Liver Oil with Lime and Soda."

Just to the north of the projected northeast corner of the house foundation, and therefore outside of the house wall, the truncated top of a mortared brick cistern was encountered. This structural subunit was designated as Structure 24. A decision was made to excavate the interior of this structure at least to the depth of its maximum diameter, which was found to be approximately 9.5 ft across (see Fig. 91). In the interest of time and because rain water had begun to collect there, no

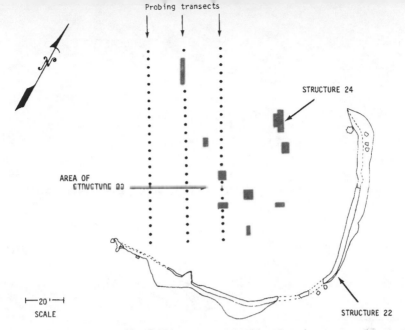

Probing transects

STRUCTURE 24

AREA OF
STRUCTURE 23

N

20'
SCALE

STRUCTURE 22

89. Probing transects and location of test excavations in the area
of Structures 22–24, the mine superintendent's residence.

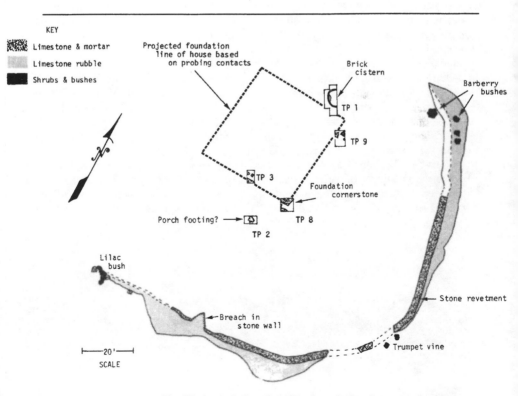

KEY

Limestone & mortar

Limestone rubble

Shrubs & bushes

Projected foundation
line of house based
on probing contacts

Brick
cistern

TP 1

Barberry
bushes

N

TP 9

TP 3

Foundation
cornerstone

Porch footing?

TP 8

TP 2

Lilac
bush

Stone revetment

Breach in
stone wall

Trumpet vine

20'
SCALE

90. Horizontal plan recording botanical and structural evidence
observed and/or unearthed in the area of the mine superintendent's residence.

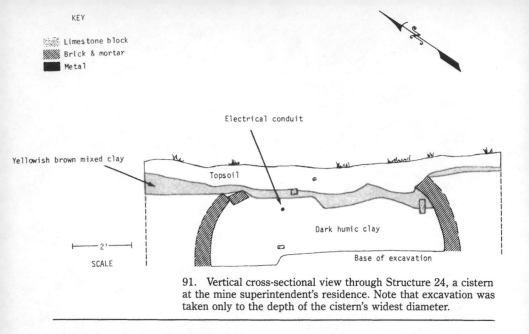

Electrical conduit

Yellowish brown mixed clay

Topsoil

Dark humic clay

├── 2' ──┤

SCALE

Base of excavation

91. Vertical cross-sectional view through Structure 24, a cistern at the mine superintendent's residence. Note that excavation was taken only to the depth of the cistern's widest diameter.

excavation within the cistern deeper than 3.6 ft below the ground surface was attempted. However, a steel probe pushed into the center of the cistern to a depth of at least 8 ft below the ground surface had not yet struck a solid floor. Structural debris and artifacts recovered from the cistern's excavated fill include cut nails, iron bolts, window glass, wood fragments, lead and copper electrical conduit, a possible fishhook, an iron door hinge, one piece of ironstone china, milk glass preserve jar lid liner fragments, a zinc preserve jar lid with rubber gasket, glass bottle segments, a four-hole milk glass button, and a walnut shell.

THE SUPERINTENDENT'S OUTBUILDINGS (STRUCTURAL COMPLEX 25)

In the spring of 1981 the archaeologists had noted a concentration of structural remains partially hidden in the grass across the fence to the north and west of the former location of the superintendent's residence. This evidence was measured and sketched, and the complex was later designated as Structure 25 (see Figs. 42 and 92). One tall, rectangular piling into which heavy iron bolts had been set was the most readily visible of the remains, and nearby lay two rather square, flat areas of limestone block capped by concrete

92. Ruins of the water tower and other outbuildings, Structural Complex 25, at the mine superintendent's residence, spring 1981. View is to the southeast. (Courtesy of the ISU Archaeological Laboratory)

(see Fig. 93). On one of the latter structural elements, in a small, squared recess that had been filled in with a thin slurry of concrete, was inscribed by hand a combination of faint Roman numerals and capital letters. These are taken to be a date and possibly some initials; if read correctly the Roman numerals form "I-X-XIV," or 1-10-14. It is quite possible that this inscription was affixed to the structure sometime after it was originally built.

Between the two flat areas was noted a small, circular depression (see Fig. 93). One short pier or pylon of mortared brick also was observed close by, and five heavy iron pipes were seen to extend up out of the ground from around the brick and limestone features. Other lengths of pipe lay on the

ground a short distance away, along with some concrete rubble. Somewhat removed from and to the north of this first group of structural elements were six low concrete pilings, arranged in two sets of three, covering an area approximately 30 ft by 30 ft in extent (see Fig. 93).

Structural Complex 25 is thought to include the remnants of one or more outbuildings, such as barns and/or garages, and the wooden water tower associated with the residence of the mine superintendent. Such structures are visible in several of the photographs taken during Buxton's heyday, two of which are reproduced as Figures 2 and 41. Along with the house of the mine superintendent, these rather obvious structures were not included

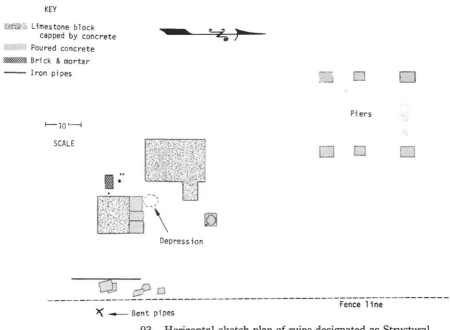

93. Horizontal sketch plan of ruins designated as Structural Complex 25, outbuildings associated with the mine superintendent's residence.

on the plat map drawn up in 1919 (Fig. 4).

THE SEWER PIPE (STRUCTURE 26)

Within the right bank of Bluff Creek in the area to the north and west of the stone warehouse was noted a large metal sewage or storm sewer pipe approximately 12 inches in diameter (see Fig. 42). Some water still flowed from this pipe in 1981, and it is assumed that this utilitarian structure had been installed during the occupation of the Buxton townsite to assist drainage of the lower portion of the downtown area.

EXCAVATIONS AT THE SOUTH END OF SITE SURVEY UNIT KP-3

INVESTIGATIVE PURPOSES AND PROCEDURES. On the basis of surface data collected in the controlled quadrat survey of Site Survey Unit KP-1 during the summer of 1980, the archaeologists had hoped to set out some test squares in that field during the summer of 1981. The purpose would have been to test hypotheses concerning the apparent locations of streets and the backs of house lots between East Fourth and East Ninth streets. As discussed previously, however, this strategy was not possible because the field designated SSU KP-1 had been sown to oats and the landowner did not want his crop damaged. Nevertheless, he was willing for the archaeologists to conduct test excavations directly across the fence on his pastureland.

The following preparations therefore were made to revise the excavation strategy for the 1981 field season: (1)

information from SSU KP-1 was extrapolated and hypothetically extended to the portion of the townsite directly to the south; this was reasoned to be the area between the former East Fourth and East Third streets; (2) probe tests were made with a solid steel rod to ascertain the nature of the subsurface deposits and the potential for buried streets and structures; and (3) a series of test holes was instituted with the use of a posthole digger. Those tests indicated (a) the presence of a relatively shallow plow zone, (b) the presence of areas of both light and heavy cinder concentrations, and (c) the presence of some cultural materials extending to depths below the modern plow zone. Those data suggested a potential for finding structural evidence and artifacts buried below the surface of the modern pasture.

Three test excavation units were staked off directly north of the fence line at the south end of Site Survey Unit KP-3 (see Fig. 94). The first three excavation units consisted of squares measuring 10 ft by 10 ft and were designated according to the grid coordinates at their southeast corners: N4200/W5100, N4210/W5110, and N4220/W5120. On the basis of the data collected in these three test squares, the excavations were extended to include two additional 10-ft squares (N4190/W5100 and N4200/W5110) and portions of four other squares— N4180/W5100, N4180/W5110, N4190/ W5100, and N4230/W5120 (see Fig. 95). Excavation techniques followed those procedures previously described. First the plow zone was stripped off and the soil was sifted through wire mesh screen (see Fig. 96). The plow zone in this area was approximately 0.6 ft in thickness. This relatively thin plow zone can probably be explained

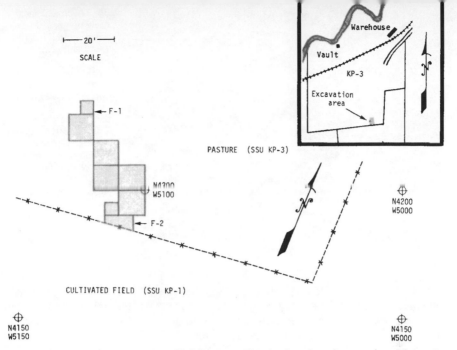

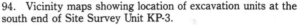
94. Vicinity maps showing location of excavation units at the south end of Site Survey Unit KP-3.

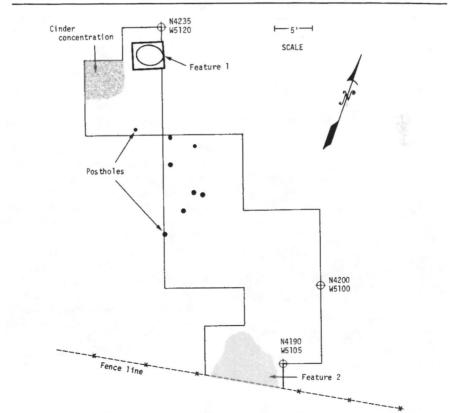

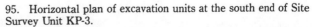
95. Horizontal plan of excavation units at the south end of Site Survey Unit KP-3.

96. Archaeological crew opening up excavation units at the south end of Site Survey Unit KP-3, 1981. View is to the northeast. This area corresponds to a former area of quarter-acre lots between East Third and East Fourth streets. The plow zone is being removed by shovel and the soil is being sifted through wire mesh screen to retain small artifacts. (Courtesy of the ISU Archaeological Laboratory)

by (a) the shoulder slope position of this part of the hillside, and (b) the fact that excessive "topsoil" erosion no doubt occurred previously at a time when SSU KP-3 was being cultivated for the growing of row crops. The contact between the plow zone and the relatively undisturbed subsoil was carefully investigated by the technique of horizontal shovel skimming (see Fig. 97). This procedure facilitated the removal of the cultural materials from the soil matrix closest to what would have been the ground surface at the time of the urban settlement of Buxton.

97. Archaeological intern shovel skimming to the base of the plow zone within Test Square N4210/W5110 during the 1981 field season. View is to the north. (Courtesy of the ISU Archaeological Laboratory)

PORTABLE ARTIFACTS RECOVERED FROM THE PLOW ZONE. Portable artifacts were abundant within the plow zone removed from the test squares at the south end of Site Survey Unit KP-3. Items cataloged include 4866 specimens, many of them small fragments of objects broken up by previous cultivation activities. Among the 1011 china tableware and container fragments are toy plates, bowls, and teapots. Stoneware crocks, jugs, and butter churns are represented by 204 sherds, while among the 57 miscellaneous ceramic objects are china doll parts, marbles, doorknobs, a drawer pull, a flowerpot, and insulators. Glass bottles, jars, stoppers and other closures, along with decorative glass containers and pitchers, are evidenced by a total of 2262 pieces of transparent glass. Milk glass jars and canning jar lid liners are represented by 227 fragments. Among the 85 miscellaneous glass artifacts are kerosene lamp chimneys, windowpane fragments, buttons, and a small, blue glass bead. There are 5 celluloid artifacts (1 button, 2 interfacing strips, and a possible pen fragment).

Within the artifact inventory from the plow zone are 842 metal artifacts, including coins (3 pennies dated 190[?], 1906, and 1912), tools (scissors, a hammer, a file, a miner's pick, and a thimble), household furniture parts (casters, clock parts, drawer pulls, escutcheons, and stove parts), construction materials (nails, screws, nuts, bolts, window fittings, and doorknobs), items of clothing (buckles, hooks, and a possible purse closure), kitchen tools and other domestic equipment (irons, enamelware pots and pans, spoons, knife blades, bottle caps and closures), weaponry (shotgun shells, rifle shell casings, and a gun part), and miscellaneous items (harness hooks, a shoe last, railroad spikes, a horseshoe, a carriage plate, a spark plug, padlock parts, a harmonica plate, pencil ends, and electrical fittings). Among the 65 fragments of leather are pieces of shoes, harnesses, and belts, while the 42 items of construction material include pieces of wood, brick, concrete, and mortar. Miscellaneous items include 6 stone objects (including a whetstone, pieces of coal, and a prehistoric waste flake), 3 carbon rods, 1 piece of cloth, and 2 hard rubber or bakelite fragments. There are 9 shell buttons and 18 pieces of unworked shell, probably representing food remains. Food remains are also represented by 22 unworked bone fragments and 5 bone segments exhibiting saw marks.

EVIDENCE FOR WOODEN POSTS AND A CINDER PATH. As indicated above, the test squares were shovel skimmed horizontally down into the virtually sterile clay beneath the plow zone. As suspected, there were several areas of soil discoloration and artifact concentrations that continued on down below the plow zone. Some soil stains encountered by archaeologists could be the result of disturbances by burrowing animals

such as rodents, moles, and badgers. Other soil discolorations are indicative of past human activities. In this case, eight circular carbonaceous stains were observed and recorded in both horizontal plan (see Fig. 95) and vertical cross section. These stains ranged in diameter from 0.5 to 0.8 ft and in depth from 1.1 to 1.9 ft below the plow zone. These eight stains are interpreted as postholes—the places where wooden posts once stood and either rotted away or were pulled up when the town was abandoned. The posts could represent a variety of things: fence posts, barriers for chicken yards, clothesline posts, etc. As such, the pattern of the posts is not clear. A larger area would have to be excavated to better ascertain their original function.

A concentration of cinders was observed and recorded in the northwest corner of test square N4220/W5120 (see Fig. 95). Although this concentration could represent the mere dumping of coal slag and clinkers cleaned out of heating or cooking stoves, it is more likely that the configuration represents a yard path that had been intentionally surfaced with cinders. In addition to the eight postholes and the concentration of cinders, two larger areas of soil discoloration and artifact concentrations were discovered. These were designated Feature 1 and Feature 2 for the purposes of further investigation (see Fig. 95).

FEATURE 1. Feature 1 was initially observed as a rectangular concentration of artifacts and cinders at a depth of 0.5 ft below the present ground surface—that is, right at the contact of the plow zone with the relatively undisturbed subsurface soil. It was obvious the plow had pulled up materials from this feature, accounting in part for the high concentrations of artifacts found in the plow zone. Continuing down into the artifact-laden mixed fill of Feature 1, the excavator noted that the concentration of materials was bordered by pieces of wood delimiting an area measuring approximately 4 ft square (see Fig. 98). Within the wooden framework was a large iron barrel hoop or wheel rim and large quantities of rusted iron objects, along with some broken china and glass artifacts. The positions of some of the larger artifacts in the fill of Feature 1 are shown here in Figures 98 and 99. Ultimately the pit was found to be 2.6 ft deep from the base of the plow zone, or 3.1 ft below the present ground surface. The walls of the pit were lined with wood, but the floor apparently was bare clay devoid of any lining. The base of the pit

98. Member of the archaeological crew excavating Feature 1, a trash-filled outhouse pit, 1981. Note the iron hoop or rim originally employed to support the wooden walls of the cesspit. View is to the northwest. (Courtesy of the ISU Archaeological Laboratory)

measured approximately 3.5 ft by 3.5 ft.

Present in the pit fill were at least 593 artifacts, some of them so highly corroded and fused together that an exact count and analysis cannot be made at present. Within the artifact inven-

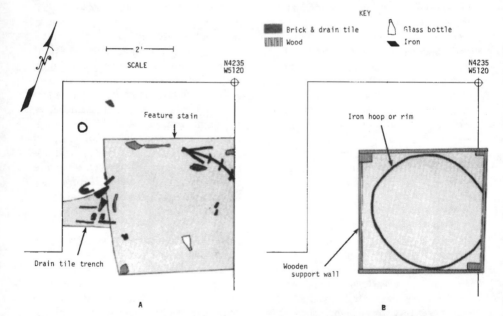

99. Horizontal plans of Feature 1: (A) pit outline and materials recovered at a depth of 0.5–0.9 ft; (B) plan view after excavation of the feature showing the wooden wall construction and iron barrel hoop within the feature.

tory from Feature 1 are 15 fragments of china tableware or other containers, 4 stoneware sherds, 11 miscellaneous ceramic objects (including a drawer pull, a marble, and drain tiles), 174 transparent bottle glass fragments (including a soda pop bottle marked "Diamond Bottling Works, Albia, Iowa," a beer bottle, a small bottle marked "Marinello," 2 small medicine bottles, a canning jar fragment marked "Cunninghams & Ihmsen, Pittsburgh, Pennsylvania," canning jars, and jelly jar fragments), 16 milk glass pieces, 10 miscellaneous glass artifacts (including a mixing bowl, a portion of a lamp base, kerosene lamp chimney fragments, window glass, and a glass tube), 308 metal artifacts (including bed springs, a bed frame fragment, a metal button, hinges, harness pieces, a horse or mule shoe, nails, bolts, hooks, iron pipes, metal pencil heads, zinc lid fragments, leaf spring parts, copper tubing, kerosene lamp parts, and the wheel rim or barrel hoop, which is approximately 3.5 ft in diameter), 1 cloth fragment, and 54 miscellaneous items (including brick and plaster fragments, pieces of asphalt shingles, bone fragments, and chunks of charcoal and wood).

The general concentration of artifacts vertically within the fill of Feature 1 is significant. Although we cannot take the exact number of artifacts too literally until all of the corroded artifacts are analyzed, the following distribution of materials is observed: 18% occur in the lowest foot of the pit filling, 13% occur in the middle foot of the fill, and 69% occur in the upper half-foot of the pit fill. We thus suggest that some artifacts were being thrown into this feature while it was being used and filled with soil of high organic content. Massive amounts of trash, however, la-

ter were dumped into the feature within a relatively short period of time. Such evidence is corroborated by the observations in 1919 of Charles Nichols, then professor at Iowa State College in charge of sanitary engineering, who inspected the conditions of several coal mining camps in Iowa, including Buxton. At Buxton he noted that

. . . in years past the Camp was regularly organized, with local authorities who maintained general sanitary order in the Camp. In its present condition, such organization, if any still exists, has become lax in its operation. . . . large quantities of litter and rubbish are evident, the privy vaults are full, and garbage has been dumped in back yards and in alleys. (Nichols 1919:20)

Yes, Feature 1 ultimately was inferred to be an outhouse, or cesspit, and the highly organic matrix was taken to be "night soil." This onetime privy was subsequently filled with trash at the time it—and perhaps the whole town of Buxton—was abandoned.

FEATURE 2. A scattering of artifacts was observed on the ground surface near a badger hole beneath the fence line separating SSU KP-1 and SSU KP-3. Removal of the plow zone from the test squares adjacent to this badger hole disclosed a rather large, irregularly shaped feature with an extremely rich fill of cinders, broken bottles and china, metal objects, and pieces of leather (see Figs. 100 and 101). This concentration was designated Feature 2, and the surrounding excavation units were expanded to reach beyond the limits of the feature to the sterile clay matrix north of the fence line. When the fill of Feature 2 was finally removed, the remaining pit had a maximum depth of 3.0 ft, measured a maximum of 8.8 ft along the fence line, and extended at most 6.0 ft north of the

100. Member of the archaeological crew brushing away soil from artifacts buried in Feature 2, a former garbage dump in Buxton, 1981. (Courtesy of the ISU Archaeological Laboratory)

101. Some of the artifacts as they were removed from the fill of Feature 2, 1981. Note that the artifacts include glass and stoneware containers and a soap dish made from a scallop shell. Behind these are paper bags filled with broken artifacts and small specimens. (Courtesy of the ISU Archaeological Laboratory)

fence (see Figs. 102 and 103).

The inventory of artifacts from Feature 2 contains 1949 cataloged items—some of which have been bagged together for further analysis as time permits. China tableware and containers are represented by 128 artifacts, including a complete small oval platter, a sugar bowl, toy doll dishes, and fragments of dishes, bowls, and cups. Among the 25 stoneware specimens are 2 complete jugs and 2 complete storage crocks. Among the 27 miscellaneous ceramic objects are doorknobs, doll parts, drainage tiles, and a portion of a lamp base. Transparent glass containers and closures are very prominent in the material inventory excavated from Feature 2. A good number of the containers are either un-

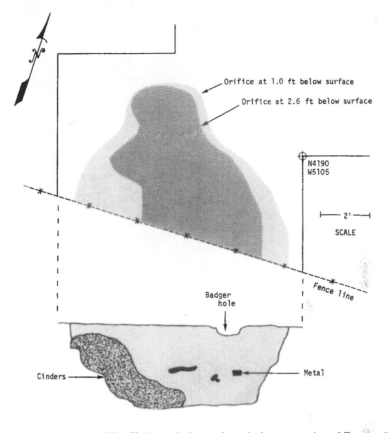

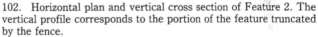

102. Horizontal plan and vertical cross section of Feature 2. The vertical profile corresponds to the portion of the feature truncated by the fence.

broken or restorable. Among the 732 items are fruit jars, jelly glasses, sauce bottles, condiment bottles, whiskey bottles, a perfume bottle, a Welch's grape juice bottle, bottles for Horlick's Malted Milk, and beer bottles (marked "Hamm, St. Paul"). Jar fragments, canning jar lid liners, and a shell-shaped soap dish are among the 36 milk glass specimens. A wide variety of objects is represented in the 117 miscellaneous glass artifacts: lamp chimneys, windowpanes, a marble, a glass lantern slide, 2 cut glass pendants or prisms for decorating lamps, buttons, and small, blue glass beads. The fill of Feature 2 also included 20 celluloid artifacts, including buttons, interfacing strips for clothing, a bracelet, comb fragments, hair pins, and an advertis-

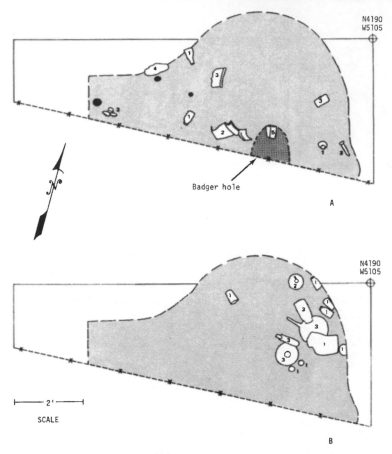

103. Horizontal plans showing selected portable artifacts in situ
within the fill of Feature 2: (A) excavation at a depth of 0–0.4 ft;
(B) excavation at a depth of 0.4–0.8 ft. Artifacts are indicated by
(1) glass, (2) ceramics, (3) metal, (4) leather, (5) brick. The darker
circles are rodent runs.

ing button marked "The Original Popcorn Confection." Shoes, boots, gloves,
and harness pieces and/or belts are
represented by the 214 fragments of
leather and rubber recovered from this
feature.

Also prominent in the pit fill were artifacts made from metal. Among the
516 metal objects are 2 coins (a 1900

penny and a 1907 nickel), a 22nd GAR
commemorative medal, tools and
equipment (a miner's pick, a sledge
hammer head, a hatchet head, files, a
wrench, a staple puller, scissors, a carbide lamp base, and an oil can), household furniture parts (stove parts, bed
post fragments, bed springs, furniture
casters, and curtain rings), construc-

tion materials (nails, screws, nuts, bolts, hinges, chain links, and pipes), items relating to clothing (a safety pin, buckles, brassiere or garter hooks), kitchen and other domestic equipment (a mophead frame, iron, washtub fragments, a spoon, frypans, zinc canning jar lids, crown cap bottle closures), weaponry (a gun trigger mechanism, shotgun shells, and casings for .22- and .38-caliber shells), and other items (including a brass harmonica plate, a crank handle, a brass escutcheon or brooch, probable clock parts, and padlock parts). Worked shell artifacts include 1 soap dish and 20 buttons, and 1 piece of bone was found that had been fashioned into a pipe stem. Unworked bone (39 pieces), some of which exhibit cuts from the butcher's saw, probably represent food remains, as do 6 unworked fragments of shell. Textiles are represented by 15 cloth fragments, and newspapers are evidenced by three scraps. Also present in the material inventory from Feature 2

are 17 fragments of nutshells and wood, 4 stone objects (including a whetstone and a sheet of mica), 1 metal brooch with glass "gem" insets, 1 bottle cork, 2 wads of horsehair stuffing, 1 hard rubber or celluloid pen fragment, and 23 fragments of construction materials (brick, linoleum, and plaster).

The form and contents of Feature 2 suggest that it was a pit excavated originally, albeit in an irregular shape, for the express purpose of trash disposal. The distribution of materials varied somewhat horizontally within the pit fill, but it was dense and more-or-less consistent vertically. This suggests that trash probably was discarded fairly steadily over a relatively long period of time.

Taken as a whole, the structural complex represented by Feature 1, Feature 2, the apparent cinder path, and the eight postholes recalls the arrangement of structures typically found at the backs of lots in Buxton (see Fig. 104). Previous residents of the town

104. Residential area shown in an historic photograph labeled "Looking S. E. From Water Tower, Buxton, Ia." Note the uniform constructional details of the company-owned frame houses, the layout of the quarter-acre lots, and the presence of associated structures such as outhouses, coal sheds, cisterns, clotheslines, and fences. (Photo credit attributed to Wilma Stewart)

mention outhouses, coal sheds, chicken coops, and other structures located at the backs of their yards, often bordering alleys between lots. Cinders would have been abundant in Buxton as a consequence of heating by coal. It is not unreasonable that this material would have been used to surface pathways through yards as well as alleys and streets. Garbage pits appear to have been one form of waste disposal in Buxton, according to some of the town's former residents. Whether or not this was the typical means of refuse disposal, however, is not yet clear from an analysis of the available interviews.

POSSIBLE HOUSEHOLD ASSOCIATED WITH FEATURES 1 AND 2. Feature 1, Feature 2, the cinder concentration, and the postholes are quite assuredly positioned at proveniences that would correspond to locations between East Third and East Fourth streets as shown on the 1919 Buxton plat map (see Fig. 40). The features, furthermore, are presently thought to be located west of the unnamed street that led up the hill from the YMCA. If those assumptions are correct, then Feature 1, Feature 2, the cinder path, and the postholes would be located at the back of Lots 7 and 8. It is also possible, but less probable, that these features correspond to the back of Lots 9 and 10 to the east of the street leading uphill from the YMCA.

Through available archival resources, an attempt was made to find the household associated with the lots in question between East Third and East Fourth streets. Unfortunately no town directory giving street addresses for all families in Buxton is known to exist. It is also unfortunate that the census takers did not record street addresses, so the location of households

is not specifically known from the census records of those days. In the face of these problems, we used the following logic and procedures to locate a household that may have been associated with the outhouse and trash pit here designated Features 1 and 2:

1. It was assumed that street addresses in Buxton usually corresponded to lot numbers indicated on the 1919 plat map. That fact was ascertained by the street address on a postcard sent to George Neal's home at 34 East Fourth Street.
2. Personnel from the ISU Archaeological Laboratory perused issues of the *Iowa State Bystander* and recorded names of people for whom street addresses were associated in various news items.
3. These names and street addresses were plotted on a copy of the 1919 plat map.
4. The 1915 census computer printout then was inspected to see if any data could be gathered pertinent to the households of people with known addresses.

Following these procedures, we have some idea of who lived on two of the four lots in question. The "Buxton Briefs" column in the *Iowa State Bystander* provides this information along with a folksy view into the goings-on in Buxton. On 12 May 1912 the *Iowa State Bystander* reported that

about midnight last Saturday or sometime thereafter, a caller came to the home of Mr. John Carter, No. 10 E. 3d St., and delivered his hen house of four nice large hens. It did not seem to matter if the coop was locked, as the person took the lock also. Several other persons have missed chickens in the last few weeks.

Thus we know that a Mr. John Carter lived at 10 East Third Street, that is, on Lot 10 in Buxton (see Fig. 40). Although other Carters are listed on a computer printout of the 1915 census, no John Carter appears. At this point nothing more is known about John Carter and Lot 10, although we did find at the townsite archaeological specimens that might represent the aforementioned purloined padlock. John Carter, however, may have moved away from Buxton by 1915, or he may have been listed in some other way on the 1915 census, or perhaps he was inadvertently not counted on the 1915 census. At this point nothing is known about Lot 9, or 9 East Fourth Street, and who may have lived there. This lack of information is perhaps not critical since it is more likely that the complex of structures represented by Features 1 and 2 are associated with lots to the west of the street running up the hill from the YMCA.

Moving across that street, then, to the west, is Lot 8, or 8 East Third Street (see Fig. 40). So far we have no information from newspapers or census data on who may have lived in the house on that lot. However, the *Iowa State Bystander* of 31 January 1913 refers to a Mr. and Mrs. Calvin Thomas, who lived at 7 East Fourth Street (see Fig. 40). We are told in the "Buxton Briefs" column that "Saturday, January 18th, the home of Mr. and Mrs. Calvin Thomas, of No. 7 East Fourth Street was blessed with the arrival of a little new girl. At this writing mother and daughter are doing well." Thus another family is fixed at an address within the lots under scrutiny along East Third Street and East Fourth Street. Further archival materials even tell something about the baby who blessed the Thomas home on 18 January 1913.

Here we are fortunate in that the 1915 state census shows that Mr. and Mrs. Calvin Thomas and their four children still lived in Buxton in that year. According to the 1915 census data, the Thomas family lived in a house they did not own. The census indicates that this family was black and belonged to the Baptist Church. Calvin Thomas, listed as the head of the household, was described as being a 49-year-old miner who had been born in Alabama, the birthplace of his parents. He had completed three years of formal education and had resided in Iowa for 20 years. His wife, Lurena Thomas, is listed as being 39 years old. She was born in Missouri, the birthplace of both of her parents; she had completed eight years of formal education and had resided in Iowa for 18 years.

The Thomases, according to the 1915 census, had a son and three daughters: Herford (or Harford), Olive, Omego, and Carmal. Herford (or Harford) Thomas was listed as 20 years old, unmarried, a miner, and a native of Missouri; he had completed seven years of formal education and had been a resident of Iowa for 18 years. Olive Thomas was 15 years old and an Iowa native; she had completed seven years of formal education by 1915. Omego Thomas, age 13, was also born in Iowa and had completed six years of formal education. Carmal Thomas was listed as two years old and as Iowa-born. It was Carmal's birth, announced in the *Iowa State Bystander*, that allowed us to place the Thomas family on Lot 7 along East Fourth Street, probably within the area of our excavation units at the south end of Site Survey Unit KP-3.

The photographic evidence and archaeological data from the area of the excavation units at the south end of SSU KP-3 are concordant with what we know of the Thomas family and the house in which they probably lived. A photograph taken from the water tower sometime after 1911 (when the second company store was constructed) shows company-style houses and associated yards on Lots 7, 8, and 10 between East Third and East Fourth streets (see Fig. 41). Looking at the artifact assemblage from Features 1 and 2 and the associated test squares, one can generally infer that the materials represent one or more households involving both adults and children. Evidence for clothing and the presence of toys justifies the latter observation. The Thomas household included four children. No doubt Olive, Omego, and Carmal played with china dolls and toy dishes. Domestic activities indicated by the artifacts include housecleaning, washing clothes and dishes, ironing and sewing, food preservation and preparation, and meal serving. Lurena Thomas undoubtedly spent much time attending to these arduous tasks.

The miner's pick and carbide lamp base probably signal Buxton's number one male occupation: coal mining. Calvin Thomas and his son were both coal miners. Other male activities re-

flected in the archaeological residue include carpentry, construction work, and perhaps machinery operation. It is not unreasonable to assume Calvin Thomas and his son were handy at these undertakings, too. While these associations are far more than can be accomplished at most archaeological sites, the individuals and activities indicated were hardly unique in Buxton. Most men in Buxton were probably miners and general handymen; most women were engaged in domestic chores typical to housewives of that day; most little girls played with china dolls and toy dishes; and young men played marbles with "crockies."

The archaeological evidence is compatible with the historical data; a definite linkage of the artifactual residue with the Thomas family, however, cannot be demonstrated beyond the shadows of doubt that always obscure, to some degree, any visions of the past. Still, on the basis of the evidence at hand, if we could go back to old Buxton we would be willing to cross the county road to Gainestown or walk down to Sharp End and wager a bet or two on that linkage.

6: Portable artifacts from the townsite

ONE GOAL of the archaeological investigations at Buxton was to ascertain something of the quantity and quality of artifacts at the townsite. As discussed previously, the sampling methods by which portable artifacts were collected included various techniques of surface survey, as well as selected subsurface test excavations aimed primarily at defining structural remains. Investigation has shown the quantity of extant artifactual remains at the townsite is large: over 25 thousand items are included in the present inventory. Concentrations of artifacts appear to be associated with the ruins of buildings, with refuse-filled garbage pits and/or cesspits below the present ground surface, with probable house sites now obscured by overlying soil and vegetation, and with old trash dumps along the several ravines throughout the townsite. In areas of the townsite that have been cultivated, of course, the materials have been distributed somewhat farther afield. Even in these instances, if we can judge from the surficial distributional data obtained in SSU KP-1, there are potential subsurface concentrations reflecting portions of the former urban settlement at Buxton.

Ground cover conditions and modern land uses, as previously noted, are not only matters that influence the visibility of materials on the ground surface; they are also controlling factors in the preservation and completeness of the artifacts. Portable objects found in plowed fields, for example, are abundant but are generally quite fragmentary. Items brought to the surface of pastures by burrowing animals are fewer but oftentimes are more completely preserved, as are the objects originally dumped into trash heaps along ravines. Most of the artifacts collected at the townsite are quite fragmentary. Even though the specimens are not typically of museum quality, however, this evidence is important to the archaeologist in interpreting past cultural patterns. Thus the archaeologist might be satisfied with a dish fragment exhibiting a design and a manufacturer's mark even though the piece of china would not impress a lay person or be a particularly suitable specimen for a museum display. Complete specimens representing artifact categories were chosen for illustration here, where possible, to supplement the following discussion. In that sense the accompanying line drawings are not typical of the total artifact inventory from Buxton, though they *do* exemplify aspects of the material culture of the town's former residents.

The quality of artifacts at the Buxton townsite – or, for that matter, at any archaeological site – also is affected by a series of depositional and environmental factors as well as by the substances from which the objects were originally

123

manufactured. The temperature, chemistry, and moisture of the surrounding soil, for example, may serve to preserve some types of information while destroying others. The alternately hot and cold, wet and dry, climatic conditions of the Midwest generally result in the destruction of organic artifacts such as bone, shell, leather, and wood, while nonorganic items such as stone and pottery will be relatively well-preserved. Iron artifacts rust quickly in this region, while china and glass specimens hold up well over long periods of time.

The preservation conditions may vary within a site according to drainage patterns and soil chemistry. This is especially true at a large site such as the Buxton townsite. Leather objects, for example, are not generally represented throughout the site; but shoes and harness fragments were found in ravines and areas where the water table was perched above bedrock or clay, thus providing a relatively consistent moist burying medium. Finally, archaeological residues are also skewed by the manner in which the material items were disposed of by humans in the past. For example, a common practice of refuse disposal at Buxton—and generally throughout the Midwest at that time—consisted of feeding some organic garbage to pigs and other livestock, burning other trash, and either burying solid wastes or dumping them into ravines or stream beds (Jacob Brown, interview 1980; Nellie King, interview 1980). Thus some material items would be recycled or at least not preserved in an easily recognizable form.

For the above reasons and others, it is common for archaeologists to summarize artifact inventories according to the materials from which the objects were originally manufactured. The subsequent discussion is therefore organized along those lines, with artifacts reviewed in this order: ceramics, glass, metal, celluloid, rubber, shell, bone, leather, hair, textiles, paper, stone, miscellaneous media, and composite materials. Wherever possible the principal functions of artifacts are indicated on the basis of Sears and Roebuck catalogs or other primary sources from the time period. These procedures follow those utilized in describing the large artifact inventory from Silcott, an early twentieth-century site in Washington (Adams et al. 1975; Adams 1977). Many artifacts, of course, may have a number of secondary uses in addition to their primary functions: "jelly jars" often were used as drinking glasses, "milk pans" were used as mixing bowls, etc. Finally in the following discussion, certain ecofacts, unworked plant and animal remains, will be summarized.

CERAMIC ARTIFACTS

Ceramic artifacts from the Buxton townsite include vessels and containers employed in the preparation, storage, preservation, and serving of food; containers associated with personal hygiene and cleanliness; various toys; decorations; and construction materials. Although pottery objects are shown occasionally in historic photographs from Buxton (see Fig. 105), the artifacts collected at the townsite by the archaeologists provide a better documentation for the range of ceramics used by residents of the former community. Representative ceramic artifacts in the present inventory are illustrated here in Figures 106–112 and 114–115.

Particularly prominent in the collec-

105. Master Wilbur Peterson taking his bath in an ironstone china basin. The child, son of Ed Peterson, manager and coach of the Buxton Wonders baseball team, died at age three. (Courtesy of Nancy Wallace)

sugar bowls, and condiment shakers. Toy dishes – plates, open bowls, lidded bowls, cups, saucers, and teapots – also are represented. Portions of china shaving mugs, wash bowls and pitchers, chamber pots, and slop jars were also collected. Most of the china sherds are undecorated white-glazed wares. Among the decorated wares in the sample are pieces with raised or embossed motifs, luster band and leaf designs, gold edge trim, various colored transfer wares, cobalt blue designs, and multicolored painted motifs.

Manufacturers' marks indicate the people of Buxton used china obtained from American pottery firms in New Jersey (Greenwood Pottery, Anchor Pottery), Pennsylvania (Wick China Co.), Ohio (Harker Pottery Co., Homer Laughlin Co., East Liverpool Potters Co-operative Co., Vodrey Brothers, West End Pottery Co., and Steubenville Co.), and Illinois (Peoria Pottery Co.). Marked, domestic china pieces are illustrated here in Figures 106*A* and 107*A*. Some imported European

tions are fragments of china tableware and food containers (see Figs. 106– 109). Here the term *china* is used in a general sense to include glazed ceramics sometimes more specifically defined as porcelain, whiteware, or ironstone ware. Tableware forms include plates, serving dishes or platters, cups, saucers, mugs, bowls, pitchers,

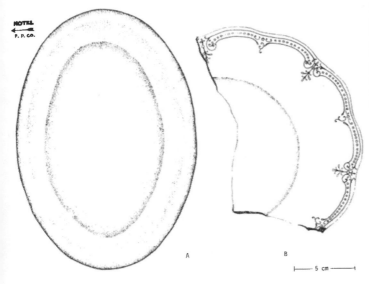

A B

|— 5 cm —|

106. Selected ceramics: white china tableware. (*A*) Small platter with trademark "Hotel P. P. Co.," KP-F2-605; (*B*) plate with scalloped edge and embossed border design, KP-F2-219.

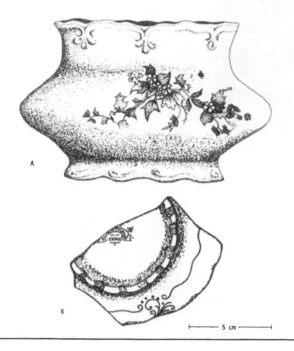

107. Selected
ceramics: decorated
china tableware with
trademarks. (*A*) Sugar
bowl with embossed
border and cobalt blue
floral design, "W. C.
Co. Semi Porcelain,"
KP-F2-350; (*B*) white
dish base with em-
bossed design, "–en-
thal China," KP-F2-501.

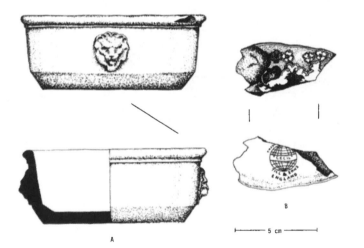

108. Selected ceramics: decorated European import ware. (*A*)
Small bowl with embossed lion heads, marked "TERRE A FEU,
UC, SARREGUEMINES," J-4-57, in front and side cutaway
views; (*B*) plate rim with cobalt blue transfer design, marked
"Cecil, Till & Sons, England," KP-XU-1410, obverse and reverse
views.

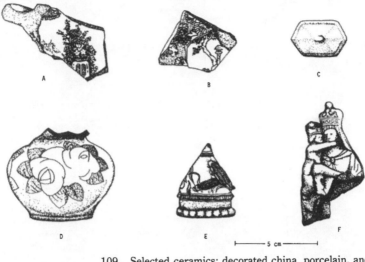

109. Selected ceramics: decorated china, porcelain, and redware objects. (*A*) China bowl base with blue floral design, KP-1-Q56; (*B*) porcelain base with "red willow" design, KP-1-Q97; (*C*) china lid for a doll's tea set, KP-F2-3; (*D*) hand-painted porcelain vase, KP-F2-1; (*E*) redware container with molded corn design, KP-F2-71; (*F*) porcelain figurine of "Madonna and Child" with traces of gilt decoration, KP-4-181.

wares are also evidenced by manufacturers' marks (see Figs. 107*B* and 108). Countries of manufacture presently identified include the Netherlands ("made in Holland"), France (Utzchneider and Co./Sarreguemines, and Theodore Haviland/Limoges), Germany (Tielsch and Co./Altwasser, and Rosenthal/?), and England (Henry Alcock Co., Thomas Till and Sons, Powell and Bishop Co., and Alfred Meakin Ltd.). Marion Carter, now of Detroit, still retains some of the tableware and glassware her parents, Dr. E. A. Carter and Mrs. Rose Warren Carter, used in Buxton (Marion Carter, personal communication 1983); among those Buxton heirlooms are china dishes imported from France (Haviland) and Bavaria. A few sherds collected at the townsite exhibit distinctly Oriental designs, but they have yet to be demonstrated to have been manufactured in China or Japan.

Stoneware sherds are numerous in the sample and represent large and small storage crocks, mixing bowls, milk pans, jugs, and butter churns. These utilitarian wares were used in food preservation, storage, and preparation for the most part. Small cheese crocks and snuff jars are also present in the sample. Representative stoneware containers are illustrated here in Figures 110 and 111. Most of the wares are mold made and covered with uniform white glazes, or bright blue, green, or red glazes. Some sponge-decorated, or "spatterware," pieces are present. These forms and glazes are

110. Selected ceramics: stoneware containers. (*A*) Mold-made jug, KP-F2-72; (*B*) mold-made container with sockets for wire handle or clamped lid, KP-F2-407; (*C–D*) wheel-turned storage crocks, KP-F2-606 and KP-F2-334, respectively.

├─ 5 cm ─┤

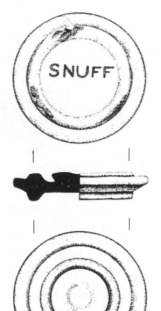

SNUFF

THE N. 2 THE WEIR. PAT MAR 1" 92 APRIL 16" 1907.

├─ 5 cm ─┤

111. Selected ceramics: stoneware and redware objects. (*A*) Snuff jar lid, KP-B-1-47; obverse, reverse, and cross-sectional views; (*B*) small crock lid, KP-1-Q100; (*C*) small jar lid with glazed Oriental design, KP-F2-610; (*D*) mold-made pipe bowl fragment, KP-1-Q32.

typical of late nineteenth- and early twentieth-century stoneware forms known in this region. The more recent containers often are fitted for wire handles and wire snap closures. Some earlier types—wheel-thrown wares with Albany slips, Bristol glazes, and salt glazes—are also represented, as are the earlier cover styles, including those with overhanging lids and lids fitted for channeled rims (cf. Gradwohl 1974:100–101). Such wares probably were manufactured within this region, but the lack of manufacturers' marks makes this impossible to demonstrate at present. Very few stoneware sherds exhibit manufacturers' marks. Those represented, however, are Red Wing from Minnesota, Western Stoneware Co., which produced pottery at several midwestern locations during the early twentieth century, and wares patented by William S. Weir of Monmouth, Illi-

nois. One small stoneware container lid exhibits a glazed Oriental motif and could represent a foreign import (see Fig. 111C). In addition to the stoneware artifacts, there are some redware pieces, most of which are unglazed. Of particular interest is a small, mold-made container decorated with a design incorporating ears of corn (see Fig. 109E). Perhaps this artifact was made in the "Tall Corn State," but the lack of a manufacturer's mark prohibits this chauvinistic identification.

Numerous other artifacts collected at the Buxton townsite were made of fired clay. Several porcelain figurines were found, including a representation of the "Madonna and Child" (see Fig. 109F). This religious figurine exhibits traces of gilt decoration over its fine, white-glazed surface. More typical in the inventory are portions of ceramic dolls (see Fig. 112). Indeed, these arti-

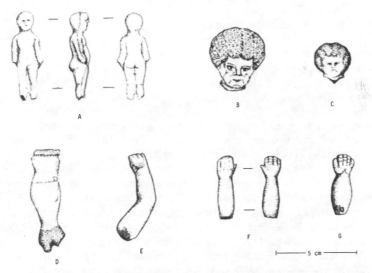

112. Selected ceramics: china dolls and doll parts. (A) "Frozen Charlotte," J-1-114, three views; (B–C) doll heads, KP-1-Q104 and KP-1-Q112, respectively; (D) doll leg, KP-F2-54; (E–G) doll arms, KP-XU-1443, KP-7-157, and KP-F2-396, respectively. F shows two views of the same arm.

facts might be considered one of the "horizon markers" characterizing this and other turn-of-the-century town and farmstead sites in this region. One doll type, shown here in Figure 112*A*, is referred to in the literature as a "Frozen Charlotte." These dolls were mold made in a single unjointed unit and, according to Desmonde (1972:71), were manufactured betweeen 1850 and 1914. Other dolls are of types referred to as glazed "china head dolls" and unglazed or bisque "parian dolls" (Desmonde 1972:10–11, 23–24). The heads of these dolls show molded hair and features and are sometimes painted (see Fig. 112*B–C*). Other dolls were fitted with natural hair. The legs and arms of these dolls consisted of molded china pieces attached to cloth or kidskin doll bodies (see Fig. 112*D–G*). A photograph of a doll of this latter type is shown in a photograph, here reproduced as Figure 113, of Dorothy Neal Collier as a child in Buxton. China dolls also appear as merchandise in an interior photographic view of the company store published in an issue of the *Iowa State Bystander* (6 December 1907). Other toys made of clay include stoneware ("crockies"), bisque, and glazed ceramic marbles.

Also represented in the inventory of ceramic artifacts are mold-made smoking pipes (see Fig. 111*D*), flowerpots, vases, kerosene lamp bases, fixtures for electric lights, sockets for fuses, and various types of insulators (see Fig. 114*B–C*). Light fixtures and electrical insulators were particularly found in and around the buildings in the downtown district of Buxton. Fragments of ceramic toilets also were recovered from the downtown area, particularly in the rubble of the boys' YMCA building and the company store. Ceramic doorknobs and drawer

113. Dorothy and Harry Neal as children, photographed with Dorothy's doll in a stroller. Photo was taken circa 1911. (Courtesy of Dorothy Neal Collier)

pulls, on the other hand, were distributed generally throughout the townsite (see Fig. 114*D*). Similarly wide in distribution were porcelain "lightning stopper" bottle closures, which are sometimes mistaken for drawer pulls or insulators (see Fig. 114*E*). Various construction materials used at Buxton also were made from clay: bricks, tiles for wells and cisterns, drain tiles, and the roof tiles used on the company's stone warehouse (see Fig. 115). The latter tiles were manufactured by Ludowici and Co. of Chicago. Several drain tiles were manufactured by the M & M Co. in Monmouth, Illinois. Bricks

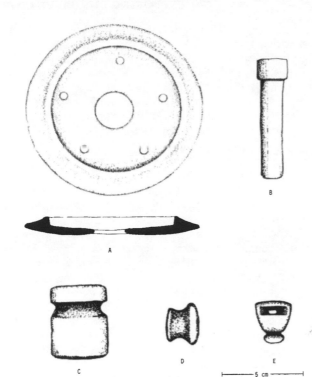

114. Selected ceramics: miscellaneous china and porcelain objects. (A) Perforated lid, KP-S6-1, interior and cross-sectional views; (B–C) insulators, KP-S4-269 and KP-1-Q27, respectively; (D) drawer pull, KP-1-Q43; (E) "Lightning stopper" bottle closure, KP-1-Q37.

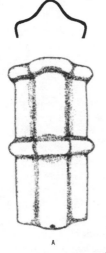

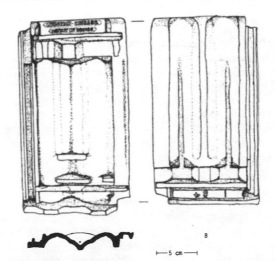

115. Selected ceramics: roof tiles from the company warehouse. (A) Ridge tile, KP-S1-18, with exterior and cross-sectional views; (B) roof tile, KP-S1-13, with interior, exterior, and cross-sectional views.

stamped "Oskaloosa" (Iowa) were found in several localities within the townsite. Also in the inventory are bricks manufactured in Boone, Iowa (Boone B. T. & P. Co.; Boone Co.), and in Missouri (A. P. Green).

GLASS ARTIFACTS

Pieces of broken glass are abundantly distributed around the Buxton townsite. Particularly numerous among the glass artifacts are jars and bottles in which food, beverages, medicine, and cosmetics were commercially distributed (Ketchum 1975; Klamkin 1971; Toulouse 1970, 1971). Dishes and containers for the serving of food also are present, as are items of clothing and decoration, electrical insulators, lighting equipment, and construction materials. Bottles and large jars are generally of transparent glass—clear, blue, lavender, green, and brown. Small bottles and jars of opaque glass and milk glass also are present. Buttons and some other items were made from black glass and carnival glass. Representative glass artifacts in the present inventory are illustrated in Figures 116 to 129.

In the late nineteenth and early twentieth centuries the soft drink industry enjoyed an expanding popularity (Gilborn 1982; Paul and Parmalee 1973). Soda pop was manufactured in Buxton and also was purchased from other soft drink companies in the region. Evidence for this commercial pattern consists of crown cap and Hutchinson closure bottles with manufacturers' marks (see Figs. 116 and 117). Bottles with Buxton marks include those from the Buxton Bottling Works and Nevins Bottling Works. Archie Harris indicated to the archaeologists that a bottling works once stood

at a location north of the railroad tracks above the right bank of Bluff Creek (personal communication 1980). Other soft drink bottles came from Albia (Albia Bottling Works, Diamond Bottling Works, and J. W. Evans), Oskaloosa (M & M Star Bottling Co. and Mahaska Bottling Works), Ottumwa (Ottumwa Bottling Works, Coca-Cola Bottling Co./Ottumwa, and Springs Bottling Works/Fred C. Caley), Keokuk (J. Burk and Co.), and Macomb, Illinois (Pure Pop Co.). Welch's grape juice, a soft drink produced in Westfield, New York, is also represented in the collection by a marked bottle. Other soda pop bottles were manufactured in other locations, although they once may have contained locally prepared soft drinks. These bottles are marked Caruthersville (Missouri), Root Glass Co. (Terre Haute, Indiana), and Pepsi Cola Co. (New Bern, North Carolina).

According to the *Iowa State Bystander* of 6 December 1907, "not a saloon is permitted on the company's ground, nor is there any whiskey sold on this ground." However, judging from the distribution of beer and whiskey bottles collected throughout Section 4 of Bluff Creek Township, the consumption of alcoholic beverages by some members of the community was not confined to the saloons reported from the outlying "suburbs" at Sharp End, Coopertown, and Gainestown. These saloons are mentioned by a number of former Buxton residents, for example, Elmer Buford (interview 1980), Dorothy Collier (interview 1980), and Mike Onper (interview 1981).

Selected alcoholic beverage bottles collected at Buxton are shown here in Figure 118. Marked beer bottles indicate at least some of the breweries supplying the community at Buxton:

116. Selected glass: soda pop bottles with crown cap closures. (*A*) Buxton Bottling Works, KP-S6-31, with basal view; (*B*) Nevins Bottling Works, KP-3-30, with basal view; (*C*) Diamond Bottling Works, KP-7-505, with cutaway and basal views; (*D*) Welch's Grape Juice, KP-F2-237.

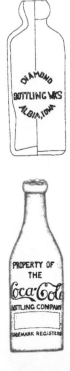

117. Selected glass: soda pop bottles. (*A*) Diamond Bottling Works, C-3-262, with Hutchinson closure and cutaway view; (*B*) J. W. Evans, KP-S4-2; with intact metal Hutchinson closure; (*C–D*) Coca-Cola bottles with crown cap closures, KP-S4-125 and KP-S6-92, respectively.

118. Selected glass: alcoholic beverage bottles. (*A*) Hamm, KP-F2-336; (*B*) J. Rieger & Co., KP-7-278; (*C*) unmarked, KP-F2-614; (*D*) full pint, unmarked, J-3-4, with cutaway and basal views; (*E*) Imperial Brewing Co., KP-7-439, with cutaway view.

119. Selected glass: large bottles. (*A*) Handled bottle with metal attachments, KP-F2-411; (*B*) stoppered bottle, KP-F2-166.

Moehn Brewing Co. (Burlington, Iowa), Hamm Brewing Co. (St. Paul, Minnesota), Conrad Seip Brewing Co. (Chicago), and the Imperial Brewing Co. (Kansas City). Other beer containers bear what appear to be bottle manufacturers' marks rather than those of brewers: American Bottle Co. (Belleville, Illinois), American Bottle Co. (Chicago), and William Franzen and Son (Milwaukee). Whiskey bottles from the townsite exhibit the following marks: J. Rieger and Co. Distributers (Kansas City) and Nivison Weiskopf Co. (Cincinnati). Many additional beer and whiskey bottle fragments bear no brewers' or manufacturers' marks.

Other bottles in the present inventory include large storage containers and smaller bottles that originally contained condiments, flavoring, oil, sauces, pickles, and relish (see Figs. 119–121). Producers of these foods, according to marks on the bottles, were Mennig & Slater (Des Moines), Watkins (Winona, Minnesota), My Wife's Salad Dressing (Chicago), T. A. Snider Preserve Company (Cincinnati), and H. J. Heinz (Pittsburgh). Bottle manufacturers' marks on containers of similar forms include Streator Bottle and Glass Co. (Streator, Illinois), Owen Bottling Company (Streator, Illinois), Illinois Glass Co. (Alton, Illinois), Leisy (Peoria, Illinois), Adolphus Busch Glass Manufacturing Co. (Belleville, Illinois), Fairmount Glass Works (Indianapolis), Louisville Glass Works

120. Selected glass: condiment, flavoring, and oil bottles. (A) Small unmarked, KP-3-25; (B–C) unmarked catsup, KP-7-281 and KP-S6-76, respectively; (D) Watkins, C-3-52; (E) My Wife's Salad Dressing, C-3-97, with basal view; (F) unmarked, KP-F2-419; (G) Marinello, KP-F1-166.

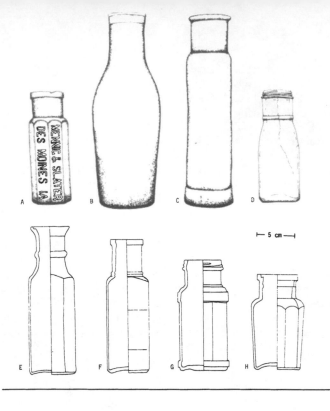

121. Selected glass: condiment, pickle, or relish bottles. (*A*) Mennig & Slater, KP-F2-335; (*B–D*) unmarked, KP-F2-355, KP-F2-84, and C-3-54, respectively; (*E–H*) unmarked, KP-F2-417, C-3-53, KP-F2-357, and KP-F2-499, respectively, cutaway views.

(Louisville, Kentucky), Brockway Glass Company (Brockway, Pennsylvania), and Fisher Bruce Company (Philadelphia). A single bottle is embossed with the word *Oklahoma.*

Judging from at least one complete specimen found at Buxton, some liquid milk was distributed in bottles (see Fig. 122*A*). The milk bottle illustrated here is of the "Common Sense Milk Jar" form advertised in the 1897 Sears and Roebuck catalog and described as "having only a slight shoulder within the neck of the jar which serves to hold the cap or cover in position when adjusted . . . the cap or cover is made of heavy wood fibre prepared so as to resist the moisture from within and without" (Sears, Roebuck and Co. 1897:146). Malted milk in powdered form was shipped in jars of various sizes marked "Horlick's Malted Milk,

Racine, Wisconsin, U.S.A./Slough, Bucks, England," apparently reflecting the merchandising of a British product through an American distributor (see Fig. 122*B–C*).

Portions of cylindrical and shouldered canning jars are numerous in the surface collections from the Buxton townsite (Fig. 123). Some of these containers have single-flanged orifices for "lightning" glass lids, which were snapped down and held in place with wire attachments. The majority of the canning jars, however, have rims threaded for closure with screw lids. Zinc lids with milk glass liners were used for capping these jars. A tight closure was insured by employing a rubber sealing ring between the lid and the canning jar. In one instance such a sealing ring was still preserved on the rim of a canning jar collected at the Buxton

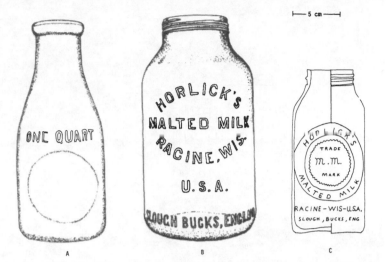

122. Selected glass: liquid and malt powder milk bottles. (*A*) Quart liquid milk bottle, KP-S6-6; (*B*) Horlick's malted milk powder bottle, KP-F2-408; (*C*) Horlick's malted milk powder bottle, KP-F2-81.

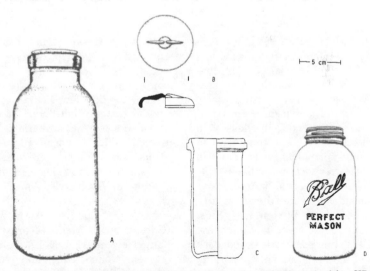

123. Selected glass: preserve jars. (*A*) Unmarked jar, KP-F2-415; (*B*) glass lid for jar type shown at left, KP-F2-747; (*C*) unmarked jar, KP-F2-615; (*D*) Ball Perfect mason jar, KP-F2-409.

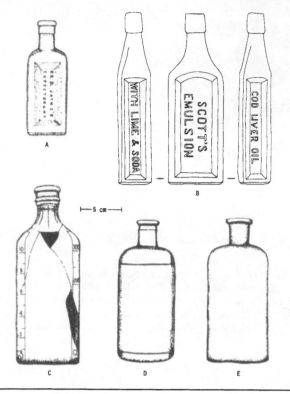

├─ 5 cm ─┤

124. Selected glass: medicine bottles. (*A*) Dr. D. Jayne's Expectorant, KP-7-40; (*B*) Scott's Emulsion Cod Liver Oil with Lime & Soda, KP-10-41, with front and side views; (*C*) graduated bottle, KP-F1-170; (*D–E*) unmarked, KP-3-1 and KP-F2-618, respectively.

townsite. Most of these glass containers are the familiar Ball mason jars produced by Ball Brothers Co. in Muncie, Indiana. One exception is a canning jar base marked "Cunninghams and Ihmsen, Pittsburgh, Pennsylvania." Smaller jars and "jelly glasses" in the collection represent containers in which food products were sold in stores and/or canned in the home.

Medicine bottles and jars are also fairly abundant among the glass artifacts collected at Buxton (see Figs. 124–126). Most of these containers are clear glass, but some are tinted dark shades of blue and brown. Unmarked, narrow-mouthed bottles for cork or glass stoppers are represented, as are wide-mouthed "pomade bottles." Such bottles are shown in the 1897 Sears and Roebuck catalog (Sears, Roebuck and Co. 1897:35), as are clear glass "ointment pots" with screw caps. Among the liquid medicines, toiletries, and ointments distributed in marked containers were Chamberlain's Cough Remedy (Des Moines), Pluto Spring Water (French Lick, Indiana), Bromo Seltzer (Emerson Drug Company, Baltimore), Dr. Pierce's Anuric Tablets (Buffalo), Mentholatum (Buffalo), Vicks Vap O Rub (New York), Vaseline (Chesebrough Manufacturing Company, New York), Lavoris mouthwash (Wilton, Connecticut), and Rubifoam for the Teeth (E. W. Hoyt and Co., Lowell, Massachusetts). Rubifoam, it should be noted, could be ordered by

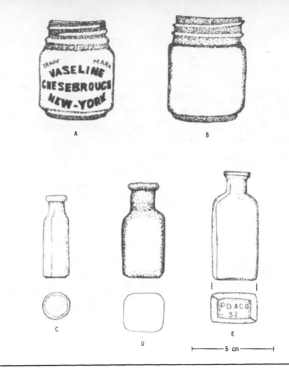

125. Selected glass: small medicine jars and bottles. (*A*) Vaseline, KP-1-Q3; (*B*) unmarked cobalt blue, KP-1-Q6; (*C–D*) unmarked, KP-S8-276 and KP-1-Q27, respectively, with basal views; (*E*) "P D & Co," KP-S8-90, with basal view.

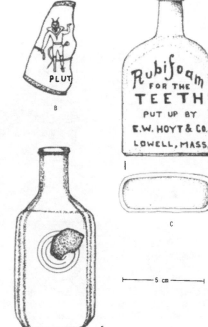

126. Selected glass: small medicine and toiletry bottles. (*A*) Dr. Pierce's Anuric Tablets, KP-7-438; (*B*) base of bottle for Pluto Spring Water, KP-1-Q63; (*C*) Rubifoam, KP-6-63, with basal view; (*D*) Bromo Seltzer, KP-1-Q101, with basal view; (*E*) unmarked, J-3-63.

mail from Sears and Roebuck (Sears, Roebuck and Co. 1897:34). The makers of nostrums marketed in bottles marked "Scott's Emulsion Cod Liver Oil with Lime and Soda" and "Dr. D. Jayne's Expectorant" have not yet been identified. Bottles marked "Watkins" (Winona, Minnesota) may have contained medicines as well as flavorings, while the original contents of bottles marked "Marinello" and "P. D. & Co." have not yet been identified. One bottle marked "J. B. Williams Co., Glastonbury, Ct." once may have contained a medicine or cosmetic lotion. Several medium and large bottles with embossed, graduated measurements were probably containers for medi-

cines or chemical compounds. Small glass containers held other products, according to the marks on bottles collected at the Buxton townsite (see Fig. 127A, F, and G). One perfume bottle is marked "Dorothy Vernon Toilet Water, Jennings Co. Perfumers" (Grand Rapids, Michigan). The former residents of Buxton used Carter's ink (Cambridge, Massachusetts) and Higgins' ink (New York), according to manufacturers' marks on small bottles collected at the townsite. Unmarked bottles of similar form no doubt also held ink, but their contents and manufacturers presumably were indicated on paper labels that have long since disappeared.

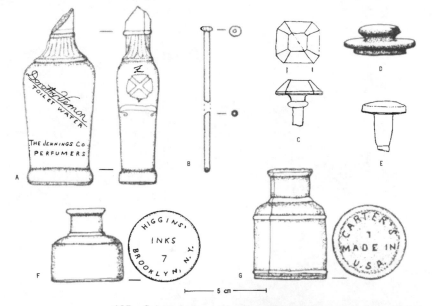

127. Selected glass: miscellaneous containers and closures. (A) Dorothy Vernon Toilet Water, KP-F2-359, with front and side views; (B) glass tube or ampule, KP-S8-203, with cross sections; (C) faceted stopper, KP-S5-199, with top and side views; (D) small lid, KP-1-Q16; (E) stopper, KP-S5-200; (F) Higgins' Inks, KP-4-74, with basal view; (G) Carter's, C-3-266, with basal view.

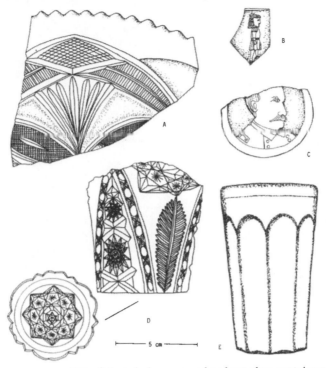

128. Selected glass: pressed and cut glass containers. (*A*) Pressed bowl fragment, J-4-30; (*B*) pressed tumbler rim fragment, KP-F2-800; (*C*) pressed tumbler base, KP-S8-60; (*D*) cut tumbler or vase, J-3-29, with side and basal views; (*E*) pressed tumbler, KP-F2-87.

Transparent glass containers also were used in serving food. Represented in the archaeological surface collection from Buxton are fragments of plates, bowls, pitchers, tumblers, and pedestalled fruit stands and/or cake plates (see Fig. 128). Plain drinking glasses are present, as are those with faceted bases. Fragments of decorative pressed glass and cut glass bowls, tumblers, pitchers, and pedestalled plates or bowls also were found. The vessel forms and designs compare closely with those advertised in the 1902 Sears and Roebuck catalog (Sears, Roebuck and Co. 1902:799–800).

Many artifacts collected at the townsite were made from milk glass, and selected milk glass objects are illustrated in Figure 129. Quite common in the collection are small jars for medicinal and cosmetic salves, ointments, and creams. Many of the containers do not bear embossed indications of the product or its manufacturer. Among those with identified products are Mother's Salve (Chicago), Musterole (Cleveland), Mum deodorant (Mum Manufacturing Co., Philadelphia), and

129. Selected glass: milk glass artifacts. (A) Feline figurine, KP-1-Q31, with top and front views; (B) preserve jar lid liner, KP-F2-753; (C) button, KP-XU-1044; (D) deodorant jar, "MUM MF'G CO," KP-1-Q9, with basal view; (E) Pond's jar, KP-1-Q97; (F) Musterole jar, KP-1-Q97, with basal view.

Pond's cold cream (Chesebrough-Pond's Inc., Greenwich, Connecticut). In addition to these objects of milk glass were liners made for the insides of zinc screw caps used on canning jars. Among the marked milk glass liners are ones produced in Bloomington, Illinois (under a patent to Charles R. Keeran) and in Philadelphia (Hero Glass Co.). Fragments of milk glass lamp globes and bases, figurines, decorative containers, soap dishes, and buttons also are present in the Buxton surface collections.

It has been suggested that the apparent high frequency of Pond's cold cream jars may be associated with the removal of coal dust and grime from the faces and hands of the mine workers in Buxton. Other observers

have suggested that the seemingly large number of glass jars for cold cream and other emollients might correlate with Buxton's relatively large population of black people (Charles C. Irby, personal communication 1982; D. Michael Warren, personal communication 1982). Today, at least, blacks often use skin creams and conditioners to prevent an undesired appearance that they refer to as "chalky" or "ashy." This condition occurs when the outermost zone of skin dries; then the small, lighter epidermal flakes show up against the deeper zones of skin, which are more darkly pigmented with melanin. Modern cosmetics are advertised for their utility in masking this condition (cf. Avon Products, Inc. 1981:68).

Fragments of glass are part of the

material evidence for the two different lighting systems in Buxton. Electrical lighting, particularly in the downtown district, is reflected by pieces of glass light bulbs and insulators. Kerosene or oil lamps are evidenced by pieces of lamp bases and globes, glass chimneys, and cut glass pendants or prisms, which often decorated the shades of fancy hanging lamps at the turn of the century (cf. Sears, Roebuck and Co. 1902:801). Several segments of glass tubing or ampules were found and, along with the bottles for nostrums and salves, they add some information to the medical practices of the people of Buxton (see Fig. 127B). Pieces of thin, clear window glass were observed throughout the townsite, while several fragments of thicker, translucent-textured, construction glass were found in the ruins of the company store.

Figurines and vases of clear glass are represented in the inventory, as are a few pieces of bowls and some buttons of carnival glass. Other colored glass buttons and beads were also collected, in addition to some multicolored glass marbles. A unique specimen is a rectangular glass slide with a colored decal or painted design. This artifact might be a lantern slide of the type described by Dorothy Collier (interview 1980): "We had toys. . . . My brother had a projector that . . . showed the little slides, you know. . . . It was a little square box, and it had a little coal lamp in it. And you pushed the pictures through and they'd reflect on the wall."

METAL ARTIFACTS

A wide range of iron, steel, zinc, brass, copper, tin, and other metal artifacts was recovered in the archaeological survey and test excavations at the Buxton townsite (see Figs. 130–134,

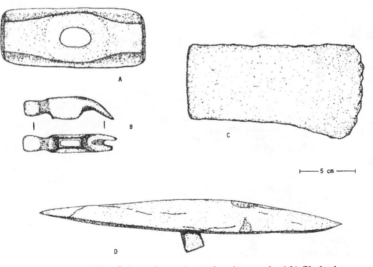

130. Selected metal: steel or iron tools. (A) Sledgehammer head, KP-F2-30; (B) claw hammer head, J-2-654; (C) single-bitted axe, KP-1-Q75; (D) pick, KP-F2-29.

136–138, 140–143, 145). Oftentimes the artifacts are broken and so corroded that they cannot be identified easily. Some "blobs" of iron rust might never be identified. At present the metal artifacts have been cleaned with water and light brushing. If time and funds are available in the future, some of these materials perhaps can be further cleaned by chemical solutions. In that case, more precise identifications will expand the present inventory.

Relatively well represented in the surface materials from Buxton are various steel and iron tools and implements (see Figs. 130–131). Tools associated with woodworking and machinery operations include claw hammers, mauls or sledgehammers, axes, hatchets, drills, files, vice clamps, pliers, socket wrenches, and a staple puller. Farming activities are evidenced by a rake and a hay fork. Picks, mattocks, and the carbide lamp base (Fig. 145D) are probably related to mining activities. Fragments of scissors and a metal thimble might have been in the tool kit of a seamstress or tailor. Interestingly enough, a pair of scissors is shown hanging on a wall of the tailor shop in which George Neal worked in 1914 (see Fig. 9). One sewing machine part has been identified in the artifact inventory (see Fig. 132). Dorothy Neal Collier recalls that her mother, Alice Mobilia Neal, had a sewing machine in their home at Buxton (personal communication 1982). At least one oil can has been identified (see Fig. 133A) and others may be rep-

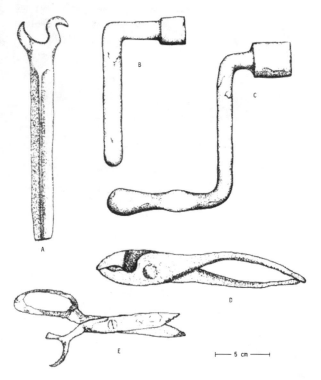

131.   Selected metal: steel or iron tools. (A) Staple puller, KP-F2-758; (B) socket wrench, KP-F2-722; (C) crank, KP-F2-762; (D) pliers, KP-1-Q72; (E) scissors, KP-F2-699.

├─── 5 cm ───┤

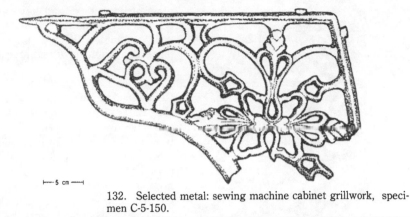

132. Selected metal: sewing machine cabinet grillwork, specimen C-5-150.

resented in flattened and badly rusted containers that have not yet been completely analyzed because of their poorly preserved condition. A shoe last is material evidence of the activities of at least one cobbler in Buxton (see Fig. 133*B*).

Metal artifacts employed in the construction of buildings are numerous in the surface collections. Of particular

133. Selected metal: tin and iron artifacts. (*A*) Oil can, KP-F2-710; (*B*) shoe last, KP-XU-879, with top and side views.

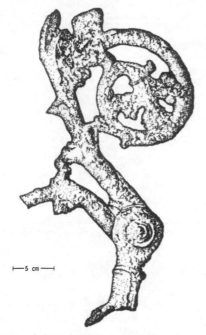

|— 5 cm —|

134. Selected metal: iron scrollwork, specimen KP-S4-286, part of iron staircase at the YMCA.

tions of door locks and keys are also represented in the collection. One door lock is stamped "W & N Co," but the place of manufacture is presently unknown.

Perhaps the largest metal objects found inside homes during the time of the Buxton urban settlement were cast-iron heating stoves and cooking ranges. The many utilitarian and fancy stoves available to people of this time period are indicated by 18 pages in the original 1902 Sears and Roebuck catalog (Sears, Roebuck and Co. 1902:812–29). One such early twentieth-century cast-iron heating stove model is pictured here in Figure 135. Cast-iron stove tops, firebox doors, and other stove parts have been identified in the archaeological surface collections from the Buxton townsite, in addition to associated accessories such as lid lifters

interest is a piece of iron scrollwork (see Fig. 134) found in the ruins of the main YMCA building along with a fragment of the iron stair treads. The iron staircases on the outside of the main YMCA building show up on photographs taken when that institution was a hub of social and recreational activities at Buxton (see Fig. 58). More mundane metal construction materials in the inventory are nails, nuts, bolts, washers, screws, hinges, angle irons, metal straps, pulleys and brackets, chain links, eyebolts, U-bolts, lead pipes, rain gutters and downspouts, a sewer trap plug, and staples. The latter items, of course, might also represent fencing materials. Wire fencing and electrical wire are both present. Por-

SEARS, ROEBUCK & CO., CHICAGO, ILL. CATALOGUE No. 117.

CORONA BASE BURNER

A THOROUGHLY GOOD SELF FEEDING, DOUBLE HEATING, RETURN FLUE HARD COAL BASE BURNER.

$20⁹⁵

PRICE REDUCED

IMMEDIATE SHIPMENT

135. Coal-burning parlor stove with mica panels, as advertised on page 651 of the Sears, Roebuck and Company catalog for 1908.

136. Selected metal: decorative iron heating stove top, specimen KP-S8-318.

and ash shaker handles (see Figs. 136–137). One stove door marked "Warm Morning" was manufactured by the Locke Stove Co. (Kansas City), and one shaker handle is stamped "Carland." A stovepipe damper is marked "Griswold. New American."

A variety of metal household appliances, utensils, and furnishings are also represented in the artifact inventory. Although only one galvanized metal coal scuttle, or hod, was preserved in a recognizable form, others may be present among the hunks of flattened metal still to be analyzed (see Fig. 138*B*). A coal scuttle and a large cast-iron heating stove appear in a photograph, here reproduced in Figure 139, taken inside the tailor shop in

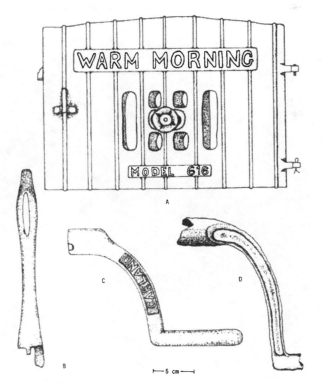

137. Selected metal: iron stove part and accessories. (*A*) Firebox door, KC-4-27; (*B*) stove lid lifter, KP-F2-757; (*C–D*) stove shaker handles, KP-1-Q63 and KP-F2-707, respectively.

A

⊢5 cm⊣   B

138. Selected metal: galvanized and enameled items. (A) Dishpan, J-3-136A; (B) coal hod, C-3-397.

139. Photograph taken inside a tailor shop in Coopertown, probably in 1914. George Neal is on the left; the man on the right is not identified. Note the tailored items of clothing, the large iron heating stove, and the galvanized coal scuttle or hod. (Courtesy of Dorothy Neal Collier)

Coopertown where George Neal worked. Utensils for the preparation and serving of food are indicated by portions of pots, pans, skillets, coffee or tea kettles, an ice cream freezer or churn can lid, and a casserole stand. One pan exhibits the mark "Brower," which is not yet identified as to place of manufacture. Enamelware cooking vessels, as well as galvanized and enamelware washing equipment (dishpans, washbasins, washtubs, and boiler tubs), were found at the townsite (see Fig. 138A). Enameled wares include white, gray, and blue-and-white mottled surfaces typical of the early twentieth century (cf. Sears, Roebuck and Co. 1902:584–87).

Another important domestic appliance at the turn of the century was the flatiron (sadiron), and this is amply represented in the surface collections from Buxton (see Fig. 140). Sewing machines are in evidence, as are churn paddles and mophead frames. Clocks and/or mechanical music boxes may be indicated by keys and balance wheels found in several locations within the townsite (see Fig. 141A–C). Other items appearing as vestiges of the furnishings inside former Buxton homes include bed frame parts and springs, furniture casters with wooden rollers, brass doorknobs (see Fig. 142B), wall or lamp hooks (see Fig. 142C), curtain rings, brackets for electric lights and/or kerosene lamps, and kerosene lamp parts such as burners and wick holders. Metal drawer pulls, as well as keys, padlocks, and escutcheon plates for drawers, closet doors, or trunks, were also found (see Fig. 141 D-E, and Fig. 143C).

Portions of knives, forks, and spoons (see Fig. 143E) were collected, as was a bottle opener. Two spoons are

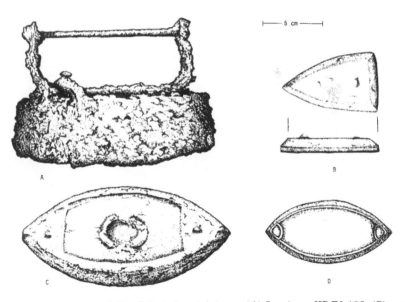

140.   Selected metal: irons. (A) Specimen KP-F2-198; (B) specimen C-5-148, with top and side views; (C) specimen KP-XU-655; (D) specimen KP-XU-1518.

141. Selected metal: lock and clock parts. (*A*) Winding key, KP-XU-1266; (*B–C*) balance wheels and/or escapements, KP-XU-1192 and KP-XU-1046, respectively; (*D*) lock cover plate, KP-F2-686; (*E*) padlock shackle, KP-1-Q57.

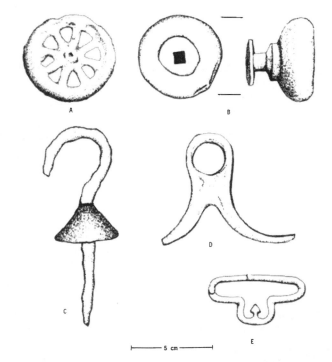

142. Selected metal: miscellaneous artifacts. (*A*) Valve regulator handle, KP-XU-656; (*B*) brass doorknob, J-2-648, with side and end views; (*C*) lamp or wall hook, KP-1-Q62; (*D*) brass harness turret, KP-XU-670; (*E*) brass harness hook handle, KP-XU-639.

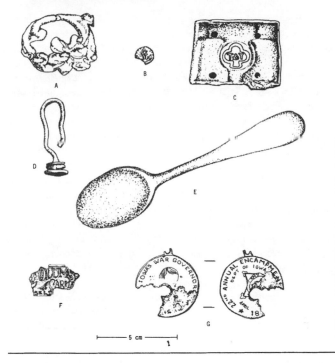

143. Selected metal; miscellaneous artifacts. (*A*) Brass escutcheon or brooch, KP-XU-644; (*B*) brass button, KP-XU-754; (*C*) brass cover plate, KP-XU-1188; (*D*) Hutchinson bottle closure, KP-S4-200; (*E*) plated spoon marked, in part, "Acorn Brand," KP-F2-281; (*F*) name plate for a "Columbus Carriage" buggy, KP-XU-221; (*G*) alloyed metal commemorative medal, KP-F2-682.

stamped "Australian Silver" and "Acorn Brand," marks that have not yet been further identified. Metal closures found parallel the different types of glass bottles previously discussed, crown caps and Hutchinson closures (see Fig. 143*D*). Zinc canning jar lids, smaller brass and zinc screw caps, and wire clamp closures for crocks and jars also are present in the inventory. Barrel hoops were observed, but the wooden staves of these containers were not. Tin cans are recognizable but for the most part are very poorly preserved, as opposed to pails or buckets, most of which were probably galvanized.

Metal items pertaining to clothing and ornaments include brooches and buttons (see Fig. 143 *A–B*), buckles, clasps, studs, grommets, brassiere or garter hooks, a safety pin, and shoe eyelets and hobnails. Portions of a pocket watch also were discovered, as was at least one commemorative medal (see Fig. 143*G*).

The several modes of transportation in Buxton — trains, horse-drawn carriages and wagons, and automobiles — are evidenced in historic photographs taken around the town. Trains, for example, are visible in Figures 18 and 33. A veritable traffic jam of horse-drawn carriages was captured in one picture (see Fig. 83). Another photograph (Fig. 23) shows a buggy in front of the Swedish Lutheran Church. During the second decade of the twentieth century, automobiles may not have been an uncommon sight in Buxton. Judging from a comment in the *Iowa State Bystander* (29 October 1909), however, some of the first cars in the town drew considerable attention: "Ruben [*sic*] Gaines and his wife have purchased their son, Ruben [*sic*] Jr., a fine two-seated automobile, the first colored man to buy a machine to our knowledge in Iowa." The truth of young Gaines' automotive leadership is not known, but the fact that the matter was worthy of publication in a newspaper out of Des Moines is, we think, socially and historically significant. An automobile, perhaps that owned by Reuben Gaines, Jr., is shown in a photograph here reproduced as Figure 144. All of the above-mentioned methods of transportation are reflected in the metal artifacts collected at the townsite: railroad spikes, a car crank, leaf spring parts, horse and mule shoes, harness pieces (see Fig. 142*D-E*), a buggy step, and a name plate for a Columbus Carriage

(see Fig. 143*F*). By the way, Columbus carriages, buggies, surries, and phaetons once could be ordered via the Sears and Roebuck catalog (Sears, Roebuck and Co. 1897:708–20).

Ice skates that clamped onto one's shoes also were advertised in the Sears and Roebuck catalog (Sears, Roebuck and Co. 1902:556). A portion of one such ice skate was found along the eastern side of the former Buxton reservoir. Several former Buxton residents, for example, Elmer Buford (interview 1980) and Odessa Brooks Booker (interview 1981), recall ice skating on the frozen reservoir when they were children in the town. Harvey Lewis (interview 1980) remembers skating on a small pond near his parents' home in East Swede town: "...Right down by the crick...there was a little pond...I don't know

144. Automobile filled with people from the Buxton community. Undated photo. (Courtesy of the Iowa State Historical Department)

whether we ever went swimming in the summertime or not, but I do know we used to go ice skating down there in the wintertime. It was just a little pond; it wasn't very deep."

Other artifacts probably associated with children's activities are wheels from toy vehicles (see Fig. 145*A*), objects thought to be harmonica plates, and lead fragments that could have been used as a source of solder and/or as a medium for making toy soldiers. Items perhaps related to school activities include metal tips for pencils, and a pencil sharpener (see Fig. 179*B*).

Miscellaneous metal items may be associated with various business and commercial enterprises in Buxton. Included in this category are a mechanical counter, valve regulator handles

(see Fig. 142*A*), lead scale weights (see Fig. 145*C*), a scale indicator arrow, and a fragment of a possible printer's plate. In addition, there is some evidence of weaponry: a rifle trigger assembly, Winchester shotgun shells, and .22- and .38-caliber cartridge casings. In that regard it is interesting to note that the "Buxton Coal Palace Gun Club" was formed early in the history of the town. To quote the *Iowa State Bystander* of 18 September 1903:

Among the many other things for which Buxton is noted is the number of crak [*sic*] shot-gun marksmen. For several years they have been known over this section of the state as marksmen of more than ordinary ability. A number of them have enviable records both in clay pigeon and live bird shooting. While ever since Buxton has been a

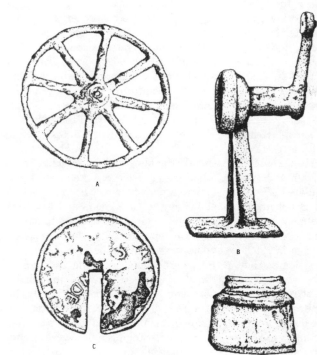

145. Selected metal: miscellaneous artifacts. (*A*) Wheel for child's toy, KP-1-Q124; (*B*) pencil sharpener, KP-1-Q44; (*C*) lead scale weight, KP-1-Q17; (*D*) carbide lamp base, KP-F2-290.

5 cm

town it has been noted for its marksmen, yet not until about ten months ago was a gun club organized in the town. At that time a number of the sportsmen got together and organized the Buxton Coal Palace Gun Club with seventeen members.

At the time B. F. Cooper, the druggist in Coopertown, was treasurer of the club, while Stewart Bingham was president and Robert Hale was secretary. A revised version of this article was reprinted by the *Iowa State Bystander* in its 17 November 1905 issue.

The archaeological crew did discover some coins at the townsite. Contrary to popular rumor, however, these finds were few and did not include any of the gold coins with which the miners reportedly were paid (cf. Swisher 1945:187). The dates on the nine coins found present a time range of 1893 to 1912. With the exception of the 1893 piece, this time range is entirely concordant with the urban occupation of Buxton. It is not unlikely, however, that a coin of that date would be among the small change in the pocket of an early Buxton resident. The nine coins, totalling 75 cents, consist of four Indian Head pennies (dated 1893, 1900, 1906, and 190[?]), one Lincoln Head penny (dated 1912), two Liberty Head nickels (dated 1907 and 1910), one Liberty Head dime (dated 1900), and one Liberty Head half-dollar (dated 1905). Now, of course, 75 cents is not much money—these days it probably would not even pay for your gas on a round trip to Albia from Buxton. But in 1902, if you shopped via the Sears and Roebuck catalog, 75 cents would buy you a five-gallon stoneware butter churn complete with stoneware cover and wooden dasher, or one dozen white china teacups and saucers and a cream pitcher "warranted not to craze, hand-

some in design," or a wooden kitchen chair and a three-pound-capacity, galvanized-metal coal hod (cf. Sears, Roebuck and Co. 1902:799, 797, 746, and 582 respectively). In those days Sears and Roebuck would accept mail orders totalling over 50 cents. Shipping costs, naturally, were extra!

CELLULOID ARTIFACTS

Celluloid, the forerunner of modern plastics, was developed during the last quarter of the nineteenth century. This transparent, synthetic material can be colored and textured to imitate a variety of other manufactured and natural media: rubber, glass, textiles, ivory, bone, amber, tortoiseshell, onyx, and ebony. Celluloid products such as combs, collars, cuffs, and films were advertised in Sears and Roebuck catalogs at the turn of the century. Surprisingly, given the poor preservation conditions at the townsite, some celluloid artifacts were collected during the archaeological surface survey and test excavations at Buxton. Hair ornaments include mock tortoiseshell hairpins and combs (see Fig. 146*E* and *F*). The latter are of a style referred to as "Ladies Vassar Back or Neck Combs" in the 1902 Sears and Roebuck catalog (Sears, Roebuck and Co. 1902:935). In addition to these there are several hair lock retainers or barrettes of the styles shown in the 1902 Sears and Roebuck catalog. Celluloid buttons and bracelets also are represented in the artifact inventory, as is an "amber" pipestem (see Fig. 146*C*) corresponding in form to those advertised by the mail-order company (Sears, Roebuck and Co. 1902:948–49). Finally, several narrow strips of celluloid exhibiting what appear to be stitching holes were found. These objects are interpreted as inter-

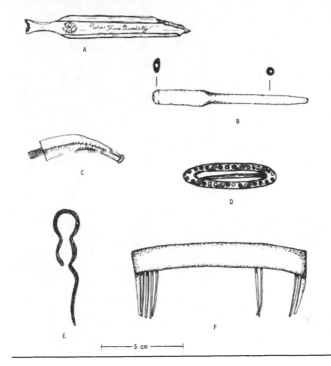

146. Selected bone and celluloid artifacts: (*A*) bone toothbrush handle, KP-7-323A; (*B*) bone pipestem for corncob pipe, KP-F2-346; (*C*) "amber" mouthpiece for pipe, KP-XU-637; (*D*) celluloid hair barrette with glass insets, KP-S8-191; (*E*) celluloid hairpin, KP-F2-375; (*F*) celluloid comb, KP-F2-374.

facing elements employed in clothing construction.

RUBBER ARTIFACTS

Only a few rubber artifacts are present in the Buxton archaeological collection. Several fragments of rubber sealing rings used on canning jars were preserved in a recognizable form, as were pieces of shoe soles and part of a rubber tire of the style used on early twentieth-century vehicles. One segment of rubber belting for a machine was collected on the surface of the site and could be from a time period post-dating the urban settlement at Buxton. Belting of similar form, however, was advertised in the Sears and Roebuck catalog (Sears, Roebuck and Co.

1897:56), and thus the fragment found at Buxton could have been associated with some of the machinery operations there.

SHELL ARTIFACTS

Shell is not well preserved at the Buxton townsite because of the fragile nature of the material, the acid content of the soil, and, perhaps, the chemicals used in modern agricultural practices there. Some shell buttons were gathered on the surface of the site, while others were obtained from the test excavations. Plain two-hole and four-hole buttons are represented, and at least one button with a carved design (see Fig. 147*B*). Similar plain and fancy "pearl buttons" could be ordered

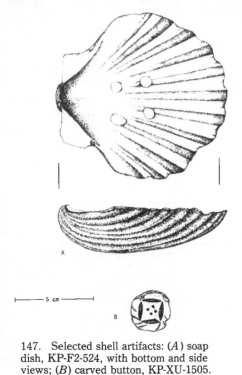

147. Selected shell artifacts: (*A*) soap dish, KP-F2-524, with bottom and side views; (*B*) carved button, KP-XU-1505.

from the 1902 Sears and Roebuck catalog (Sears, Roebuck and Co. 1902:940). The valve of a scallop was discovered during the excavation of Feature 2. This shell exhibits perforations, presumably for attachment to a metal stand, and is interpreted as a soap dish (see Fig. 147*A*). Interestingly enough, a portion of a similar dish made from milk glass was also recovered from the fill of Feature 2.

BONE ARTIFACTS

Very few bone artifacts were collected by the archaeologists at the Buxton townsite. Bone probably was not used extensively as a source material for artifacts during the early twentieth century. Furthermore, bone is a relatively fragile material and the same conditions that destroy shell will destroy bone. Presently identified worked-bone items in the archaeological inventory are a disc-shaped button or gaming piece, knife handles, and a toothbrush handle marked "Pure Fine Quality" and exhibiting a manufacturers' mark of an N inside a star circled with the words "Qualite Superieure" (see Fig. 146*A*). A delicately fashioned pipestem, presumably used in conjunction with a corncob pipe bowl (see Fig. 146*B*), also was found.

LEATHER AND HAIR ARTIFACTS

As indicated previously, some leather artifacts were recovered from the Buxton townsite, especially in locations where the surrounding soil has been consistently moist. Selected leather artifacts are illustrated here in Figures 148 and 149. Several types of footwear can be identified. In adult sizes are lace-tied, high-top dress shoes, low-cut oxfords, and work boots. In children's sizes are a hook-and-lace-tied, high-top shoe and a low-cut sandal or slipper that fastened with a buckled or snapped strap. Children's sandals of a similar style are shown in a photograph, here included as Figure 150, taken of Harvey, Howard, and Dorothy Lewis when they were children in Buxton. Several fragments represent the major portion of a red-stained leather shoe. Isolated metal eyelets and hobnails are also associated with footwear. Other items of leather clothing are gloves and belts. Some of the belt-like strips of leather and heavier straps with brass fittings are obviously harness fragments and other livery pieces. Several circular leather washers in-

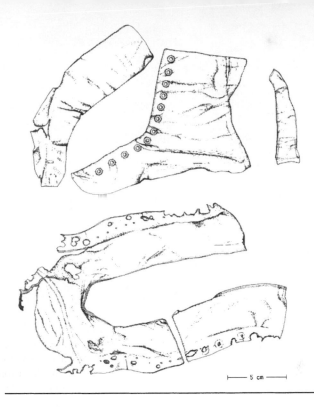

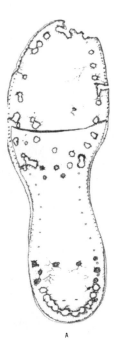

148. Selected leather: child's high-top shoe; segments of a single shoe, KP-F2-141/146.

149. Selected leather: shoe segments. (*A*) Man's shoe or boot sole with hobnails, KP-7-512; (*B*) child's slipper upper with strap, KP-F2-457; (*C*) woman's shoe sole and heel, KP-F2-152.

150. Howard, Harvey, and Dorothy Lewis as children at their home in West Swede Town in the summer of 1913. Note the children's leather sandals and Dorothy's parasol. (Courtesy of Harvey Lewis)

cluded in the archaeological inventory are presumed to be associated with machinery. A few wads of horsehair were discovered in the refuse-filled pit designated Feature 2. This material is thought to represent horsehair stuffing, which was widely used in upholstered furniture at this time period (cf. Sears, Roebuck and Co. 1902:775).

TEXTILE ARTIFACTS

Characteristically, textiles are poorly preserved in the archaeological record, and the Buxton townsite is no exception to this rule. Even in historical archaeological sites in this region, one does not expect to find many surviving specimens of cloth. In that respect the textile fragments collected at Buxton are significant. Several pieces of thin black cloth associated with some pieces of wire are thought to be the remains of an umbrella. The other textile specimens found at the Buxton townsite are thicker and more coarsely woven. These appear to be pieces of burlap, canvas, and asbestos sheeting

associated with industrial and commercial enterprises. They could, however, represent storage bags and other domestic items found in a house of this time period. Asbestos sheet stove mats and toasters, for example, are advertised in the 1902 Sears and Roebuck catalog (Sears, Roebuck and Co. 1902:582–83). In addition, the archaeological inventory contains some rings of asbestos that are probably heat-resistant washers or insulators.

PAPER ARTIFACTS

Generally, paper products are even less well preserved than textiles in the archaeological record. The archaeologists therefore were surprised and gratified that any evidence of paper products survived at all at the Buxton townsite. In one instance the scraps of paper appear to be remnants of wallpaper. In several other instances fragments of newspapers have been preserved. In processing these specimens in the laboratory, the archaeological technicians observed the similarly shaped edges of the scraps as well as the differential preservation of the material. They suggested that these pieces of paper represent several tightly rolled or folded pages of newspaper that were wet and only partially burned when they were discarded (James Gifford and Martha Williams, personal communication 1981). At present neither the date nor the place of publication of the newspaper or newspapers represented by the scraps can be identified. Several possibilities, however, exist.

Given the coverage the *Iowa State Bystander* gave to Buxton, it is reasonable to assume that residents of the community were subscribing to that Des Moines–based newspaper. That newspaper, incidentally, still publishes today as the *New Iowa Bystander*, with a logo proclaiming its role as "A Black American Tradition Serving Iowans Since 1894." It is also quite probable that the residents of Buxton were subscribing to, or at least obtaining copies of, other newspapers being published in the region: the *Albia Union*, the *Albia Republican*, the *Oskaloosa Herald*, the *Ottumwa Courier*, and the *Centerville Iowegian*.

The scraps of paper found by the archaeologists at the townsite might also be from one of the newspapers intermittently published in Buxton. Contrary to Rutland's (1956:41) statement that "there appears to have been no newspaper published at Buxton," the *Advocate*, the *Bulletin*, and the *Gazette* published in Buxton at different times, as several secondary sources note (Swisher 1945:182; Shiffer 1964:343). At least two pages from the *Buxton Gazette* are in the collection of documents in the Olin papers at the Iowa State Historical Department. An even earlier newspaper published in Buxton was

the *Eagle*. The welcome the *Iowa State Bystander* gave its sister newspaper and fellow journalists in its issue of 21 August 1903 is worth noting:

The Buxton Eagle is soaring high and promises to be a first class paper. 'The Buxton Eagle' is the name of a new paper just reached our sanctum, published in Buxton, Iowa. It is a 7-column folio, well filled with interesting news, well edited. The salutatory sets out its motto and aim, which is good. Therefore we welcome the Eagle. The editor is Rev. R. H. Williamson, a [*sic*] able writer and a good man. The Bystander has been plodding along as the only colored journal printed in Iowa for the past ten years, except where some men get the newspaper fever, would start up, then suspend. We know there is room for the Eagle and wish it success on the troublesome journalistic sea.

Another publication produced for a time in Buxton was the *Iowa Colored Woman*, whose "editress," according to the *Iowa State Bystander* (29 October 1909), was Mrs. A. L. DeMond. It is hoped that a thorough archival search eventually will locate copies of some of these local and regional newspapers. They no doubt contain valuable information about the community, and they might facilitate a linkage with the archaeological specimens of newspapers found at the townsite.

STONE ARTIFACTS

Stone was a source material utilized for the manufacture of a few artifacts collected at the Buxton townsite. Several whetstones for sharpening knives and other cutting tools were found. These compare in form with those advertised by Sears and Roebuck as "Emery Oil Stones" (Sears, Roebuck and Co. 1897:71). Fragments of slate found in several localities throughout the townsite may represent blackboards of the kinds Sears and Roebuck offered as "suitable for home, Sunday and private schools" (Sears, Roebuck and Co. 1897:356). Sheets of mica or muscovite were also collected in several find spots at Buxton. Some of these fragments probably represent transparent panels placed in the doors of fancy iron heating stoves during the early twentieth century (Sears, Roebuck and Co. 1902:820–21). Mica panels can be observed in the heating stove illustrated in Figure 135. Mica was also used in goggles, lamp chimneys, electric toasters, and fuses. This shiny, white, tabular-fracturing stone has also been used for ornaments and for simulated snow in Christmas decorations. Other stone materials associated with the urban settlement at Buxton are coal and cinders, or slag, the source materials for and waste products from heating and cooking in the iron stoves throughout the town.

A few objects represent prehistoric American Indian activities in what is now Section 4 of Bluff Creek Township: one biface fragment and two waste flakes. At present these materials are not sufficient to justify designating a prehistoric archaeological component within the townsite. It is not unlikely, however, that additional American Indian artifacts might be found within this section. At least one former Buxton resident, Paul Jackson, recalled finding Indian artifacts: "Oh, we used to . . . when we got out of school, we'd go down to the woods and shoot slingshots, and cut our initials in a tree, and pick up Indian arrowheads . . . wade in the creek, stuff like that" (interview 1980). On this basis perhaps one could ask other former residents about similar archaeological finds. Although relatively few prehistoric archaeological sites have been designated in Mahaska and Monroe

counties, it is not unreasonable to suppose that such cultural resources do exist here given site distributions northwest along the Des Moines River valley in Marion, Warren, and Polk counties (cf. Gradwohl 1974).

ARTIFACTS OF MISCELLANEOUS MEDIA

Various other source materials are represented in the artifacts collected at the Buxton townsite. Molded carbon cylinders and graphite rods may be portions of railroad fusees and/or electrodes for drycell batteries. Others are probably electrodes for arc light moving-picture projectors. This type of movie projector and its "carbons" are advertised in the 1902 Sears and Roebuck catalog (Sears, Roebuck and Co. 1902:171). It is interesting to note that some carbon rods were found in and around the ruins of the main YMCA building. A large auditorium, used for a variety of cultural activities, was located on the second floor of the YMCA building. An interior view of this room is shown in the *Iowa State Bystander* of 6 December 1907. In this auditorium movies were shown by the "Langlois sisters," also referred to as the "French women" (Swisher 1945: 185).

Many former residents of Buxton comment about the evening movies shown at the YMCA. Recalling her own childhood in Buxton, for example, Marjorie Brown reminisced that the YMCA was "boys' territory," but that she and others could go to the YMCA to watch the movies (interview 1980). In her words, "I had the thrill of my life because my Aunt Eva played for the movies. And when she would take her breaks, all 11 years old, I got to play. . . ." Vera Olson Fisher, a former resident of the East Swede Town neighborhood of Buxton, also remembered attending the moving pictures at the YMCA during her youth: "We went to shows when we got a little older because mother wouldn't let us go unless we went with some of the older ones" (interview 1980). Such comments bring some life to the carbon arc light rods found in the now-quiet ruins of the main YMCA.

A good many items used by former Buxton residents may have been manufactured from wood and cork. Today, however, there are few surviving artifacts made from these media. Several pieces of cut and planed wood were found as structural elements in and around the ruins of buildings in the downtown area. In addition to the box in which the dog was buried alongside the main YMCA building, smaller pieces of wood in several excavation units also may represent containers. One cylindrical wood fragment from an excavation may have been the handle of a shovel or broom. Some cork stoppers for beverage and medicine bottles are present, and there are also a few remnants of cork linings in the crown cap closures for soda pop bottles.

Materials associated with the construction of buildings include a number of media not yet discussed. Poured concrete served as the foundation for the company store, the White House Hotel, and several other buildings in the downtown district. Poured concrete sidewalks—some with initials and other graffiti—also were present in portions of the downtown area, although photographs show and informants recall that wooden sidewalks were more typical throughout this part of town. Plaster fragments were noted in the ruins of the company store, the YMCA buildings, and several other structures

in the downtown area. Cement mortar for stone foundations and for brick foundations and chimneys is more widespread in its distribution around the townsite. Asphalt shingles were observed in the ruins of the main YMCA building, while concentrations of tar and pebble roofing were found in the rubble of the company store. In several other locations small pieces of linoleum floor covering were collected.

ARTIFACTS OF COMPOSITE MATERIALS

Many artifacts are made from a combination of materials, and their description is not particularly facilitated by a separate consideration of each medium. Selected objects of this nature are illustrated here in Figures 151 and 152. Several fragments of knives include bone handles and portions of the metal knife blades (see Fig. 151A–B).

151.　Selected composite artifacts: (A–B) bone and metal knife handles, KP-F2-697 and KP-F2-345, respectively; (C–D) celluloid and metal advertising buttons, KP-F2-270 and KP-XU-1508, respectively; (E) metal and porcelain spark plug, KP-1-Q18.

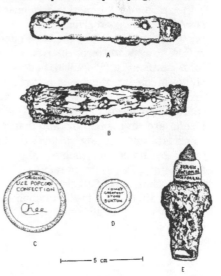

An umbrella is probably represented by some segments of wire and associated fragments of black textile, while the end of a pencil includes wood, metal, and a trace of a rubber eraser. A pot handle includes a shank of metal surrounded by wood, and a thin piece of wood capped with brass is probably a remnant of an engineer's folding ruler. Several furniture casters are also made of wood and metal. Metal door-locking mechanisms and ceramic doorknobs have been described separately, but in one instance the entire complex was found together as a unit (see Fig. 152).

Several decorative pieces also combine different media. One metal brooch has clear and green glass "gems," while a celluloid barrette has red glass insets (see Fig. 146D). Two advertising buttons combine metal and celluloid in bragging their messages to the world (see Fig. 151C–D); one advertises "Iowa's Greatest Store, Buxton." One wonders if such advertising is unique among company-owned stores in mining towns throughout the United States! Another button pushes the consumption of the "The Original UCE Popcorn Confection."

Electrical and automotive equipment combine glass, porcelain, metal, rubber, and perhaps other media. Found within the downtown district were fuses, broken light bulbs, and segments of insulated wire. One fuse is marked "D & W Fuse Co." Several spark plugs combining metal and porcelain are evidence of automative transportation existing in addition to travel by horse and buggy. Marked spark plugs were manufactured by "Bergie National" of Rockford, Illinois (see Fig. 151E), and by "Champion X," whose place of manufacture is not ascertained at this time.

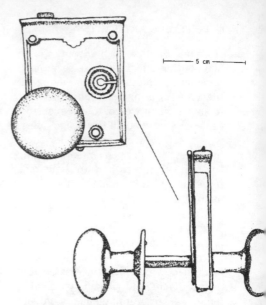

5 cm

152. Selected composite artifact: ceramic doorknobs and metal locking mechanism; specimen KC-4-28, with front and side views.

PLANT REMAINS

During the archaeological reconnaissance survey of the Buxton townsite, crew members observed various plants that appeared to be out of their present natural context and are probably vestiges of gardens and landscaping from the urban settlement of the area. Plants producing edible foods included asparagus, mint, strawberries, and grape vines. Among the flowering plants and shrubs were irises, lilac bushes, trumpet vines, barberry bushes, and certain groupings or alignments of rose bushes. Catalpa trees and some groupings of cedar trees appeared to be intentionally planted as landscaping along the sides of houses or lots. Examples of plant remains collected in the subsurface test excavations are few: some walnut shells, several peach pits, and an almond shell.

Photographs taken from the Buxton water tower show yards with garden plots (see Fig. 3). Lester Beaman (interview 1980), Elmer Buford (interview 1980), Dorothy Collier (personal communication 1982), and Nellie Lash King (interview 1980) mention having had vegetable gardens on their house lots when their families lived in Buxton. Among the garden plants mentioned by these people and other former Buxton residents are tomatoes, potatoes, corn, beans, mustard greens, turnips, collard greens, cabbage, carrots, cucumbers, peppers, peas, and onions. Hazel Stapleton (interview 1980) also commented that "we had a lovely strawberry patch, and we had lovely gooseberry bushes, and blackberries, and raspberries. Then we had a few plum trees, few apple trees and cherry trees, on the place." Gooseberry bushes were observed throughout Section 4 during the archaeological reconnaissance, but it is possible they are natural rather than introduced plants from old Buxton gardens.

Given the archaeological, photographic, and oral historical information on Buxton gardens, it is significant to note that the Consolidation Coal Company once published a garden book for mine workers. This booklet was described by a reviewer in the journal *Coal Age* (Anonymous 1916:810):

The brilliant pictures of the Consolidation Coal Co.'s Garden Book are the brightest things which have appeared on the *Coal Age* desk this spring. The illustrations are in eight or more colors.

The preface ascribes the book to the activities of the Welfare Department, and adds: "This, our first, garden book is written for the employees of the Consolidation Coal Co. with the hope that it will help in making homes more beautiful and surroundings more attractive."

The booklet suggested flowers for massing in front of porches and sheds (castor bean plants, sunflowers, cosmos, and hollyhocks), for borders in beds (zinnias, marigolds, scarlet sage, nasturtiums, geraniums, and bachelor buttons), along fences (morning glories, nasturtiums, hops, gourds, and grape vines), and plantings in flower boxes (nasturtiums, wandering jew, geraniums, and coreopsis). The booklet also recommended growing vegetables, in addition to flowers, for economic and aesthetic reasons, as well as for the maintenance of health: "Working out of doors in a garden, seeing things grow, breathing clean, fresh air is good for us all." Dorothy Collier recalled that in Buxton her mother and grandmother grew "flags," or irises, plus yellow roses and pink roses (personal communication 1982). The archaeological evidence and the advice of the Consolidation Coal Company garden book, then, provide an additional historical context for Dorothy Neal Collier's recollections of the gardening pursuits of Alice Mobilia Snead Neal and Sally Snead (later Reasby) back in Buxton.

ANIMAL REMAINS

Some animal bones were recovered from the archaeological reconnaissance survey as well as from the test excavations at Buxton. Both unworked and sawed bones of pigs and cows have been identified, as have unworked bones of rabbits and the complete skeleton of a dog (the one found buried in a box along the wall of the main YMCA building). Pet dogs are included in photographs taken of people in Buxton during its heyday—the mascot pictured with the YMCA basketball team (Fig. 63), the Neal family's pet dog named Kid (Fig. 8), and the Carter family's pet dog named Duke (Fig. 156). Evidence of pet dogs at the Buxton townsite occurs in the form of paw prints observed in the sidewalk east of Structure 8.

In addition to the company store and several grocery stores in Buxton, at least two butcher shops were present in the town. Hobe Armstrong operated one butcher shop up the little hill to the northeast of the company store (Archie Harris, personal communication 1980). Armstrong's store is shown in a photograph in Chapter 5 (see Fig. 83). Another butcher shop was located at Sharp End and was run by John Baxter, who became Hobe Armstrong's son-in-law by marrying Lottie Armstrong (Mike Onper, interview 1981; Dorothy Collier, personal communication 1981). The sawed bones found archaeologically could represent cuts of meat purchased at one of these butcher shops. Meat also was brought out into the neighborhoods from the meat market, according to Dorothy Collier (interview 1980): "We'd go to the meat market sometimes . . . and they did have meat wagons that went around the camp. . . . It drove through the neighborhoods and you could buy your meat off the wagon. It had the scales, and was iced, you know. . . ." Dorothy Collier's statement is interesting to the archaeologists not only in explaining the distribution of sawed animal bones throughout the townsite, but in providing a possible reason for the finding of several scale weights in areas that had been residential neighborhoods.

On the other hand, various informants have indicated that livestock was kept by some Buxton residents. Dairy cows were kept for milk and butter; pigs, for meat; and chickens, for eggs and meat. Lester Beaman (interview 1980), who lived in Buxton during his childhood, noted:

We raised our own hogs. . . . We had a man, Mr. Van Arsdale, he used to kill our hogs for us, butcher 'em, you know. Cut 'em up and then cure 'em for us. . . . We had a big old white Poland China. And we used to ride it like you would a pony. . . . He was real tame. And boy, you talk about some crying. When they killed that hog, we cried our heads off, my youngest sisters and I. . . . We really cried when they killed that hog. I guess we ate him. We called him 'Boy.' That's what we called him, big old hog.

At any rate, judging from the distribution of pig bones and teeth at the townsite, pork was not unusual fare at Buxton dinner tables.

The apparent paucity of bones of small animals and fish is worth noting because Buxton residents reportedly engaged in fishing and hunting activities. For example, Hazel Stapleton (interview 1980) recalled: "My oldest brother . . . he's just crazy about hunting . . . rabbits. Oh, yes, he was a very good, very good hunter. He loved to go fishing. And there'd be a place where he used to catch bullheads . . . then there was a little red fish that the ponds were full of that he'd catch." Hazel Stapleton also described how her mother prepared and served the rabbits as food. In addition, she mentioned that her brother used to hunt quails. Rabbit bones found archaeologically may indicate the hunting of small game; but other small animals have not been identified, and fish bones seem to be absent in the collections. Such bones, however, are small and would probably only be recovered from sealed trash pits. The apparently small number of these bones may be due to the relatively small area of the townsite sampled by subsurface methods. It is also possible that the remains of small hunted animals and fish were consumed by hogs, dogs, and other scavenging animals about the town.

7: Social and cultural patterns from an archaeological perspective

ARCHAEOLOGICAL evidence can shed light on various social and cultural patterns of the past. In general, it has been said that the following cultural activities represent ascending levels of difficulty in reconstructing behavior from material remains: technological activities; economic and subsistence patterns; social and political patterns; and the most difficult, religious and belief systems (Hawkes 1954). In general, this model is probably true given the nature of archaeological evidence and the factors of preservation. In the case of reconstructing prehistoric human behavior, the archaeologist is essentially left with the material residue alone, although ethnographic parallels and analogies can widen the scope of inferences. When the archaeologist works within the period of written records, however, the material evidence can be interpreted with the historical data as a framework (Adams 1977; Deetz 1977; Noel Hume 1969; South 1977; Weitzman 1976). In the case of Buxton, historic photographs, plat maps, census data, published information from such sources as economic geological reports and commercial gazetteers, newspapers, and oral communications from the community's former residents assist the archaeologist in interpreting

the material residues remaining at the townsite. By the same token, the archaeological evidence acts as a cross-check against the historical data and can fill in the gaps that exist in the available archival and oral historical sources.

These examples will serve to illustrate the interdisciplinary nature of the present project's goal of understanding the former Buxton community:

1. Photographic evidence and oral historical information indicate the general location of the former White House Hotel and the previous residential complex of the mine superintendent, neither of which show on the 1919 plat map of the town. With these data as a guide, the archaeologists were able to pinpoint the location of these structures and evaluate the nature of the extant remains via reconnaissance survey and subsurface excavation techniques.
2. Similarly, the cemetery is not shown on the 1919 plat maps, and photographs of the cemetery area at the time Buxton was an urban settlement have not yet been obtained, if indeed these ever existed. The location of the cemetery, of course, is known to many former Buxton resi-

dents and to others still living in the vicinity of the abandoned town. On this basis the archaeologists were able not only to verify the present extent of the cemetery by surface reconnaissance but also to record material evidence ultimately relating to mortuary patterns, kinship relationships, sodality affiliations, occupational statuses, and religious symbolism associated with the inhabitants of the former community.

3. A final example of the interrelationship of archival data, oral historical information, and the material residues obtained by archaeology consists of identifying the particular products purchased and used in the daily lives of former Buxton residents. Apparently no extant records document the range of specific products available at the stores in Buxton, although there are general references in issues of the *Iowa State Bystander* and in the reminiscences of the town's previous inhabitants. Similarly, living informants recall and describe generally such domestic activities as canning foods, serving meals, taking baths, and washing clothes. To a large degree the material remains collected and observed by the archaeologists can specify the types of jars and crocks former Buxton residents used in preserving foodstuffs, the kinds of china tableware and eating utensils that graced their dinner tables, and the forms of equipment they used for housekeeping, laundering, and maintaining personal hygiene. These are, as James Deetz (1977) puts it, "the small things forgotten," bits and pieces of the past that can help objectify written documents and human memories of bygone years.

MAKING IT: THE BUSINESS, COMMERCIAL, AND OCCUPATIONAL ENTERPRISE

As a company town of the Consolidation Coal Company, Buxton was dominated by the mining and transportation industries. A perusal of information from the *Iowa State Bystander*, former Buxton residents, and other sources indicates that many business and commercial facilities in Buxton were owned and/or managed by the company, its officers, and their relatives. The magnitude of the Monroe Mercantile Company store was indeed noteworthy, being hailed by the *Iowa State Bystander* (6 December 1907) as "perhaps the greatest commercial enterprise in all Iowa."

The "company store," however, did not completely monopolize Buxton's economic system. Other businesses are known from advertisements and references in various newspapers. While few, if any, complete issues of Buxton newspapers have been preserved, a single page from the *Buxton Gazette* edition of 2 July 1908, here reproduced as Figure 153, may serve as a good example of the commercial activities promoted in the town. Among the businesses indicated, aside from the Monroe Mercantile Co., are H. A. Armstrong's meat market, Samuel Johnson's restaurant, E. G. Lowe's clothing store, the Thomas Drug Co., the Williams drug store, the Warren and Co. meat market and grocery store, and the Coopertown Livery Co. E. G. Lowe's merchandising of women's fine wearing apparel, as advertised, was linked to Chas. A. Stevens and Brothers in Chicago. The fact that some Buxton businesses changed ownership and/or management throughout the years is reflected in the notice that a livery business of E. Lob-

153. Commercial advertisements run in the *Buxton Gazette*, 2 July 1908. (Courtesy of the Iowa State Historical Department)

bins had been bought out by the Coopertown Livery Co.

Another perspective of Buxton's business, commercial, and occupational enterprise comes from issues of *Polk's Iowa Gazetteer,* published by the R. L. Polk Company. These gazetteers, admittedly, cannot be used as a city directory in isolation from other sources. They may be skewed by the listing of paid patrons in the way that the Yellow Pages in modern telephone books reflect those individuals and firms paying for telephone service. Nevertheless, the gazetteers are useful in portraying a picture of firms and individuals involved in business, commercial, and occupational roles over time. In that regard it is interesting to note that issues of *Polk's Iowa Gazetteer* contain 9 listings for 1903–1904, 16 for 1905–1906, 38 for 1914–1915, 37 for 1916–1917, 36 for 1918–1919, and 23 for 1922–1923.

Figure 154 shows the 38 entries for Buxton, on page 239 of the *1914–1915 Polk's Iowa Gazetteer.* Among the business, commercial, and occupational firms and individuals listed are two companies of coal miners, five general stores (some of which, we know, contained grocery departments), one grocery, two meat markets, one bank, one telephone and telegraph office, one postmaster, four drug stores, one jeweler, two tailors and milliners, one musical instrument distributor, one cigar manufacturer and confectioner, four liveries, one restaurant, one bakery, one hotel, five physicians, two dentists, and two lawyers. Listings included in

other issues of the gazetteer include the following additional entries for Buxton: printer/publisher, theater proprietors, saloons, shoes, bottler, express agent, and fuel company. Notably lacking in these entries are listings for jobs such as blacksmiths, machinists, and carpenters, as well as for many occupations, including ministers, teachers, and undertakers. Other economic roles accomplished from people's homes—for example, the activities of seamstresses, cooks, and boardinghouse operators—likewise are not listed in the gazetteers.

From the standpoint of archaeology, a good deal of the economic system is reflected in the material residues present at the townsite. The railroad bed, the massive ruins of the company store and the vault, and the subsurface indications of the pay office, the warehouse, the foundations of the hotel, and other structural remains are, taken together, dramatic evidence of the primacy of the Consolidation Coal Company and the Chicago and North Western Railroad. Portable artifacts such as railroad spikes, miners' picks, and a carbide lamp base are also evidence of these business and industrial interests. Additionally, the inventory of portable artifacts can be associated with at least the following occupations, jobs, and other economic pursuits: butchers, druggists, physicians, tailors, seamstresses, purveyors of livery and drayage, blacksmiths, farmers, plumbers, electricians, carpenters, machinery operators, bottlers of soft beverages, jewelers, moving picture pro-

154.   Buxton advertisers in the 1914 *Polk's Iowa Gazetteer* (adapted from p. 239). Note that the population, rightly or wrongly, is listed as six thousand. (Courtesy of the ISU Archaeological Laboratory)

BUXTON. Population 6,000. A mining camp on the C. & N. W. Ry., in Bluff Creek township, Monroe county, 12 miles n. of Albia, the county seat. Has Baptist and Methodist Episcopal churches and a bank. Tel., W.U, Exp., Am Tele phone connection. A.E. Thomas, postmaster.

Armstrong H A, meats
Baxter John, meats
Buxton Savings Bank (capital $10,000),
   B C Buxton pres, T R Coles cashr
Byrd A T, r r, tel and exp agt
Carter A E, physician
Consolidated Coal Co, miners
Cooper B F, drugs
Co-operative Store, W H London mngr
Crawford Coal Co, miners
Cross J R, physician
Fitzgerald S H, jeweler
Godshall O, dentist
Granberry Bros, tailors
Harris Joe, livery
Jeffers Bros, restaurant
Larson J E, general store
Larson W W, physician
Lobbins E M, livery
London & London, musical instruments
Lowe E G, tailor and milliner
M M Company, bakery
M M Company Hotel, E M Hammond
   propr
Mater R V, physician
Monroe Mercantile Co, general store
Neely J W & Co, grocers
Roberts James, cigar mnfr and confr
Robinson C G, physician
Ross George, livery
Roush Edward, livery
Spears James A, lawyer
Standard Drug Co
Standard Mercantile Co, general store
Thomas A E, Postmaster
Thomas Drug Co
Williams Drug Co
Williams D, general store
Willis L E, dentist
Woodson George H, lawyers

jectionists, and perhaps newspaper publishers, as well as manufacturers and/or distributors of musical instruments.

Judging from the range of artifacts, one could assume that the company store and several other general stores sold a large variety of china, stoneware, glassware, foods, tools, metal containers, toys, furniture, smoking paraphernalia, cosmetics, and items of personal hygiene. The products represented in the archaeological collection came from sources literally close at hand and others ultimately far and wide. At least five trade networks can be identified: town/local, statewide, Midwest regional, national, and international.

The *town/local* trade network is proclaimed by an advertising button bragging that Buxton has "Iowa's Greatest Store." Even more extensive evidence are bottles of the Buxton Bottling Works and the Nevins Bottling Works. A. E. Larson (interview 1981), who ran a bottling works in Buxton, provided a good deal of information about the soda pop factory there. Larson stated that pop in lemon, strawberry, orange, cream, and grape flavors was bottled, with syrup extracts obtained from Chicago. Other products such as milk, meats, eggs, fruits, and vegetables also were part of the town/local trading system.

Statewide network trade patterns are evidenced by marked products manufactured and/or distributed from Albia, Oskaloosa, Ottumwa, Des Moines, Burlington, and Keokuk. The *Midwest regional* pattern is demonstrated by marked items from Minnesota, Wisconsin, Illinois, and Missouri. Represented in the *national* network are products from Michigan, Indiana, Ohio, Kentucky, Pennsylvania, Mary-

land, North Carolina, New Jersey, New York, Connecticut, Massachusetts, and California. This trade network is essentially oriented toward the East, a fact probably reflecting not only the distribution of American industries at this time but the importance of the Chicago and North Western Railroad as the primary transportation link of Buxton with the "outside world." Finally, an *international* trade network is reflected by foreign-manufactured products found at the Buxton townsite. Items from England, France, the Netherlands, and Germany have been identified among the artifacts in the archaeological inventory. The decoration of some items suggests products ultimately acquired from the Orient, but this fact cannot be demonstrated at present.

Many of the products mentioned above, of course, probably were sold at the company store or at other stores right in the community of Buxton. The patterns of trade reflected in the artifact assemblage give credence to this statement in the 1907 *Iowa State Bystander* (6 December 1907):

The wants of the people are catered to as in no other camp in Iowa. Mr. E. M. Hammond, as purchasing agent, is constantly in the field, buying exclusively for this store, with headquarters at 1111 Masonic Temple, in Chicago. . . . He keeps the store stocked with the latest styles and fads from the great market centers of the United States. Every three months a trip to New York is made to select seasonable merchandise. Philadelphia, St. Louis and other large manufacturing centers are regularly visited for the purpose of selecting merchandise at the factory, not waiting until it is put in the hands of the jobber or middle man and get the "leavins." In this manner the stock is always clean, fresh, and up-to-date. This fact alone brings many customers from towns of larger populations within a radius of thirty miles to make selections such as could not be supplied by their home merchants.

This statement is significant not only in pointing out the trade networks exploited by the merchandisers for the Monroe Mercantile Company but also in indicating that the Buxton store itself may have been a hub for regional trade. The national and even international trade networks represented in the artifacts collected at Buxton could also reflect mail-order trade from such supply houses as Sears, Roebuck and Co., headquartered in Chicago. Both domestic and imported products were advertised by that company in its turn-of-the-century catalogs (Sears, Roebuck and Co. 1897; 1902). Mail-order china, for example, included wares from potteries in Ohio, Pennsylvania, and West Virginia, as well as in England (Wood and Sons; W. H. Grindley and Co.; Alfred Meakin; and Upper Hanley Pottery Co.) and France (Theodore Haviland/Limoges). Various former Buxton residents mention mail-order catalogs. Dorothy Collier (interview 1980) recalled that "Mama used to order a lot from the Sears and Roebuck catalog or the Montgomery Ward . . . and then there was somebody came down and took grocery orders. They did that through the catalog, too." Sister Marene Sofranco (interview 1981) also mentioned having Montgomery Ward and Sears and Roebuck catalogs. Her family used the pages to wrap up apples for winter storage in their "cave," or root cellar. In addition, merchandise was brought to Buxton by peddlers. According to Dorothy Collier, travelling salesmen and saleswomen brought dresses, jewelry, and eyeglasses to the residents of the community (interview 1980).

Certain items, it should be noted, apparently were not sold in the company store. According to the *Iowa State Bystander* (6 December 1907):

There are two articles one cannot purchase at this store, revolvers and alcoholic patent medicines, the kind in which the alcohol is so prevalent that it becomes a cheap grade of whisky. The sale of a certain patent medicine was withdrawn when a miner was found drunk with two bottles (empty) at his side.

Patent medicine bottles, of course, were found by the archaeologists throughout the townsite. Perhaps the original contents of these nostrum bottles were not, indeed, alcoholic. Even so, some former residents of Buxton did consume beer and whiskey within the limits of the company town, as evidenced by the marked glass containers found throughout Section 4 of Bluff Creek Township. "Home brew" also was available in Buxton. Paul Jackson recalled that his parents made corn whiskey in Buxton during the town's second decade (interview 1980):

My folks made home brew but it was just for the house. "Chalk" they called it. That was the drink that a lot of people came from Oklahoma, coal miners, drank. They brought that with them. . . . They never bottled it or nothing. They just left it in a crock, and we just had a dipper hanging on it, and you just drank it right out of the crock.

The stoneware crocks, abundantly represented in the artifacts collected from the townsite, are of the type that could have been used for making "home brew." This sort of specific linkage, of course, cannot be made at the present time.

HOME, HOME BY THE RANGE: THE DISTAFF AND DOMESTIC DOMAINS

The nature of Consolidation Coal Company rental houses is fairly well known from historic sources. In their day these houses were hailed as more than a cut above the kinds of domestic structures usually observed in the region's coal mining camps. The *Iowa State Bystander* (18 September 1903), for example, stated that

most of the dwelling houses are five and six room, one and one-half story houses, all uniform in size, architecture and color. They are painted a bluish slate color, clean and bright, which is clean and striking on first appearance, thus doing away with the old red or white-washed miner's house so generally seen in mining camps. Too much praise cannot be given to this company for raising the life, tone and building for the miner where he and his family can at least have some of the home comforts.

Most company houses had two bedrooms upstairs and three rooms—a kitchen, living room or "front room," and a dining room or third bedroom—on the first floor. Other company houses had a fourth room, usually a kitchen, on the first floor at the back of the house. Architectural plans for such a six-room house for miners were drawn up by Frank E. Wetherell for the Consolidation Coal Company. Portions of those plans are shown here in Figure 155. Company-owned houses of the five-room and six-room styles can be seen on a number of panoramic photographs taken in Buxton (see Figs. 3, 12, 29, 41, and 104).

The company also leased land to the town's residents for the purpose of building their own homes. Privately owned homes often were larger and of more elaborate design than the company houses. Over the years, issues of the *Iowa State Bystander* pictured with pride a number of these privately owned homes in the main residential part of Buxton as well as in East Swede Town. Photographs of two of these larger, domestic-style structures appear as Figures 26 and 74; the foun-

dation of another such privately owned house was mapped in the field and described in Chapter 5 (Structure 11). The house of the mine superintendent appears to have been the largest of the homes in Buxton (see Fig. 86).

Structures associated with houses in Buxton included summer kitchens, coal sheds, chicken coops, and outdoor toilets. Odessa Brooks Booker remembered the structures clearly (interview 1981): "We had outhouses, you know. We had to walk from here out to that alley. . . . We used to take lamps and walk out to the outhouse. . . . Oh, boy, and we had to get out and shovel snow before you went to go to the coal house or to the chicken coop." Cisterns and/or wells also were present on many of the town's lots. Elmer Buford, for example, reported that his family "had a well and had a cistern. . . . Water run off the roof into the cistern. That's what they call soft water. And you get it out of the well; that was hard water" (interview 1980). A cross-sectional plan for a cistern was included on Frank Wetherell's architectural plans for the miners' homes (see Fig. 155). Old photographs of Buxton typically show company-owned houses with roof gutters and downspouts leading down into cisterns (see Figs. 3, 41, and 104). Various former Buxton residents, as discussed previously, also remembered "caves," or root cellars, for the storage of fruits, vegetables, and other foodstuffs.

In general, the archaeological survey data and limited excavated evidence corroborate the archival and oral historical information. House foundations appear to be associated only with privately owned houses. Construction materials of various media indicate frame houses with windows, brick chimneys, metal gutters, and downspouts. Cis-

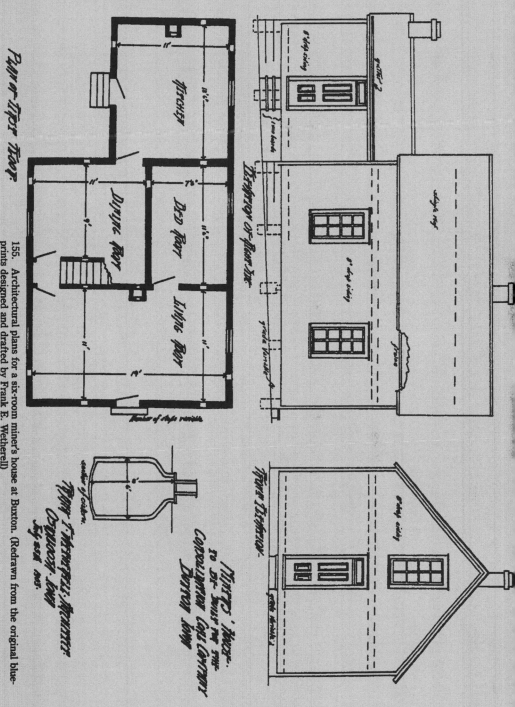

155. Architectural plans for a six-room miner's house at Buxton. (Redrawn from the original blueprints designed and drafted by Frank E. Wetherell)

terns and/or wells were observed in the downtown area of Buxton and at the superintendent's house, as well as in residential neighborhoods throughout the various site survey units investigated by the archaeological reconnaissance crew. A storage cave (Structure 10) is associated with a privately owned house (Structure 8) and several root cellars were noted throughout the townsite during the surface survey. Feature 1, located in the main test excavation unit at the south end of SSU KP-3, is interpreted as a cesspit subsequently filled with trash, probably as the townsite was being abandoned. As previously described, Feature 2 also is located in the excavation unit at the south end of SSU KP-3 and is regarded as a large garbage pit. While garbage pits are not clearly indicated on any photographs at hand, burial of garbage is mentioned as one means of waste disposal by former residents of the town.

Inside the houses, cast-iron cooking ranges and heating stoves were important among the necessary furnishings. A number of former residents of Buxton described the heating and cooking appliances they remembered from their previous homes. Lester Beaman (interview 1980) recalled that

we had one big heater in the dining room. I think that's where it was located. Then in the kitchen we had a cookstove, they call 'em. One that had the hot water tanks on one side, and all that, that would heat. . . . It's almost got an oven-like thing on top. That was the warming oven, we called that. It's got five or six lids here, and a firebox right here.

Mr. Beaman went on to discuss the problems and strategies of heating a Buxton home with a coal stove:

That stove'd be cherry red, man. It'd be cold. . . . You see, we'd be burning up front,

freezing behind. See at night, they'd bank the fires, they call it, or put some slack or something on top of the coals, so it wouldn't burn. And in the morning someone would get up and stir it up until it'd get warm, you know.

A cast-iron stove, along with a coal scuttle or hod, appears in a photograph taken in 1914 inside the tailor shop where George Neal worked (see Fig. 139). During the archaeological survey of the Buxton townsite, the archaeologists collected a good deal of material evidence of the use of cast-iron ranges and stoves: decorated stove tops, firebox doors, grates, and other parts along with lid lifters, ash shakers, and other range appurtenances.

Specific data on furniture in the homes is less easy to obtain. Informants refer to obvious categories of furniture in general terms—beds, chairs, cupboards, tables, curtains, rugs, etc.—but usually do not describe them in more definite terms. For example, Odessa Brooks Booker (interview 1981) recalled:

We had a rug on our living room but we had linoleum on the kitchen and dining room. . . . Our tables were bare, those wooden tables. Boy, that table was so pretty and bright 'cause they just scrub that thing, you know. I'm telling you, yeah, we had linoleum 'cause we had so many kids. Mother said it was clean and sanitary. And she used to take those mattresses, used to have those straw mattresses, and she used to empty them things every year, and wash those ticks out, and order more hay and straw or whatever it is, and fill them things up. And we'd have more fun getting on one of them great big high beds!

Apparently very few photographs were taken inside homes, so interior furnishings are not well known from that line of evidence. A picture of Dr. E. A. Carter and his associates (see Fig. 156) shows three carved wooden chairs—a straight chair, an armchair,

156. Informal portrait of Dr. E. A. Carter and associates at Buxton. Carter is seated second from the left. The man on the extreme left is his brother-in-law, Jim Warren, who cleaned his
medical office and barn, and the dog on the right is Duke. The
man second from the right has been identified as a Dr. Powell.
The identities of the man on the right and the dog on the left are
unknown. (Courtesy of the Iowa State Historical Department)

and a rocking chair. Fancy rattan
chairs, ornate tables, and carved
wooden pedestals show up in many
photographs of Buxton's former residents. These pieces of furniture, however, are obviously props in the studios
of professional photographers. In the
archaeological collections there are artifacts that provide some basis for the
consideration of the interior furnishings of Buxton's homes: doorknobs,
drawer or cupboard pulls, escutcheons,
casters, curtain rings, clock parts, wall
or lamp hooks, linoleum fragments,
bed frame parts, bed springs, and
horsehair stuffing for upholstered
furniture. Mophead frames are part of
the material evidence for the distaff activity of house cleaning mentioned in

interviews with a number of the town's
former occupants.

Food preparation and the serving of
meals were general topics of discussion
in interviews conducted with former
Buxton residents. For the most part,
the interviews do not reveal in specific
terms the kinds of china tableware,
glassware, and metal eating utensils
that obtained in former Buxton homes.
In this sense the previously discussed
archaeological specimens give the
clearest picture of the forms and styles
of dishes, glasses, and silverware used
in the community. Food preparation in
stoneware mixing bowls, iron skillets,
enamelware pots, pans, teapots, and
coffee kettles is further objectified and
specified by the archaeological evi-

dence. Specimens of butter churns and storage crocks found during the archaeological investigations corroborate informants' memories of milking cows, churning butter, and storing the product. For example, Hazel Stapleton (interview 1980) commented:

We made our own butter. . . . We'd churn our milk. Had a little churn about that high. I'd be churning, churning, churning, then maybe Jeanette [her sister, now Jeanette Adams], she'd take over. She'd churn, take a turnabout. Then my mother would churn. Then when it'd begin to get hard, we would look down and see butter on it about the stick. Then when we got through, when we could hardly churn, she'd take it out and put it in a big crock. And she had a paddle, and she'd just work it, work all the white out of it . . . until it just got right down.

The archaeological data also provide evidence of extensive food preservation and storage activities. Glass canning jars, wide-mouthed bottles, stoneware crocks, and stoneware jugs were used for "putting up" a variety of fruits, vegetables, pickles, sauces, and juices. Bessie Lewis (interview 1981) reminisced about making tomato juice and grape juice and canning fruits and vegetables: "I used to can tomatoes. I used to can greens, too, peaches, apples, pears, make jelly." Asked how she preserved them, she answered, "Put them in glass jars." Dorothy Collier (interview 1980) also recalled her mother's preserving food in stoneware crocks and glass jars:

I can remember Mama making, what'd they call it? Chow-chow or piccalilli. She'd fix hers in a big crock, and cover it up. . . . It was a relish. And then she would stuff green peppers and sew the tops of 'em on with relish and put that in a crock. And apple butter was put in a crock. And so the rest of the stuff was in jars, you know.

Certainly the canning of vegetables

and fruits was an important household economic activity in Buxton, as elsewhere in the United States, during the early twentieth century. The large number of fragmentary food preserving containers found at the townsite is witness to that fact.

Personal health and hygiene are represented by many items in the artifact inventory collected at Buxton: dishpans, washbasins, washtubs, wash pitchers, boilers, laundry tubs, soapdishes, a toothbrush, shaving mugs, glass containers for patent medicines, mouthwash, salves, and lotions. Toiletries are represented by containers for cosmetics, perfumes, and deodorants. Attention to grooming is evidenced by remains of combs and hair ornaments. Bathing and body cleanliness were concerns in this town, especially for the coal miners, whose work was literally a dirty business. Marjorie Brown (interview 1980) explained in detail:

My Lord, those miners took a bath every day. Every day! That was part of the evening routine. To put that great huge kettle of water on the stove so it would be hot. The miners took a bath every day. They couldn't come in the house if they didn't, with those dirty black clothes. And the children, we went barefoot. . . . My land, there was a bucket sat under the pump and . . . you had to wash your feet before you came into the house to take a bath. I didn't know we were supposed to be dirty. Because you had to wash your feet before you could come in the house. Take a bath, go upstairs, and get in that bed with the sheets.

Dorothy Collier recalled that her mother heated bath water in the reservoir on the kitchen coal stove and then she and her brother were bathed together in a "big tin tub" (interview 1980). In several overview photographs of the town, one can see large metal washtubs hanging near the back doors of many houses. Understandably, there probably are no photographs of adults performing their bodily ablutions. We have, however, a photograph of master Wilbur Peterson taking his bath (see Fig. 105). Of particular interest to the archaeologist is the large ceramic washbasin similar to those advertised in the 1902 Sears and Roobuok catalog. It is a whole vessel, as compared to the broken pieces collected during the reconnaissance survey of the townsite.

Photographs provide a good deal of information about the clothing styles in Buxton (see Figs. 8–10, 157–160). Children's garments shown in photographs include christening gowns, "Sunday best" attire, and play clothes (see Fig. 159 and Figs. 8, 113, and 150). Most of the photographs of adults are formal and show people clothed in relatively "dressy" attire. One suspects that the tailors and milliners in Buxton

158. Formal portrait of a man identified as Leonard Walker by Dorothy Collier. Mr. Walker is seated in a fancy rattan chair shown in other formal portraits taken by a professional photographer in or around Buxton. (Courtesy of the Iowa State Historical Department)

157. Rose Warren Carter and daughter Marion, taken circa 1913 in Buxton. (Courtesy of Marion Carter)

were busy people! Men were usually photographed wearing suits, sometimes vested, with white starched shirts, either bow ties or four-in-hand ties, high-topped laced shoes or oxfords, and felt or straw hats with cloth hatbands. Pocket watches, watch chains, watch fobs, and possibly medals are also exhibited in the photographs. In Figure 156, Jim Warren (Dr. E. A. Carter's brother-in-law and handyman) is shown wearing what appear to be one-piece overalls and work boots. Few clear pictures exist of coal miners in their mining clothes around town (see *Iowa State Bystander* 6 De-

178

cember 1907), but there are views of these men in their working apparel with lamps and other equipment at the mines or otherwise on duty (see Fig. 18). Available pictures also show men in uniforms for playing baseball (see Fig. 10) and basketball (see Fig. 63). Available pictures of women show them dressed in tailored suits with long skirts or else gowns with pinched waists, lace cuffs, collars, and bodices. Kid gloves, necklaces, lockets, brooches, chatelaine watches, rings, and bracelets are also observed in the photographs, as are broad-brimmed felt and straw hats, sometimes ornamented with large ostrich plumes, bows, and what appear to be cloth flowers.

The archaeological evidence of all this finery is present, but the view into the looking glass is indeed clouded. Artifacts representing clothing and ornamentation include shoes, boots and other footwear, belts, gloves, studs, safety pins, brassiere or garter hooks, buttons (shell, metal, glass, celluloid), buckles, grommets, celluloid interfacing, brooches or pins, beads, bracelets, and barrettes. Scissors, flatirons, sewing machine parts, and a thimble indicate the activities of the tailor and the seamstress. Both were present in Buxton. For example, George Neal was a tailor and made men's clothing, while his wife, Alice Mobilia Neal, made most of her own clothes rather than buying them from Mrs. Vance, a travelling saleswoman from Des Moines. As explained by their daughter, Dorothy Neal Collier (interview 1980):

I know my Mama used to say safety pins and things like that was alright, but she never wanted none of Mrs. Vance's botched up clothes. So evidently she made a lot of clothes. She made a lot of her own clothes. . . . As far as clothing, the people

159. Formal portrait of Lottie Armstrong Baxter. Identified by Dorothy Collier, Mrs. Baxter was a cashier for the Monroe Mercantile Co., the daughter of H. A. "Hobe" Armstrong, and the wife of John Baxter. (Courtesy of the Iowa State Historical Department)

dressed real well. They were really dressy, you know. 'Cause I can think of a dress my mother had . . . a beautiful knit. Oh, I can remember it so plainly. Blue dress, and instead of being scalloped at the bottom, it had little tiny heavy silk embroidery squares. And she had blue satin slippers with rosettes on 'em. Oh, I thought she was so pretty with that.

According to Dorothy Collier, however, her mother also bought dresses at the company store and ordered them by catalog from Montgomery Ward and Sears and Roebuck.

GETTING AROUND: TRANSPORTATION, UTILITIES, AND FACILITIES

Buxton was located on the Chicago and North Western Railroad, an important transportation and communication link with the world beyond Bluff Creek. Available photographs show the railroad depot, freight trains, and the trains that took the miners to and from the coal mines each day (see Fig. 33). Today, as archaeological evidence, the bed of the railroad can still be observed, although the ties and rails long since have been dismantled. Some railroad spikes are found scattered throughout the townsite. Evidence for horseback riding and horse-drawn carriages exists in photographs (see Figs. 14, 23, and 83), in information from the oral interviews, and in the material residue collected by the archaeologists: horseshoes, metal harness fittings, leather harness fragments, several identifiable buggy parts, and the name plate for "Columbus Carriages." Automobiles are pictured in photographs (see Fig. 144), mentioned in the *Iowa State Bystander*, and evidenced by a fragment of a rubber tire for a car, at least one car crank, dry cell battery electrodes, and spark plugs. The leaf spring parts could be for either automobiles or horse-drawn buggies.

Getting around town, of course, was facilitated by a well-planned street system. While the pattern of streets was functional and reasonably thought out, the streets were not paved or surfaced with crushed stone materials as county roads in Monroe and Mahaska counties are today. The streets were often difficult to travel, particularly in wet weather. Former Buxton resident Lola Reeves (interview 1980) recalled that when it rained, there was

Mud! You had to tie your boots or your shoes on. If you walked out, then you'd fall. They never did pave the streets. They used to have a road down there called "Cinder Road." I don't know whether it was any better than the rest of them or not. But we lived up the hill from the store and, I'm telling you, it was something else when it rained!

Various former inhabitants of Buxton

refer specifically to a street they call the "Cinder Road." It is not entirely clear which of the unnamed streets on the 1919 plat map is meant. The Cinder Road may be the street that once followed the ravine in what is now the property of the Raymond Carter family. That linkage, however, demands further analysis before it can be verified.

Former Buxton residents also recall walking a lot from their houses to the company store, to the YMCA, to the saloons in Coopertown or at Sharp End, or to the reservoir. In Elmer Buford's comments to his interviewer he exclaimed, "I got around, buddy. I got

160. Formal portrait of the Sears sisters in Buxton. Marion Carter identified these young women as "Mac" (Macnola) and "Peggy" (Vascilla) Sears, her maternal first cousins. Peggy Sears was born in Muchakinock, later lived in Buxton, and as of 1983 resided in Baton Rouge, Louisiana; Mac Sears is deceased. (Courtesy of the Iowa State Historical Department)

around. There wasn't a place there I didn't go" (interview 1980). Perhaps the worn out and discarded shoes found by the archaeologists are mute evidence of getting around via "shank's mare." Wooden sidewalks for pedestrians show up on photographs of the downtown area and are recalled by several former Buxton residents. Some concrete sidewalks around the YMCA building and the company store were also verified in the archaeological investigations.

It is interesting to note that good evidence for the two different lighting systems is present in the archaeological collections. Ruins of the power plant (Structure 17) have been identified, although the nature of the building awaits more extensive subsurface investigations. Broken light bulbs, light sockets, fuses and fuse sockets, glass and porcelain insulators, and insulated wire fragments are the material evidence of the electric lighting utilities that served the downtown district of Buxton, the superintendent's house up on the hill above Bluff Creek, and perhaps some of the dwellings south of the downtown area. The base of a lamppost was discovered in the archaeological investigation of the company store (see Fig. 52). Photographs of the second company store, of course, show five of these iron lamps on the sidewalk facing out onto East First Street (see Figs. 47 and 48). The distribution of materials relating to electrical lighting appears to be concentrated in the downtown area. Insulators, however, were found in areas of former residential neighborhoods, and available photographs show what appear to be power lines beyond the business/commercial district per se.

Most, if not all, of the homes in the residential neighborhoods, however,

seem to have been without electric lighting. When asked about the lighting in his former home in Buxton, Lester Beaman (interview 1980) replied, "Regular old kerosene lamps. No electricity." Similarly, Vera Olson Fisher, presently of Newton, Iowa, recalled that when she was a young girl and woman in Buxton, "we didn't have electricity there and everything was pitch dark. They didn't have street lights like they do here" (interview 1980). Kerosene lamps were used in Coopertown, as evidenced by the hanging lamp shown in the shop where George Neal worked (see Fig. 9). The archaeological inventory includes many specimens of kerosene lamps: clear and milk glass lamp bases, clear glass chimneys, milk glass globes, metal burners, and wick holders. Several cut glass pendants or prisms also were found, suggesting that at least some houses in Buxton were illuminated by fancy oil lamps in addition to the "regular" kind.

Central water, heating, and sanitary facilities also are evidenced in the downtown area of Buxton and at the superintendent's house perched above the town. The latter residence had its own water tower, as shown on photographs and observed in the surface ruins noted during the preliminary archaeological survey. (The foundation remnants of the water tower and associated buildings were subsequently designated as the Structure 25 complex.) Water was supplied to the town via at least one water tower, located near East Fourth Street, and probably by the water control devices observed at the eastern end of the dam at the reservoir. Water pipes were recorded in several structures in downtown Buxton, although the full extent of the system of running water is not known at present. Associated with the ruins of the White House Hotel (Structure 6) were a well and a cistern, suggesting that this downtown building was not serviced directly by the municipal water system (see Fig. 72). According to several past Buxton residents, however, cisterns sometimes were filled by water wagons. Based on the field data at hand, steam for heating was generated at the power plant (Structure 17) and was conveyed by pipes to at least the company store (Structure 2) and the two YMCA buildings (Structures 4 and 5). The large house of the mine superintendent was heated by a central furnace and had at least two inside bathrooms, according to Marvin Franzen, who, as son of the caretaker for the estate, had been inside the home many times (interview 1981). The archaeologists found evidence of indoor flush toilets at the company store and at the boys' YMCA building. The latter facility had at least three toilet stalls available to the public.

HAVING FUN: RECREATION AND RELAXATION

Most of the people who once lived in Buxton recall toys and games that amused them when they were children in the town. Dominoes, dolls, toy wagons, ice skates, and sleds were mentioned by Hazel Stapleton (interview 1980). Odessa Brooks Booker remembered ice skates, wagons, roller skates, kites, and jacks (interview 1981); Elmer Buford thought back on playing baseball and marbles (interview 1980). A photograph from Dorothy Neal Collier's collection shows her as a child with a large doll and a toy baby carriage (see Fig. 113). Dolls are shown in an interior view of the first company store as pictured in the *Iowa*

State Bystander of 6 December 1907. Frozen Charlotte dolls and china head dolls are well represented in the archaeological collection from the townsite, as are glass and stoneware marbles. One ice skate was found along the edge of the former reservoir. Also in the collection are pieces of lead (possibly for "tin" soldiers), a probable slide for a lantern slide projector, parts of pencils, ink bottles, and portable blackboards. One former Buxton resident mentioned collecting Indian arrowheads as a boy; several prehistoric artifacts discovered by the archaeologists lend support to that informant's statement.

Both children and adults attended moving picture films at the YMCA. Archaeological evidence for this entertainment consists of carbon rod arc light cathodes. Some men, at least, were members of the Buxton Coal Palace Gun Club and disported at shooting clay pigeons and live birds. Portions of a gun trigger mechanism, along with shotgun shells, might be associated with that activity. Other men fished in the reservoir and hunted small animals in the surrounding woods and fields. The rabbit bones found by the archaeologists might represent the latter sport. It is unfortunate that no archaeological evidence was collected to verify the Buxton Wonders baseball games or the basketball players, boxers, or gymnasts at the YMCA, but proof of those activities lies in photographs.

The ruins of the YMCA buildings themselves, of course, are monuments to the extensive recreational and cultural facilities available to members of the Buxton community. They offered a gymnasium, an auditorium, pool tables, a place for roller skating and dancing, a swimming pool, and other forms of amusements unique, or nearly so, in Iowa "mining camps" and other settlements in the region. The main YMCA building had a reading room, and presumably reading books and newspapers was a form of education as well as of recreation. As Mike Onper (interview 1981) described the layout of the main YMCA building:

When you come in, they had a reading room. They had books. . . . They got the paper. No, it wasn't no library, it was just, you know, just a place with big chairs. . . . You go in there and read the papers. . . . Some of them older guys, they play checkers. The older guys, you know, they belong to it too, but they just played checkers and, you know, read in there.

In that regard, the fact that newspapers were published in Buxton, and the finding of pieces of newspapers and a portion of a possible printer's plate, are significant. Playing pianos and other musical instruments, and listening to the Buxton Concert Band, were also amusements in Buxton (*Iowa State Bystander* 18 September 1903 and 6 December 1907). Musical instruments are not well represented so far in the archaeological collections. Items identified as harmonica plates and pieces of a possible mechanical music box were collected; other possible musical instrument parts need to be further documented.

Voluntary associations and lodges are referred to in issues of the *Iowa State Bystander* and in the interviews with former Buxton residents. A medallion in Dorothy Collier's personal collection is material evidence for the existence of the Order of Calanthe, a black women's sodality in Buxton. Some other fraternal organizations are represented materially by the symbols on gravestones in the cemetery: Ma-

sons, Eastern Star, Odd Fellows, and United Mine Workers of America.

Finally, it can be noted that the archaeological evidence does document the practices of pipe smoking and snuff sniffing or sucking. No material evidence was discovered, however, for James Roberts' cigar manufacturing firm. That evidence, so to speak, must have gone up in smoke.

PRAYING AND PASSING: RELIGIOUS AND MORTUARY PATTERNS

At least seven churches once existed in Buxton. Along the northern entrance road into the community were two large Methodist churches: the First Methodist Church and the African Methodist Episcopal Church, also referred to as St. John's Church (see Fig. 27). In East Swede Town there was the Swedish Lutheran Church, a structure moved from Muchakinock to Buxton, where it stood until it burned down in 1954 (see Fig. 23). The Mount Zion Baptist Church was located on East Sixth Street on a lot adjoining that of the elementary Fifth Street School. Another church was located on West Eleventh Street, according to the 1919 plat map and information from former Buxton residents; those references, however, are equivocal as to the denomination of that congregation. In West Swede Town there were two churches, a Swedish Methodist church and a Slavic Lutheran Church.

Other religious congregations worshipped together in Buxton, but they seemed to have been shorter-lived than the larger, established congregations with church buildings. These congregations apparently met in private homes and other buildings in Buxton.

According to Sister Marene Sofranco, the Catholics held Masses in the auditorium on the second floor of the YMCA building (interview 1981). In this regard it is significant to note that the only portable, obviously religious artifact collected by the archaeologists at the Buxton townsite appears to be associated with Catholicism. This artifact is a representation of the "Madonna and Child" in white porcelain (see Fig. 109F). In it the Virgin Mary is depicted wearing a cape and a crown with a veil, while the nude Infant Jesus also is wearing a crown. It has been suggested that this molded figure is specifically a depiction of the "Infant of Prague" motif not uncommon in Catholic art at the turn of the century.

Mentioned frequently in interviews with former Buxton residents, the churches were obviously among the focal points for people in the community. Even after the abandonment of the urban settlement at Buxton, the Swedish Lutheran Church building continued to serve its congregation until the unfortunate fire of 1954 (Mabel Blomgren, personal communication 1981). From an earlier day during her childhood in Buxton, Vera Olson Fisher (interview 1980) reminisced:

> In East Swede Town where we lived . . . they had a Swedish Lutheran Church . . . and services were all in Swedish. . . . When we were all kids at home, why we'd go to English school in the wintertime, and as soon as that school was out we had to go to Swedish school. In the summer, us kids went to school, studied Swedish, studied the catechism and Bible history and things about the Bible.

Today there are no demonstrable structural remains of the church. Perhaps subsurface archaeological test excavations could relocate the foundations of this building. In the meantime, Mabel Blomgren's piece of blue stained glass and a church record book written in Swedish are the only known artifactual remains of the Swedish Lutheran Church.

Similarly, the former location of the Mount Zion Baptist Church is now a cultivated field in Site Survey Unit KP-1. During his youth in Buxton, Elmer Buford was a participant, albeit not always a willing one, in the Mount Zion congregation (interview 1980):

> Mount Zion Baptist Church . . . I had to go. Sometimes I didn't want to go. I had to go. . . . I went to Sunday school. Then my grandmother'd take me . . . back into church. . . . Yes, never missed a Sunday, only when I was sick or something.

Hazel Stapleton also attended the Baptist church, and she related the following (interview 1980):

> I went with my mother, with my aunt. You had to get down on your knees and pray, you know. And I was down on my knees, praying, trying to get religion . . . and I remember I got so tired down on my knees, I wasn't praying, I was just wasting time. And all at once, I jumped up, and said "Mama, I got it! I got it!" . . . I ain't had nothin' but I got tired gettin' down on my knees!

Today perhaps the only people kneeling in this area are the archaeologists stooping over to look for the remains of the former buildings along East Sixth Street.

Except for some scattered bricks and mortar, along with some construction materials in an adjacent ravine, there are no apparent surficial remains of the First Methodist Church and the African Methodist Episcopal Church. Lola Reeves, a former elementary school teacher in Buxton, recalled that she "used to play for the people's choir at St. John's all the time I was in Buxton" (interview 1980). The African Meth-

184

odist Episcopal Church apparently had a considerable reputation for its organ and choir. Of particular interest in the archival records is a photograph showing the large congregation of the A. M. E. Church assembled outside the church building (see Fig. 161). In addition to the fine clothing and the American flag proudly proclaiming the congregation's patriotism, note the background structure made of logs and branches. This structure is apparently a ramada-like building to shade picnickers. To archaeologists familiar with similar American Indian structures used for social and religious gatherings, this construction by Afro-Americans at Buxton appears to be something of an anachronism, if not a striking example of cultural borrowing. Such significant but temporary buildings usually do not leave much archaeological evidence, but then, neither did the imposing "permanent" structure of the African Methodist Episcopal Church. It, too, did pass.

Many people who "passed" now lie buried in the Buxton cemetery. Some former residents of the town recall the cemetery and the funeral processions that sometimes paraded with pomp and circumstance to this otherworldly spot. For others the trip to the final resting place was more earthly. Odessa Brooks Booker (interview 1981) remembers burying her father, George William Brooks, in the Buxton cemetery:

They were all dirt roads, you know. . . . Everybody had a horse and buggy 'cause I remember when they buried my father, they had this hearse and everything. And, boy, it was raining bad and we didn't know if we were going to make it to the cemetery 'cause, you know, the ground was soft going there.

Among the 37 extant gravestones observed in the Buxton cemetery, the ar-

chaeologists found none marked George William Brooks; perhaps he lies in one of the many unmarked graves. He shares an epitaph, however, with John W. Williams, whose memorial inscription and mortal span of life from March 7, 1882, to March 18, 1914, were preserved for posterity in chiseled stone. He is "Gone But Not Forgotten."

161. Photograph of the African Methodist Episcopal Church (St. John's) and its congregation gathered for a festivity. Note the American flag and the arbor, or ramada-like structure, between the people and the church. (Courtesy of Dorothy Neal Collier)

ARCHAEOLOGICAL EXTENT AND QUALITY OF THE TOWNSITE

As an archaeological unit the Buxton townsite (13M010) is rich in historical context and material manifestations. The downtown area of Buxton, for the archaeologist, has abundant structural remains relating to the commerce of the town, as well as to the industrial and transportation systems linking this community to regional and national networks. Data pertaining to the mine superintendent and other elite of the community are available at the locations of privately owned homes, while information on the people living in company-owned houses to the south of the commercial district was revealed in test excavations and the reconnaissance survey of the greater portion of Section 4 of Bluff Creek Township. Despite a variety of adverse circumstances, both structural remains and portable artifacts are present to some degree throughout the townsite. Artifacts found in fields presently being cultivated are broken, but they are scientifically and historically significant. Surface reconnaissance suggests the potential for finding remains of structures now masked by vegetation or buried below the ground.

The archaeological data are important, if not essential, to a full understanding of the Buxton experience. To be sure, the primary and secondary archival sources are vital in providing a great range of information pertaining to this town. The oral historical mate-

rial obtained from many of Buxton's former residents also provides insights into what members of that now-abandoned community thought and did in their everyday lives. The material cultural evidence, however limited and skewed, can nevertheless provide additional objective data from which the previous patterns of life in Buxton can be seen. In the words of James Deetz (1977:160–61):

Material culture may be the most objective source of information we have concerning America's past. It is certainly the most immediate. When an archaeologist carefully removes the earth from the jumbled artifacts at the bottom of a trash pit, he or she is the first person to confront those objects since they were placed there centuries before. When we stand in the chamber of a seventeenth-century house that has not been restored, we are placing ourselves in the same architectural environment occupied by those who lived there in the past. The arrangements of gravestones in a cemetery and the designs on their tops create a *Gestalt* not of our making but of the community whose dead lie beneath the ground. If we bring to this world, so reflective of the past, a sensitivity to the meaning of the patterns we see in it, the artifact becomes a primary source of great objectivity and subtlety.

So it is that in quantity and quality the archaeological resources from the Buxton townsite—the trash from Feature 2, the basement chambers of the White House Hotel, and the gravestones in the cemetery—provide primary data for understanding the gestalt, or system, of Buxton as a town in the physical sense and as a community of interacting people.

in retrospect and prospect

Undoubtedly such evidence also occurs outside Section 4, the section owned by Consolidation Coal Company and here designated as 13M010, the Buxton townsite. The larger Buxton community certainly included ancillary "suburbs" such as Sharp End and Tait's Corner, south of Section 4, and perhaps Miami and Whiteburg, to the west. To the north, in Mahaska County, were Coopertown, Gainestown, and Hayestown. These commercial and residential developments were part of the Buxton community, too. For example, George Neal lived in Gobbler's Nob on East Fourth Street in Buxton, but he worked in a tailor shop several blocks north in Coopertown, Mahaska County. Similarly, Reuben Gaines had his various establishments in Gainestown in Mahaska County, but he figures largely in newspaper accounts of Buxton, as well as in the memories of people who once lived in that community. Furthermore, the parents of Reuben Gaines now lie buried in Monroe County, at the Buxton cemetery in the northwest corner of Section 4 of Bluff Creek Township.

BUXTON'S RELATIONSHIP TO NATIONAL TRADE NETWORKS

The manufacture marks and patents on artifacts recovered in the archaeological investigations reveal not only an intensive local and regional trade network (Oskaloosa, Albia, Des Moines), but also extensive national

(Minneapolis, St. Louis, Chicago, New York) and international exchange systems (England, the Netherlands, France, Germany, and perhaps the Orient). Marked ceramic and glass containers provide the most information in this regard (cf. Baugher-Perlin 1982; Godden 1978; Honey and Cushion 1956; Kovel and Kovel 1953). Given the primacy of the railroad at Buxton this wide network is not surprising, but it emphasizes the fact that this community was part of the national and international urban/industrial complex superimposed on the countryside of Iowa. It was born and quickly grew because of these factors. It also died, apparently, as a consequence of shifts relating to a whole series of matters involved in the exploitation of regional, geological resources as well as the reorganizations of the American economy during and after World War I.

REGIONAL AND NATIONAL SIGNIFICANCE OF BUXTON

Judging from the available and potential materials on Buxton, along with the interest and feedback we have obtained from individuals studying black communities in North America, we suggest that this case study is not only of regional, but also of national, significance. Whether Buxton is "typical" or "unique" is perhaps less important than the fact that it provides an unusual opportunity to focus on interethnic relations and black history in the United States. As yet the history of black peo-

187

ple in Iowa has not been studied and summarized adequately. Leola Nelson Bergmann's (1969) monograph entitled *The Negro in Iowa* is a decent enough start, but the range of data located in the Buxton project alone shows how much wider and deeper we must go in investigating this subject. If the role of blacks has not been well documented in historical studies, it has been less well explored through archaeology. The few studies of blacks from an archaeological or material cultural perspective have been primarily of urban dwellers in the Northeast and of slave settlements in the South (for example, Baker 1980; Bridges and Salwen 1980; Geismar 1982; McDaniel 1979, 1982; Schuyler 1980; and Singleton 1980). Virtually no archaeological resources pertaining to blacks have been tapped in the prairies, plains, and western portions of the United States.

In addition, the Buxton townsite is significant as an interethnic community of many European-derived national groups: Swedish, Slavic, Austrian, English, Welsh, Irish, and others. It is also significant, we suggest, as a facet of the regional coal mining industry and the importance of the railroad transportation and communications system in this area. It is, finally, significant as an example of the superimposition of the urban/industrial pattern on the rural countryside and the subsequent shifts that occur as regional economic exploitive systems change. These processes occurred in the past; still, they are parts of our lives today as railroad systems are being abandoned, new systems of mining coal are being explored, and urban communities increasingly are encroaching upon the region's agricultural lands.

Buxton is significant in terms of the many foreign countries and American states from which its residents came. Buxton is also significant in terms of the many places to which its former five thousand or so residents dispersed after the demise of the town. As one looks around the country, one finds the many more thousand descendants of people who once lived in Buxton. They are not only in Iowa but also in California, Arizona, Colorado, Nebraska, Arkansas, Louisiana, Texas, Illinois, Wisconsin, Michigan, Ohio, New York, and elsewhere around the United States. The network extends throughout the country; the threads go back to the townsite in northern Monroe County, Iowa.

Considering the nature of the former community at Buxton, its role in the industrial and social development of Iowa and the Midwest, its broader linkages to the history of the United States in the post–Civil War period, and the demonstrated cultural resources extant on the land where the town once stood, the archaeologists proposed that the townsite (13M010) more than met the criteria for inclusion on the National Register of Historic Places. After due consideration, the U.S. Department of the Interior officially placed the townsite on the National Register during the fall of 1983, thus formally recognizing the significance of Buxton and its former residents in American history.

BUXTON'S SETTLEMENT PATTERN

The settlement pattern of Buxton appears to be unusual, if not unique, for coal mining communities, and indeed perhaps for many other communities that sprang up in the American West at the turn of the century. Buxton was certainly a carefully planned settlement—a *town* and not a *mining camp* in the sense that the term often has been used in the literature. The business and commercial enterprises were centralized, to a large degree, along the Chicago and North Western Railroad tracks. While this organization is not unique, it reflects the primacy of the transportation and coal mining industries (that is, the Consolidation Coal Company and the Chicago and North Western Railroad) over the community. The range, number, and size of communal/public buildings is impressive for this type of community. The fact that the Consolidation Coal Company engaged the services of Frank E. Wetherell, a well-known architect, to draw up plans for miners' houses, two churches, and a high school is a notable indication of urban planning and social humanitarianism in the organization of Buxton. The structure of the community appears to have been planned in considerable detail beforehand and then quickly established upon the initial movement of the population from Muchakinock and elsewhere. While some streets may have been routed according to local topography, the system is essentially a grid pattern superimposed upon the landscape. Archaeological evidence and archival data indicate the situation was emphatically *not* that described by J. A. Swisher (1945:185), who said "the streets were irregular, 'following the lay of the land.' " Materially this system represents a superimposition of the urban/industrial pattern upon rural countryside.

The separation of the mine superintendent's residence on an isolated scenic hilltop across the Bluff Creek valley from the main part of town is a striking spatial pattern. The distance, in fact, was as much social as geographical. When Ada Baysoar Morgan lived in Buxton as the daughter of mine superintendent E. M. Baysoar, her forays into the town were few; her social contacts with the townspeople were even more limited. In reminiscing about her life in Buxton, Ada Morgan (interview 1981) stated, "I never had any associations with any colored people except Macnola [Sears] and a laundress. . . . I didn't know any white miner families either. That meadow seemed to separate us, I guess."

In all these respects, the material remains and the multi-faceted dimensions of the Buxton townsite offer many opportunities not only for cultural resource management and public interpretation but also for continuing field research programs, internship sessions, and archaeological field schools. In James Deetz's terms, artifacts represent "the small things forgotten." He points out their potential for public education and interpretation (Deetz 1977:161):

It is terribly important that the "small things forgotten" be remembered. For in the seemingly little and insignificant things that accumulate to create a lifetime, the essence of our existence is captured. We must remember these bits and pieces, and we must use them in new and imaginative ways so that a different appreciation for what life is today, and was in the past, can be achieved.

In the case of the data from Buxton, for example, museum displays could incorporate artifacts, along with reproductions of documents, photographs, and even sound track portions from the taped oral interviews in presenting and interpreting the Buxton experience to the general public. In these ways and others, the material cultural remains from Buxton could be employed to help achieve an understanding of American people today in terms of what they have been in the past.

ETHNICITY IN BUXTON

One dimension of U.S. history that most Americans are still struggling to understand and cope with is the fact that the country is made up of people of various ethnic groups and many different national origins. In that respect Buxton was a microcosm of the general American scene. The dimensions of ethnicity in Buxton are revealed by the documents in public archives and personal collections and by former residents through oral interviews. Ethnicity is also reflected to some degree in the material remains collected at the townsite or otherwise observed during the recent investigations.

The gravestone of Andrew Jackson is tangible evidence of the presence of blacks in Buxton (see Fig. 39). Data chiseled into the marble monument tell us that Jackson was a member of Company K of the 5th United States Colored Infantry. In addition it may be that the presence of black people at Buxton can be correlated with the apparently large number of cold cream jars and containers for other skin conditioners and emollients represented in the artifact inventory from the townsite. Although not collected from the townsite, a medallion and ribbon in the collection of Dorothy Collier is further material documentation of Buxton's black population. The medallion's embossed ribbon, marked "Hermione Court No. 256, O.O.C., Buxton, Iowa," refers to The Order of Calanthe, a women's auxiliary of the Knights of Pythias of North America, Europe, Asia, and Africa. These organizations were sodalities for black people, in contrast to the Knights of Pythias and the

Pythian Sisters, whose memberships were restricted to whites (Schmidt 1980:183–86).

Several artifacts from Buxton also reflect the ethnic diversity of whites in the town. The molded figure of the Madonna and Child is a Catholic representation. The manufacture of the figure in the "Infant of Prague" style is suggestive of Slavic affiliations, although that linkage may not be entirely warranted without further study. Another artifact is tangible evidence of the Lutheran community in East Swede Town: the church record book, written in Swedish, in the personal collection of Mabel and Loren Blomgren. Members of the Blomgren family were among the first residents in Buxton, where they attended the Swedish Lutheran Church until it burned down in 1954 (Mabel Blomgren, personal communication 1981). Mabel and Loren Blomgren still live in Section 4 of Bluff Creek Township and represent a linkage of the Buxton townsite with people of Swedish ancestry for over eight decades.

Further ethnic identifications on the basis of the presently collected archaeological inventory are more difficult to discern at this time. More extensive collections from East Swede Town and/ or West Swede Town would be advisable, if not absolutely necessary, to look for these kinds of variations. It is probable, however, that (a) the material inventories from the different ethnic neighborhoods will not differ much because all Buxton residents may have obtained most of their items at the company store or by mail-order catalogs, and (b) ethnic differences may not have been significantly expressed in the material culture of these peoples at that time. Ethnic differences in material culture are not very obviously exhibited, if indeed at all, in the available photographs from the period. Trash dumps from specifically identifiable persons or families probably would be necessary to fully demonstrate any hypotheses regarding ethnic variations in the material culture of Buxton residents.

It is quite possible, of course, that the artifactual remains might be just as varied and mixed as the associations and interactions of the former Buxton residents. According to Marion Carter (letter to H. L. Olin, 7 January 1963), in Buxton there were "all white affairs, all colored affairs, and all all affairs."

WHAT ABOUT BUXTON AS UTOPIA?

The original interdisciplinary research proposal made to the Heritage Conservation and Recreation Service was entitled "Buxton, Iowa: A Black Utopian Community." The title, for better or worse, captured a feeling and perception in the minds of many members of the Buxton, Iowa Club Inc., as well as the Iowa State University researchers who wanted to undertake a study of the now-abandoned community. Admittedly we archaeologists, approaching the situation as anthropologists, were somewhat cautious, maybe even cynical, about the grandiose statements heard and read about Buxton. Was the town really as large as people said—a "metropolis," as occasionally labelled in print. Were there really as many colored, or black, people there as reported in newspapers, in journal articles, and by former residents of the community? Were things really as "good" as people recalled— "like a heaven to me"—or were they just memories of an embellished past?

Many of these questions, of course,

involve cognitive perceptions, if not material matters. Since perceptions as well as "realities" are important here, we mention an incident that challenged our own questions, if not biases, upon beginning the project. During our first meeting with the Buxton, Iowa Club Inc., a gentleman who had been a miner in Buxton turned to us and said, to the best of our recollection, "Buxton was a good place to live. We had our own doctors. We had our own dentists. We had our own lawyers. Things were good there. And then we moved Des Moines and stepped back one hundred years." Since this was an essentially informal situation, we were not sitting there with tape recorders or notebooks to take down our conversations verbatim. Pondering and further discussing the magnitude of this man's statement, we did not even think to ask his name. But his "utopian" recollection of Buxton and the contrastive statement of what life had been for him in Des Moines have remained as a powerful philosophical viewpoint for us to consider. There was no question in our minds as to the reality this man carried in his mind. Those sorts of realities must be dealt with whether or not they square with our own preconceptions.

Chapter 1 of this book quoted portions of two "utopian" statements from former Buxton residents. Those statements were made by Dorothy Neal Collier and Jesse Frazier on the television production entitled *You Can't Go Back to Buxton,* produced by the Iowa Public Broadcasting Network (IPBN) in 1979. Similar statements were made in the videotape by Marjorie Brown, Paul Wilson, Carl Kietzman, and Reuben Gaines, Jr., all former residents of Buxton. Such utopian evaluations appear to prevail in many statements made about Buxton at the time the town was thriving and by former residents thinking back on their lives in the community there. A few examples will suffice to indicate the nature of these perceptions. In 1909 the editor of the *Iowa State Bystander* (29 October 1909) referred to Buxton as "the Negro Athens of the north" and stated:

The population will number about 5,000, of which 3,000 are colored people, and I can truthfully say that here live some of the race's most successful and business men. Here one can study the race from a viewpoint that no other large community offers to the Negro. Here he has absolute freedom to everything that any other citizen has. Here you can see well trained doctors, lawyers. Here you can see the public schools with mixed teachers, mostly colored, with a colored principal. . . . Here you can see colored men officers administering the law, providing the punishment and inflicting the penalty; here you can see colored men building the buildings, operating the electric plant, riding in automobiles and carriages; here you can see them farming; here you can see them owning amusements, parks, baseball parks and their own bands. Here we have the church bells ringing from the colored churches and the YMCA, owned and operated on business basis by colored men, and many other things too numerous to mention.

Such was the message of the editor of the region's leading Afro-American newspaper, speaking primarily to the community of black people in Iowa.

The utopian aspects of Buxton were also noted nationally. An issue of *The Southern Workman* in 1908, for example, noted the efforts of B. C. Buxton in establishing the town: ". . . he has not attempted to build up a democracy. On the contrary he has built up an autocracy and he is the autocrat, albeit a benevolent one" (Wright 1908:494). Beyond that, the article generally waxes luxuriant on the organization of the town and the manner in which various racial and ethnic groups lived in har-

mony. In that discussion, Wright (1908:497) stated:

. . . the relation [*sic*] of the black majority to the white minority are most cordial. . . . The Negroes do not fear the whites and the whites do not try to make them fear them; there is mutual respect. Both races go to school together; the principal and most of the teachers are colored; they go to the same soda-water fountains, ice-cream parlors, and restaurants; work in the same mines, clerk in the same stores, and live side by side.

Similar themes are seen in the statements former Buxton residents made in interviews during the recent project. In the words of Bessie Lewis (interview 1981):

I'm telling you, Buxton is the place that really give the colored person a chance. Give them a chance to do anything that they wanted to do. They had a chance to do it and they helped them to do it. They helped them to go to school. They helped them to learn different trades. And they sent them away. They sent a clerk out of the store. They wanted him to work in an office or something, they'd send him to school somewhere and get a training and come back, pick up a stenographer job and go off.

These sentiments are mirrored in the comments of Lola Reeves (interview 1980), a former schoolteacher in Buxton:

You know, Buxton to me was a new experience and I really enjoyed it. . . . I had been raised in a white surrounding. . . . I was the only colored child in the town. . . . Going to Buxton with all the people of my own race was a great experience for me. I learned a lot and I acted shy and timid first. But after I got there, I could exercise my feelings, my potentials, my talent . . . and I think Buxton brought a whole lot of joy to me, just to be able to live and, a colored girl, in a colored area, and feeling like I was one of them and I was happy.

The feeling of group solidarity apparently was not limited just to black people interacting with black people. While the following statement may not represent a unanimous opinion of former Buxton residents, it is certainly loud and clear. Elmer Buford (interview 1980), responding to a pointed line of inquiry by the interviewer, retorted:

I told you, there wasn't no discrimination down there. . . . Well, you just keep asking me about the black and white. They worked together. They ate together. And if they wanted to, they slept together. And they did everything together down there.

These sorts of statements and perceptions are typical of what we have heard in our discussions with black people who once lived in Buxton. A good number of white people who lived there express similar viewpoints; others do not.

To the degree that utopian concepts can be related to material objects, the archaeological evidence accords with the idea that the people living in Buxton seemed to be rather well off economically and socially. Judging from the portable artifacts collected during the surface reconnaissance and test excavations, the residents of Buxton appear to have prospered materially. They acquired products from a wide network of manufacturers nationally and internationally. In addition to abundant mundane and utilitarian wares are what might be considered luxury items. These observations are supported by photographs and by statements made in the oral interviews. Furthermore, in regard to the archaeological specimens, many potentially reusable or recyclable items were thrown out. It may be that this was a consequence of the termination of the community, although our impression is that a relatively free disposal of usable materials may have occurred through-

out the urban occupation at Buxton. There was, perhaps, a relative surplus of economic resources and limits to the frugality of the town's inhabitants.

In a broader anthropological perspective, perhaps the utopian perception among blacks may be explained, at least in part, by their antecedents in coming into the Muchakinock community and then on into Buxton. Many of these people or their parents were just three or four decades removed from slavery. Equally important are the subsequent scenes into which black people moved upon leaving Buxton. In many instances they appear to have gone to cities where they worked in jobs, businesses, and occupational roles less advantageous than those they had enjoyed in Buxton. In Buxton there was no Ku Klux Klan. In Buxton black people could eat in any restaurant they wished, swim in *the* town swimming pool, and try on clothes in any of the stores. Could they do all of those things freely in Des Moines, Waterloo, Omaha, or Chicago?

As anthropologists analyzing the archaeological residues and looking to the historical and sociocultural systems beyond, we have no difficulty in believing the utopian statements and sentiments we hear former Buxton residents expressing. There will of course be other perceptions, and those are social realities too. If we accept the uniformitarian principle that "the present is the key to the past," however, we should not have problems in this regard. Today one can pick up copies of *The New Iowa Bystander* and the *Des Moines Register* and see different expressions of "reality" pertaining to events in Des Moines. We can also imagine the problems future archaeologists and other researchers might have in deciding whether Des Moines was a "good" place to live during the twentieth century. Different perceptions might arise depending upon which people they interview, what sources they read, and where they conduct their surface reconnaissance and archaeological excavations.

Returning to Buxton for a final perspective, however, we offer a last photographic image, which we feel encapsulates a good deal of the spirit of the Buxton experience. The dubbed studio photograph, here reproduced as Figure 162, shows four of the Carter brothers (Edward Albert, Davis, Clinton, and Clayborne) in a balloon "Flying High in Buxton" over the railroad station, the post office, and perhaps the Perkins Hotel. The image is admittedly corny, but it has serious value as an analogy.

The Carter brothers obviously are dressed up and having a good time. They may not be "in heaven," but they are closer to it than if they were on the ground. Buxton probably was not a total utopia, if indeed such has ever existed; but Buxton may have been closer to that concept than are many towns today. Furthermore, the residents of Buxton may have understood, or at least tolerated, each other in a more productive manner than do those in many places today. The sources for evaluating these possibilities—and for learning from them—exist not only in people's memories, photographs, old newspapers, and population statistics, but also in the concrete rubble of former buildings and in fragments of china and glass.

162. Professional photographer's mock photograph of the Carter brothers "Flying High in Buxton" in the basket of a hot air balloon. *Left to right:* Edward Albert (E. A.), Davis, Clinton, and Clayborne. (Courtesy of the Iowa State Historical Department)

Adams, William H. 1977. *Silcott, Washington: Ethnoarchaeology of a rural American community.* Reports of investigations, no. 54. Pullman: Laboratory of Anthropology, Washington State University.

Adams, William H., Linda P. Gaw, and Frank C. Leonhardy. 1975. *Archaeological excavations at Silcott, Washington: The data inventory.* Reports of investigations, no. 53. Pullman: Laboratory of Anthropology, Washington State University.

Andreas, A. T. 1875. *A. T. Andreas' illustrated historical atlas of the State of Iowa.* Chicago: Andreas Atlas Co.

Atkinson, R. J. C. 1953. *Field archaeology.* London: Methuen and Co. Ltd.

Atlas of Monroe County, Iowa. 1937. (Available at the Monroe County Courthouse, Albia, Iowa.)

Avon Products, Inc. 1981. *Looking good, feeling beautiful: The Avon book of beauty.* New York: Simon and Schuster, Inc.

Baker, Vernon G. 1980. Archaeological visibility of Afro-American culture: An example from Black Lucy's Garden, Andover, Massachusetts. In *Archaeological perspectives on ethnicity in America: Afro-American and Asian American culture history.* Robert L. Schuyler, ed. Pp. 38–47. Farmingdale, N.Y.: Baywood Publishing, Inc.

Baugher-Perlin, Sherene. 1982. Analyzing glass bottles for chronology, function, and trade networks. In *Archaeology of urban America: The search for pattern and process.* Roy S. Dickens, Jr., ed. Pp. 259–90. New York: Academic Press.

Bergmann, Leola Nelson. 1969. *The Negro in Iowa.* Iowa City: The State Historical Society.

Beyer, S. W., and L. E. Young. 1903. Geology of Monroe County. *Iowa Geological Survey Report* 13:354–422.

Bridges, Sarah T., and Bert Salwen. 1980. Weeksville: The archaeology of a black urban community. In *Archaeological perspectives on ethnicity in America: Afro-American and Asian American culture history.* Robert L. Schuyler, ed. Pp. 38–47. Farmingdale, N. Y.: Baywood Publishing, Inc.

Brown, P. E., C. L. Orrben, H. R. Meldrum, and A. J. Englehorn. 1936. *Soil survey of Iowa: Monroe County soils.* Soil survey report 78. Ames: Iowa Agricultural Experiment Station.

Clark, Grahame. 1960. *Archaeology and society.* London: Methuen and Co. Ltd.

Deetz, James. 1977. *In small things forgotten: The archaeology of early American life.* Garden City, N. Y.: Doubleday Anchor.

Desmonde, Kay. 1972. *Dolls and dolls houses.* New York: Crescent Books.

Dethlefsen, Edwin, and James Deetz. 1966. Death's heads, cherubs, and willow trees: Experimental archaeology in colonial cemeteries. *American Antiquity* 31(4):502–10.

Dethlefsen, Edwin, and Kenneth Jensen. 1977. Social commentary from the cemetery. *Natural History* 86(6):32–39.

Garden Book for Mine Workers. 1916. *Coal Age* 9(19):810.

Geismar, Joan H. 1982. *The archaeology of social disintegration in Skunk Hollow: A nineteenth-century rural black community.* New York: Academic Press.

Gilborn, Craig. 1982. Pop pedagogy: Looking at the Coke bottle. In *Material culture studies in America.* Thomas J. Schlereth, ed. Pp. 183–91. Nashville: American Association for State and Local History.

Godden, Geoffrey A. 1978. *Godden's guide to English porcelain.* London: Hart, Davis, and MacGibbon.

Gradwohl, David M. 1974. Archaeology of the Central Des Moines River Valley: A preliminary summary. In *Aspects of Upper Great Lakes anthropology: Papers in honor of Lloyd A. Wilford.* Elden Johnson, ed. Pp. 90-102. St. Paul: Minnesota Historical Society.

Gradwohl, David M., and Nancy M. Osborn. 1972. *Stalking the Skunk: A preliminary*

References cited

survey and appraisal of archaeological resources in the Ames Reservoir, Iowa. Papers in anthropology no. 1. Ames: Department of Sociology and Anthropology, Iowa State University.

———. 1973. *Site seeking in Saylorville: An intensive archaeological site survey of Reconnaissance Units 1 and 3, Saylorville Reservoir, Iowa.* Research report. Ames: Iowa State University Archaeological Laboratory.

Hawkes, Christopher F. C. 1954. Archaeological theory and method: Some suggestions from the Old World. *American Anthropologist* 56(2):155–68.

Hedge, Manoah. 1906. *Past and present of Mahaska County, Iowa.* Chicago: S. J. Clarke Publishing.

Hester, Thomas R., Robert F. Heizer, and John A. Graham. 1975. *Field methods in archaeology.* 6th ed. Palo Alto, Calif.: Mayfield Publishing.

Hinds, Henry. 1909. *The coal deposits of Iowa.* Iowa Geological Survey report 19:21–396.

Honey, William Bowyer, and John Patrick Cushion. 1956. *Handbook of pottery and porcelain marks.* London: Faber and Faber.

Joukowsky, Martha. 1980. *A complete manual of field archaeology: Tools and techniques of field work for archaeologists.* Englewood Cliffs, N. J.: Prentice-Hall Inc.

Ketchum, William C. 1975. *A treasury of American bottles.* New York: Bobbs-Merrill.

Klamkin, Marian. 1971. *The collector's book of bottles.* New York: Dodd, Mead, and Co.

Kovel, Ralph M., and Terry H. Kovel. 1953. *Dictionary of marks: Pottery and porcelain.* New York: Crown.

Lees, James H. 1909. *History of coal mining in Iowa.* Iowa Geological Survey report 19:521–97.

Lohmann, Karl B. 1915. A new era for mining towns. *Coal Age* 13:799–800.

Magnusson, Leifur. 1920. *Housing by employers in the United States. Bulletin of the United States Bureau of Labor Statistics. Miscellaneous series no. 263.* U.S. Department of Labor.

McDaniel, George W. 1982. *Hearth and home: Preserving a people's culture.* Philadelphia: Temple University Press.

———. 1979. *Preserving the people's history: Traditional black material culture in nineteenth- and twentieth-century southern Maryland.* Unpublished Ph.D. diss. Durham, N.C.: Duke University.

Nichols, Charles Sabin. 1919. *Report on inspection of housing and sanitary conditions at various coal mining camps in Iowa.* Ames: unpublished manuscript prepared for Iowa State Board of Health.

Noel Hume, Ivor. 1969. *Historical archaeology.* New York: Alfred A. Knopf.

———. 1974. *All the best rubbish—Being an antiquary's account of the pleasures and perils of studying and collecting everyday objects from the past.* New York: Harper and Row.

Nutty, Colleen Lou. 1978. *Cemetery symbolism of prairie pioneers: Gravestone art and social change in Story County, Iowa.* Master's thesis. Ames: Iowa State University.

Olin, Hubert L. 1965. *Coal mining in Iowa.* Des Moines: State Mining Board, Iowa Department of Mines and Minerals.

Orrben, C. L., and W. E. Tharp. 1931. *Soil survey of Monroe County, Iowa.* U.S. Department of Agriculture, Bureau of Chemistry and Soils, report no. 9, 1931 Series.

Oschwald, W. R., F. F. Riecken, R. I. Dideriksen, W. H. Scholtes, and F. W. Schaller. 1965. *Principal soils of Iowa.* Iowa State University Department of Agronomy, special report no. 42. Ames: ISU Cooperative Extension Service.

Pammel, L. H. 1903. *The forest trees and shrubs of Monroe County.* Iowa Geological Survey report 13:423–33.

Paul, John R., and Paul W. Parmalee. 1973. *Soft drink bottling: A history with special* reference to Illinois. Springfield: Illinois State Museum Society.

Plat Book of Monroe County, Iowa. 1896. Philadelphia: Northwest Publishing.

Polk, R. L. and Company. 1903–1923. *Polk's Iowa State gazetteer.* Volumes 12–20. Des Moines: R. L. Polk and Co.

Prior, Jean Cutler. 1976. *A regional guide to Iowa landforms.* Iowa Geological Survey Educational Series 3. Iowa City: Iowa Geological Survey.

Rutland, Robert. 1956. The mining camps of Iowa. *Iowa Journal of History* 54(1):35–42.

Rye, Stephen. 1972. Buxton: Black metropolis of Iowa. *Annals of Iowa* 41:939–57.

Schmidt, Alvin J. 1980. *Fraternal organizations.* Westport, Conn.: Greenwood Press.

Schuyler, Robert L. 1980. Sandy ground: Archaeology of a 19th-century oystering village. In *Archaeological perspectives on ethnicity in America: Afro-American and Asian American culture history.* Robert L. Schuyler, ed. Pp. 48–59. Farmingdale, N.Y.: Baywood Publishing, Inc.

Schuyler, Robert L., ed. 1978. *Historical archaeology: A guide to substantive and theoretical contributions.* Farmingdale, N.Y.: Baywood Publishing, Inc.

Sears, Roebuck and Co. 1897. *The 1897 Sears, Roebuck catalogue.* Abridged reprint 1968, Fred L. Israel, ed. New York: Chelsea House.

_____. 1903. *The 1902 edition of the Sears, Roebuck catalogue.* Abridged reprint 1969. New York: Crown.

_____. 1908. *Sears, Roebuck and Co. catalogue no. 117: The great price maker.* Abridged reprint 1969, Joseph J. Schroeder, Jr., ed. Chicago: The Gun Digest Co.

Shiffer, Beverly. 1964. The story of Buxton. *Annals of Iowa* 37:339–47.

South, Stanley, ed. 1977. *Research strategies in historical archaeology.* New York: Academic Press.

Singleton, Theresa A. 1980. *The archaeology of Afro-American slavery in coastal Georgia, a regional perception of slave household and community patterns.* Unpublished Ph.D. diss. Gainesville: University of Florida.

Standard Atlas of Monroe County, Iowa. 1919. Chicago: Geo. A. Ogle and Co., Publishers and Engravers.

Swisher, Jacob. 1945. The rise and fall of Buxton. *Palimpsest* 26:179–92.

Toulouse, Julian Harrison. 1971. *Bottle makers and their marks.* New York: Thomas Nelson, Inc.

_____. 1970. *A collector's manual of fruit jars.* New York: Thomas Nelson, Inc.

Towson, Charles R. 1915. Replacing the saloon in mining communities. *Coal Age* 8(7):264–66.

U. S. Department of Agriculture Soil Conservation Service. 1981. *Monroe County, Iowa, advance field sheet #5 and soil survey interpretations.* Lincoln, Nebraska: USDA Soil Conservation Service.

Weitzman, David. 1976. *Underfoot: An everyday guide to exploring the American past.* New York: Charles Scribner's Sons.

White, Charles A. 1870. *Geology of the coal counties.* Report of the Geological Survey of the State of Iowa 2:254–74.

Wright, Richard R., Jr. 1908. The economic condition of Negroes in the North: Negro governments in the North. *The Southern Workman* 37(9):486–98.

INTERVIEWS

Adams, Jeanette. 1980. Interview by Elmer Schwieder and Joseph Hraba. 21 June 1980.

Ambey, Naomi Tobin. 1981. Interview by Dorothy and Elmer Schwieder. 16 June 1981.

Beaman, Lester. 1980. Interview by Joseph Hraba. 17 November 1980.

Booker, Odessa Brooks. 1981. Interview by Dorothy and Elmer Schwieder. 5 June 1981.

Brown, Jacob. 1980. Interview by Joseph Hraba. 18 November 1980.

Brown, Marjorie Lee. 1980. Interview by Joseph Hraba. 19 August 1980.

Buford, Elmer. 1980. Interview by Joseph Hraba. 30 June 1980.

Collier, Dorothy Neal. 1980. Interview by Dorothy and Elmer Schwieder. 17 October 1980.

Fisher, Vera Olson. 1980. Interview by Elmer Schwieder and Joseph Hraba. 30 August 1980.

Franzen, Marvin. 1981. Interview by Joseph Hraba. 9 September 1981.

Jackson, Paul. 1980. Interview by Joseph Hraba. 20 August 1980.

King, Nellie Lash. 1980. Interview by Joseph Hraba. 23 December 1980.

Larson, A. E. 1981. Interview by Joseph Hraba. 23 July 1981.

Lewis, Bessie. 1981. Interview by Joseph Hraba. 17 January 1981.

Lewis, Harvey. 1980. Interview by Joseph Hraba. 29 December 1980.

Morgan, Ada Baysoar. 1981. Interview by Dorothy and Elmer Schwieder. 2 June 1981.

Oliper, Mike. 1981. Interview by Joseph Hraba. 23 June 1981.

Pernot, John. 1981. Interview by Joseph Hraba. 19 June 1981.

Reasby, Harold. 1980. Interview by Dorothy and Elmer Schwieder. 19 August 1980.

Reeves, Lola. 1980. Interview by Elmer Schwieder and Joseph Hraba. 21 June 1980.

Sofranco, Sister Marene. 1981. Interview by Dorothy and Elmer Schwieder. 8 May 1981.

Stapleton, Hazel. 1980. Interview by Elmer Schwieder and Joseph Hraba. 24 June 1980.

Index

Adams, Jeanette, 101, 176
"Adaptive reuse" of structural remains, 36, 65
Advertising. *See also* Montgomery Ward catalog; Sears, Roebuck and Company catalog
  archival source for archaeological reconstruction, 146–47, 166–71
  buttons, 117–18, 161–62, 170
Aerial photographs
  archaeological survey, 17–19, 25, 62
  evidence of former surface features, 12, 17–19
African Methodist Episcopal (AME) Church. *See* Churches, African Methodist Episcopal
Agricultural practices. *See also* Buxton, townsite, present land use
  effect on archaeological evidence, 26, 30, 44–45, 112, 123, 155, 186
Albia Bottling Works (Iowa), 51, 132
Alcock, Henry, Co. (pottery, Eng.), 127
Alcoholic beverages, selling restrictions, 132, 171
Ambey, Naomi Tobin, 78, 102
American Bottle Co. (Ill.), 135
American Indian artifacts, 160, 181
Anchor Pottery (N.J.), 125
Archaeological evidence, and historical data, 6, 110, 120–22, 165, 172
Archaeological excavation techniques, 15, 57, 59–66, 70–72, 75–76, 78, 84–91, 93–103, 106, 110–20
Archaeological grid system, 12, 13, 62–64
Archaeological laboratory techniques, 13–16, 65, 144, 158–59
Archaeological survey techniques, 12, 15, 25, 44, 48–49
Architectural plans, major buildings, 23, 189
Archival studies, and archaeological finds, 6, 15, 159, 163, 165–66, 186
Armstrong, H. A. (Hobe), 30–32, 37, 39, 43, 51–52, 102, 164, 166–67, 169, 178
Artifacts
  categories, based on material and primary function, 28–29, 124
  factors in preservation, 123–24, 140, 144, 155–56, 158
  portable, definition, 6, 7
  structural, definition, 6, 25
Ashby, Howard, 56
A Street. *See* Streets, A
Automotive parts and supplies, 152, 155, 161–62

Bakery, 13, 18, 88, 100–09
Ball Brothers Co. (preserve jars, Ind.), 137–38
Ball park, 23, 55
Bandshell, 42, 48, 102
Barns, 42, 48, 61, 95, 100, 102, 105, 109
B Street. *See* Streets, B
Bataille, Gretchen, 53
Bathing and personal hygiene, 125, 176–77
Bathrooms, 105, 181
Baxter, John, 33, 164, 169, 178
Baxter, Lottie Armstrong, 164, 178
Baxter family, 22
Baysoar, E. M., 50, 104, 189
Beamon, Lester, 101, 163–64, 174, 180
Bergie National (spark plugs, Ill.), 162
Bingham, Stewart, 154
Blacksmith shop, 47, 50, 168
Blomgren, Emanuel, 26
Blomgren, Loren, 8, 26, 42, 190
Blomgren, Mabel, 8, 26–27, 42, 183, 190
Blomgren family, 22, 30
Bluff Creek, 9, 17–18, 20, 24, 41–42, 47–50, 52, 55–61, 63, 68–69, 73–74, 103–4, 110, 132, 178, 180, 189
Bluff Creek Township, 1, 6, 17–19, 20–23, 25, 27, 62, 132, 160, 169, 171, 186–87, 190
Booker, Odessa Brooks, 152, 172, 174, 181, 184
Boone B. T. & P. Co. (bricks, Iowa), 72, 132
Bottle and jar closures, 129–30, 132–33, 136–38, 140, 142, 151, 155, 161
Bottles. *See also* Milk glass containers
  alcoholic beverage, 132, 134–35, 171
  food and milk, 135–37
  medicine, 138, 140, 143, 171, 176
  preserve jar, 136–38, 176
  soft drink, 132–33, 170
  toiletry and emollient, 139–40, 176
Brockway Glass Company (Pa.), 136
Bromo Seltzer, 138–39
Brooks, George William, 184
Brown, Marjorie, 160, 176, 191
Buford, Elmer, 132, 152, 163, 172, 179, 181, 183, 193
Burk, J., and Co. (bottling, Iowa), 132
Burkett, Maggie, 56
Busch, Adolphus, Glass Manufacturing Co. (Ill.), 135
Butcher shops. *See* Meat markets
Buxton, Ben C., 20, 22, 50, 56–57, 63, 104, 169, 192
Buxton, John E., 20

Trade and transportation networks, evidence, 25, 166–71, 186–87

Travel
automobile, 151–52, 155, 179
foot, 179–80
horse-drawn carriage, 13, 28, 102, 151–52, 179, 184
train, 20, 49, 151–52, 179

Travelling salesman/saleswoman, 171, 178

Twelfth Street. *See* Streets, Twelfth

Umbrellas and parasols, 160, 162

United Mine Workers of America (UMWA), 54, 182

Upper Hanley Pottery Co. (Eng.), 171

Utzchneider and Co./Sarreguemines (pottery, Fr.), 126–27

Vaseline, 138–39

Vault, 11, 43, 48, 59–60, 72–77, 168. *See also* Pay office, company

Vernon, Dorothy, Toilet Water, 140

Vicks Vap O Rub, 138

Vodrey Brothers (pottery, Ohio), 125

W & N Co., 146

Walker, Leonard, 177

Wallace, Nancy, 14, 41

Wallpaper, 158

Warehouse, stone company, 7, 11, 42–43, 48–49, 59–60, 65–68, 100, 103, 108, 110, 168

Warehouses, general, 42, 48

Warren, D. Michael, 142

Warren, Jim, 175, 177

Warren and Co. (meat market/grocery store), 166–67

Waste disposal. *See* Garbage pits; Outhouses; Sanitation

Water supply for town, 90, 94, 104, 172, 180–81. *See also* Cisterns and wells; Reservoir and dam; Water towers

Water towers
behind superintendent's residence, 3, 60–61, 105, 108–9, 180
on Fourth Street, 2–3, 11, 59, 119, 122, 163, 180

Watkins (bottled food, Minn.), 135, 140

Weeksville site (Brooklyn, N.Y.), 6

Weighing devices, 153, 164

Weir, William S., 129

Welch's (bottling, N.Y.), 117

Wells, W. A., 23, 56

Wells. *See* Cisterns and wells

Well's Hill, 56. *See also* West Swede Town

West End Pottery Co. (Ohio), 125

Western Stoneware Company, 35, 51, 129

West Swede Town, 24, 55–56, 158, 182, 190

Wetherell, Frank E., 23, 172–73, 189

Wever, Charles, 12

Whiteburg, 187

White House Hotel, 7, 11, 41, 43, 48, 59–61, 63, 68–69, 86–91, 161, 165, 168–69, 181, 186

Wick China Co. (Pa.), 125–26

Williams, J. B., Co. (Conn.), 140

Williams, John W., 184

Williams family, 22

Williamson, Rev. R. H., 159

Wilson, Paul, 191

Wood and Sons (pottery, Eng.), 171

Woodson, George H., 56, 169

YMCA, boys'
activities in, 84, 181–82
historic location and photographs, 2, 41–42, 48, 59, 63
restroom facilities, 84–86, 130, 181
structural evidence, 7, 11, 43, 59–60, 64, 82–86, 90, 161, 181
swimming pool, 64, 84–86, 181, 193

YMCA, main
activities in, 77–78, 160–61, 179, 181–83
historic location and photographs, 2–3, 13, 41–42, 48, 59, 78, 86–87
pool hall, 78, 181
structural evidence, 7, 11, 43, 59–60, 64, 77–83, 90, 146, 161, 180–81